MAN

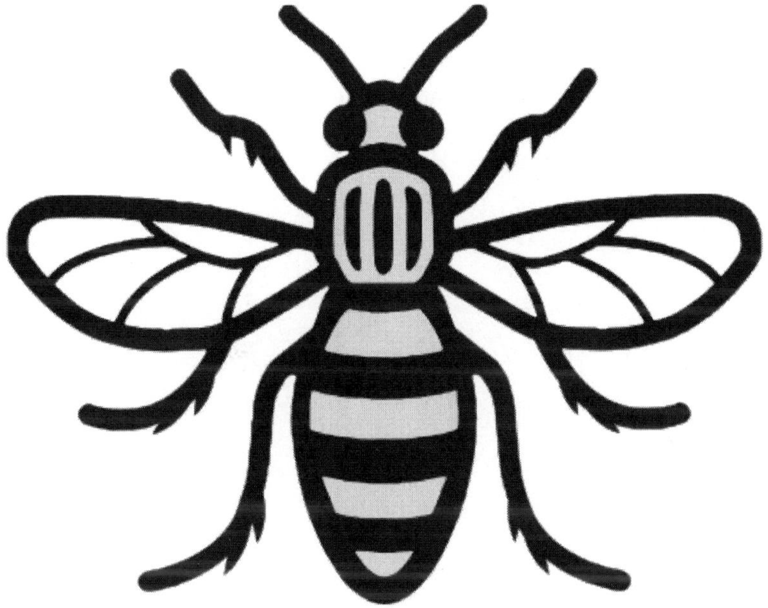

MAVERICKS

COLIN BLANEY

First published in 2019

This book is copyright under the Berne Convention. All rights are reserved. Apart from any fair dealing for the purpose of private study, research, criticism or review, as permitted under the Copyright Act, 1956, no part of this publication may be reproduced, stored in a retrieval system, or transmitted, in any form or by any means, electronic, electrical, chemical, mechanical, optical, photocopying, recording or otherwise, without the prior permission of the copyright owner. Enquiries should be sent to the publishers at the undermentioned address:

EMPIRE PUBLICATIONS
1 Newton Street, Manchester M1 1HW
© Colin Blaney 2019

ISBN: 978-1-909360-64-8

Printed in Great Britain.

CONTENTS

FOREWORD BY BILL HOPKINS	5
INTRODUCTION	9
1. BILL HOPKINS	40
2. SYLVIA BLANEY	49
3. ALAN HANCOCK	60
4. KATH RILEY	74
5. BILL KEITH	79
6. GEORGE SMITH	97
7. BRIAN HUGHES	112
8. ROUFY	123
9. ERIC BARKER	136
10. ANDY BARKER	142
11. SIMON WOLSTENCROFT	147
12. ALAN LORD	153
13. ANTHONY DONNELLY	161
14. KAREN WOODS	166
15. TOMMY DUNN	169
16. SUE CUNDALL	181
17. RAY BANKS	188
18. STELLA GRUNDY	193
19. IAN HOUGH	202
20. LEON AND HIS MUM	227
21. GED THE RED	241
22. DAVID BLATT	255
AFTERWORD	274

A FRUITFUL RETIREMENT

Some years ago I retired afier a forty-year career in Education, one half of it in Britain (Manchester, Liverpool and Glasgow) - the other half in teacher training in African universities (Kenya, Zimbabwe, Malawi).

When I returned to England, my family prevailed upon me to write my life story. "What a fascinating life you've led," they said. "You simply must get it down on paper for the sake of posterity Start with your childhood in Collyhurst Manchester." I did as I was told writing under the pen-name of Tim Lally. It took me a year. Then they said, "This is amazing stuff. Why not make it into a novel? It's bound to be a best-seller." Once again, I did as I was told

and, using the pen-name of Billy Hopkins, wrote a 150,000-word story entitled 'Our Kid'.

Next they commanded, "Now you must go about getting it published and hit the bookshops with it. First, you need an agent." I looked through 'The Writers' Handbook' and picked out thirty likely looking agents. Since it takes some of them six months to answer a letter, I realized that it would take about

fifteen years to get round the list. So I decided to write to them all at the same time, enclosing a sample chapter and a synopsis, to see if anybody wanted to promote my "masterpiece".

Eighteen did not answer but after a year, I had a dozen replies. The responses were worth a book in themselves.

The first one said "Charming story - charmingly told. What a pity you're not a little girl. Why not write it again and pretend that you are?" The second said simply "You should try to write sideways." (Meaning? The only time I wrote sideways was when I was teaching in a tough Manchester school and writing on the blackboard was a hazardous exercise). The next reply stated bluntly, "There's no demand for stories about nostalgia, northern slums, and trouble int' mill stuff." (Pace 'Coronation Street' and Catherine Cookson!) A third sent me a note in illegible scribble which we only managed to decipher with the aid of a magnifying glass and after prolonged debate. It said, "Someone left this stuff on my desk. I don't know Why. But I certainly do not have time to read it. I'm swamped." I was assured that any kind of comment was a bonus since most agents answer with a cryptic 'No thanks'.

One agent answered after a year: "I have just found your manuscript. It had fallen behind the radiator. Pity, as it has great potentia and I'm sure I could have done something Wlth it".

Needless to say I rushed off a copy of the whole book to her. I heard no more. 3 months later I discovered that she had gone bankrupt! Hope I wasn t a contributory factor but maybe she has a cornucopia of masterpieces hidden behind her radiator.

In the end I decided to publish the book myself. l bought desktop equipment (Amstrad) and learned how to use it. First l had three copies printed and bound in rexine_ and it cost me nearly £40 per copy. They were so well received by the people who read the book that I splashed out and had 100 printed and results exceeded all my expectations. Family, friends and colleagues were most appreciative. Perhaps it had something.

I eventually had 500 copies of the book printed and after advertising in magazines like The Oldie and Practical Gardening, I sold the lot. Not much of a profit but I'd got my book out there being read.

One copy landed on the desk of a man who had been born in Salford but had worked at every major studio in Hollywood as "creative and script-writing consultant" on such productions as Peyton Place, Dynasty, Dallas. He liked OUR KID so much, he recommended it to a London agent who loved it and persuaded Headline Publishing to publish it. It was slow to get started but then the news spread by word of mouth and sales rose dramatically.

OUR KID has sold well and in the year 2000 was on the best-seller charts for

several weeks. The World Book Club chose it as its star book of the month for May 2000. A sequel entitled HOPES followed and this too reached the best-seller list. Finally a third book KATE'S STORY (based on my mother's life story) was published in 2001 and sold well, especially in the North West. Since then I have written two other books: GOING PLACES and recently

INTRODUCTION

ANYTHING GOES. OUR KID has since been translated into Spanish ("Nuestro pequefio Billy") while this month, both KATE'S STORY and OUR KID have been transcribed into Braille by the National Library for the B1ind.

So in retirement, I have written five novels since the age of 70. Goes to show: it's never too late to start a new career! You can't keep a maverick down!

Bill Hopkins

INTRODUCTION

The word "maverick" made me think (or "tink," as the Irish Mancs and Moss Side lads say) of the likes of cowboys and untamed ponies. Yet the word also brings to mind images of wild, untamed and free-roaming spirits. A maverick is a trailblazer, often imitated, yet never equalled. In Manchester, the word "mav" is used to describe a person who's over  the top. Instead of saying, "you're mad," it's just "Mav". Simple as.

Manchester has always been made up of a mixed league of nations and Mancunians are known as the most bohemian people in Europe. To describe many of the city's unique characters as "wild spirits" would be fitting and with this book I aim to tell the stories of those who appear within its pages.

I have interviewed more than twenty of Manchester's mavericks – those who have achieved fame, or those who've simply had an affect on me, or made waves in the city and beyond. A few of them are well-known, several of them are infamous but most are people I feel pretty confident most people will not have heard of. With their input and that of my own, I'll try to paint a picture of the city's history using memories of families, friends, neighbours and events.

To be considered you didn't necessarily have to be born in Manchester. After all a lot of Manc icons were born elsewhere, I'm thinking about people like Friedrich Engels, Alan Turing, Alex Higgins and Matt Busby. This being Manchester outsiders are always welcome and many have made outstanding contributions to the renown of the city.

I'll delve into their backgrounds and upbringing and we'll learn about how things were back then, how much has changed and the speed at which those changes have occurred and continue to do so. For example, people are now beginning to live, on average, to the age of 80. Fantastic.

Out of all the lads I grew up with, at least 90 per cent took the crooked road, and most have paid a heavy price. When I got married in a German jail in 1998, I was forever ringing home, finding the main topic to be, "So-and-so's on his way out. Run over on his doorstep, peppered with bullets, got jail". Add to this the physical harm we did to ourselves via the drink and drugs we got involved with and it's really no wonder we're dropping like flies. But I'm lucky - I've still got the chance to put something back into the area in which I grew up.

When I came to ask about the mavericks' childhood and early schooling memories, many came to a stumbling halt and there were times when we'd have to return to the topic. I spent a good few hours telling my own tales, which always helped to jog their memories.

My earliest personal memory are of moving, in 1959, from the cobbled streets of Miles Platting to the huge Collyhurst Flats. If these flats were still standing, there's no doubt they'd have been converted to yuppie apartments by now. But before this could happen, one block simply sank overnight in the mid-Sixties. It was a funny sight, with all the media present and the families escorted out on council wagons. Mining in the nearby pits had weakened the foundations and the council had their work cut out, wedging the balconies with thick, wooden beams. It was even worse inside, where the gaping holes and cracks were so big, you could fit your arm in them. The council tried to fill the cracks with a kind of super glue, but green fungus would ooze out when it got damp.

The decrepit flats became the last slums to be demolished in Manchester and when I speak in libraries and at writers' meetings I explain how coming from the last slum generation has given me many advantages. The fact is, when I started writing I needed to do a lot of research and it was only then I realised how many people from my estate, Collyhurst, have broken through in all walks of life. There's Freddie Garrity from 'Freddie and The Dreamers' and Bruce Jones, who plays Les Battersby, the comical star of 'Coronation Street'. He was in St Oswald's Boys Brigade

INTRODUCTION

with me in the mid-Sixties and he got his big break in 'Raining Stones', playing alongside Ricky Tomlinson. It was filmed on the Langley estate and the story follows Bruce's character as he tries to buy the full rig-out for his daughter's first Holy Communion.

Another Collyhurst chap who appeared in Corrie was Jack Smethurst, who got his break in Carry on Sergeant in 1958. He was better known for his lead role as Eddie Booth in 'Love Thy Neighbour', playing the part of a Union Jack-waving bigoted Labour man, who finds himself living next door to a West Indian couple. Jack was also in the Oscar-winning film, 'Chariots of Fire' and later starred in 'Last of the Summer Wine'.

The reason I believe the slums worked in our favour is because you can't get any lower when you're at the bottom of the ladder. So you graft your way up, you bond and help each other out. All the doors to the homes of the big families were never closed and when I'd get home from school, it was normal for some of my wagging mates to be making sugar butties in each other's flats. Butties with jam and sauce were a real treat and the girls dipped theirs into condensed milk, while the older folk used dripping. The first time I saw my Nana Nellie dip hers, she did a buzzard of a swoop into the crusty chip pan with the bread, which hit the juice and went straight down her Gregory Peck (neck) in one gulp. I was well impressed.

Nana worked in the White City canteen and in United's chippie and I was always boxed off with top scran when I worked, selling the Evening News and the football pinks at Old Trafford. My patch was the United Road, as the Cantilever stand had just been built for the World Cup. My Granddad took me to see all the games in this section and I was smitten with Eusebio, the Black Panther from Benfica. We even travelled down in his Ford Pop to see Portugal versus Brazil at Goodison Park.

There wasn't much St George merchandise in the Sixties, unlike nowadays, with the hit tune Three Lions still going strong after it gripped the nation in 1996. England supporters are a mass of bulldogs now, draped in the George and Dragon, outnumbering the fans of every nation we play, friendlies or not.

In our day, we just had beer and songs, which we'd sing in the streets. But this is a thing of the past. If a kid were caught singing in the street today, he'd get attacked for being too happy. The main song from our area is Collyhurst Road, which has the best chorus you could wish for: "My old man said be a City fan," sang to the tune of "Don't Dilly Dally on the way". It's Manchester's most popular pub tune and it's still sung at all the big Manchester United games 30 years on.

My best mate in the flats was Eric Hostey. He was the only City fan in our crew, but he came to all the big United games just for the aggro. He was influenced by the Glaswegian mob from Mary Hill, who began moving into the flats around that time. All were heavy drinkers who would carve each other up at weekends and I got hooked on watching these brutal battles sat on the roof on Central Drive. Eric soon got involved and he started carrying a blade. We called these blades 'chivs' because they were the size of steak knives, but machetes were also favourites. Most of the fighters were heroin addicts, who would always be jacking up, and a few smoked it in cigs, as chasing the dragon on silver foil only became common in Manchester during the late-Seventies.

Vinny Healy was the cock of our school and he took Eric down Collyhurst Road to his old man's scrap yard, where there was gossip about a family feud with some outsiders. The kick-off was reported in all the Sunday papers, as one fella was killed with a shotgun and a huge amount of weapons were seized. Eric had seen someone's face get ripped apart during the fight. His cousin, Richard Tchaikovsky (we called him Chike), was the biggest rogue in Collyhurst at the time - he was on par with Robin Hood, robbing from the rich and getting pissed with the poor. We all looked up to him as he'd been through the prison system and was the first real grafter we knew who was a career criminal, serving more than a life sentence before he'd hit his forties.

Chike's old man had a barny with his missus in Eric's flat. Just as he was ducking his holy ghost (toast) into his chucky egg, his mum was stabbed in the throat and her blood spurted all over Eric's breakfast. This had a major effect on him and from then on he carried a loaded gun and began visiting Moss Side shebeens.

Most lads from the north side used a shebeen in Cheetham

INTRODUCTION

Hill called Banjos, where they'd do ten-bob weed deals. Uppers and Downers were the main drugs, but what amazes me now is the state of hash and weed today. It's all a bag of shite that makes you ill. The skunk's sprayed with chemicals and a block of solid will be made up of only ten per cent hash. It's a sad state of affairs. The Red Lebanese we used to buy in weights came from the PLO with guns stamped into the hash. We used to boil the cloth it came wrapped in, making a jug of tea to rival Irish Poteen.

Both Eric and myself had big ambitions to make the grade in football. Eric had City trials coming up and I was supposed to sign a schoolboy contract with Oldham, alongside John Duddy, but we were both sent to young offenders units and in those days no club would take you on with a record, even if you were a red-hot player.

There was an endless amount of footballing talent coming out of every school and later, when I was sandblasting the Blue Coats School in Oldham, I called into the club for a natter with Duddy who gave me a signed photo of the team line-up. It was great to see his grin but it got me thinking what a fucking dickhead I'd been, having lost the opportunity of a pro career. Although it's easy to say now, I believe I was given the choice between being a pro footballer and being a criminal, with the plus side to a life of crime being the chance to become the writer I am today. Looking back, I would have chosen the option of pro footballer, but that's like saying, "If shit was rice pudding, you'd never go hungry".

Eric learned to play snooker in Rose Hill and was the dog's bollocks at telling jokes. Bernard Manning, also being a City fan, took a shine to Eric who passed on all the latest street jokes, which Manning then polished up and fired out at weekends. Bernard would have the club in stitches, ripping into Joe Public, the doorman or the bar staff. I'd be bursting for the karzy, having to squeeze my nuts waiting for the break because Bernard got anyone who moved. Women were executed on the way to the toilets and it got even better when they'd try to heckle back.

Bernard worked the local clubs and was known originally as a comedy compère. In 1959 he bought the Embassy Club on

MANCHESTER MAVERICKS

Rochdale Road from his old man (The Beatles played there) and in 1971 he got his TV break on 'The Comedians', then became a compère in the 'Wheeltappers and Shunters Club' on Granada.

People say Bernard was a racist bigot, and things got heated after his agent booked him for a BNP conference in Burnley. He'd performed for the Labour and Tory parties, so why the big fuss? Wisely he cancelled it. He let out a stormer once, saying the English, Irish, Jocks, Welsh, West Indians and Chinks should all come together and give it the Pakis. He even travelled over to film in Bombay but after working at the MGM Grand in Vegas, nothing could faze him. Apart from the opening night of the Hacienda club where he stormed out after a barney with 'the faggot Factory staff', as he called them, sensing that he'd been set up.

The Salvage pub on Collyhurst Street was rumoured to have been built with bricks salvaged from the city's bombing but this isn't true, as those bricks were used to build pigeon courts. TV comedian Les Dawson began his career there telling jokes and playing the piano. He'd been a dab hand at boxing, which left him with a cracked jaw. But this enabled him to pull all those grotesque faces. He actually strived to be a poet and writer but in those days writing poetry was as good as coming out of the closet. Any gay person in Collyhurst around that time would have been in serious shite but Les's diaries contained lots of poems, which remained unseen until he died. I loved his comic attacks on his mother-in-law, who told him that when he died, she'd dance all over his grave, to which his response was, "Fantastic! I'm being buried at sea". He also used to say his wife was a sex object, as "when he'd ask for sex, she'd object!"

The Salvage became the swanky Manhattan in 1972, when it opened as a disco with music functions on each night. Foo Foo Lamar was top of the bill and two years later it became the first pool club in Manchester. Alex Higgins put in an appearance as the special guest on the opening night. These days, sadly, it's a run-down hostel with just one small, sweaty bar.

My Granddad ran the Locomotive Tavern on Rochdale Road which was built next to the Manchester-Leeds railway line.

INTRODUCTION

Locals nicknamed it The Loco and a blind fella would sit by the door saying hello to whoever passed through, as he knew every person by the sound of their footsteps. Another fella, Tiny Tim, who stood over seven feet tall, would clean the lights for a free drink and whenever he fancied another, he'd simply lean over, pull his own pint, open the till and pay for himself.

There's a book called 'The Pubs of Rochdale Road' and my family are so proud to be in it. Today there's only one pub left on Rochdale Road, The Marble Arch, which recently won Manchester's Pub of the Year title. It's like walking into the past, as the marble arches and window frames are still in tip-top condition and it still serves the old cask ales.

My Granddad's ales were always winning prizes. He was really proud when Billy Green, who ran his own pub, The Vauxhall, would come over Rochdale Road to his. When Billy passed away in the Seventies, they changed the name of The Vauxhall to Billy Green's. The 'blood tubs' were all over Manchester in those days and Billy Green's had one – these were small rings in which mismatch fights would take place every weekend. Usually it was an old pro against a young urchin and, with a full turn out, the boxers shed plenty of blood, hence the name.

In 1952 my old man was on home leave from the RAF, where he was a PTI in charge of the boxing squad, and had just been chosen to box for the United Services. When he called into The Loco my mother was working away behind the beer pumps and later that same night, he told her he wanted to marry her. It may sound silly now, but that kind of true romance was common back then.

Only a few days later my Mam was booked onto a boat which set sail from Southampton around the Bay of Biscay through the Suez Canal and past Aden where a war was in full swing before docking in Hong Kong. They were married the next day and continued to live the high life for three years with servants at their beck and call but after losing their first child and missing Blighty they set sail for home. I was conceived somewhere between the Red Sea and the Dead Sea, which is fitting as I've been a life-long Red and have only just avoided winding up Dead on many occasions.

Before I entered St Malachy's Catholic School, I went to Sharp Street, Manchester's oldest ragged school, which opened in 1853. It's still there today as a listed building and the tobacco factory next door has been converted into leisure apartments, with a swimming pool and palm trees.

The school ran on charity and even today, on Sunday mornings, they give out free brekkies for the homeless. In our day you could attend during the day or at night as it was run like a youth club. We played crab football in the cellar and the flagstones were always freezing, even in the summer. With the porridge we were given a teaspoon of black stuff, which was supposed to be some kind of Marmite. For dinner, we were given apples and if we stayed there late we got a buttie or black pudding, while the teachers tucked into tripe. My old man swore tripe was the UK's pasta and said all the coal pit grafters ate it regularly, with plenty of pepper and onions.

We were given two yearly treats, the first of which was a trip to Blackpool in November for the Illuminations. Once there, we'd all pile out on the pier for a piss. It would blow back all over us and everyone else, but it was such a thrill to watch that long jet going like a good 'un into the dark sea. Then we'd be back on board to cruise the golden mile. The highlight of the trip was the chippie before the main road back to Manchester, where we'd all get a bag of Jockeys Whips and piles of scrapings, all soaked in Sarson's Vinegar, which we'd drink out of the bottom of the newspaper it was held in.

The bumper day out came when the buses took us down Oxford Road to the big cinema, which had been converted for the day in order to ship in 1,000 kids from all over Manchester whose families were 'on the penny'. There we had a ball with yo-yo competitions followed by cartoons and a huge feast of butties, sweets and Tizer drinks. To crown it all, on the way out we'd visit Santa, who'd give out chocolate selection boxes (definitely not Cadbury's) and Snakes & Ladders or Draughts game sets. We were thrilled to bits.

My clearest memory of St Malachy's school was looking at the

INTRODUCTION

huge, grey blanket of dank fog, while peering out of the frosted windows at the trains. The noise of the trains were intoxicating, with steam shooting up high over the Victorian viaducts as they entered the tunnels with an ear-piercing whistle. Every now and then, on the way to Monsall's Red Rec for a game of football, we'd jib the quick way via a few tunnels. And when a rattler steamed into the tunnel, we'd all shag the wall, crying out, "Mam!" as the wind would get you from behind, almost dragging you under.

We looked like the Black & White Minstrels when we emerged, full of bravado. Some of us would have a go at the others, saying we'd heard them shout for their mums. Once a kid called Spamhead admitted he'd shouted out "Mumsie!" instead and, my God, did he come in for some stick after that. Even today we shout "Mumsie!" whenever we see him.

We used to climb inside the top part of the arches on Collyhurst Street, waiting for the trains to pass overhead. The pigeons never blinked an eye as the rattlers coming over the top of us made the entire arch shake. The lines were full of detonators, which meant you had to have a firm grip on the metal frames due to the kick back you'd get when they'd explode. They were used to direct the train drivers as they came towards the sheds. We would pinch the detonators from the tracks when it came close to Bonfire Night, throwing huge slabs on them to sound out a warning if another gang were on their way to raid our bommie.

We had our own steam train, Puffing Billy, parked under the biggest railway viaducts you've ever seen. Only the Stockport viaducts, which LS Lowry described as the veins into the country, are bigger. But ours were more like the veins into hell. Lowry's grandparents lived locally and later, following his years of study at the Manchester College, he painted the area. My favourite work of his is Irk Place, but his most well known piece is 'Britain at Play'.

Puffing Billy was situated next to the foul-smelling, rat-infested River Irk and on Sundays we'd leave the flats en masse, dressed up as cowboys, singing, "We are the Collyhurst Kids. Oi! Oi! We are the Collyhurst kids. Oi! Oi! We learn all our manners by knocking off tanners. We are the Collyhurst kids. Oi! Oi!"

MANCHESTER MAVERICKS

We'd head down the dip into Irk Valley, past the Tin School (made out of actual tin so that when we rattled and banged on it, you'd swear the whole thing was about to come out off its foundations), then over the River Irk. Here we'd pile on board Billy, throwing a sack-full of coal into the engine, followed by a can of petrol. And soon we'd have her going like a good 'un!

There were times when we'd use industrial coke and, my God, that shite gave off some wicked fumes. But this would add to the thrill. I remember a funny incident when the black smoke got going and the kid in charge of the cabin was struggling like fuck, choking away. He had to blow his sports whistle to get attention, as all us cowboys were yelling, "Let's get the hell out of Manchester!" and "No stoppin' 'til Texas!" We'd be wearing our caps, with our water pistols and slug guns blazing away to let the enemy know we were ready to rumble.

The enemy was a crew from the cobbled streets off Collyhurst Road, The Red Indians, led by their top kid, Sitting Bull. He'd wear a full headset and had a sling for chucking duckers. The rest wore painted faces with mud or lipstick stripes and snake belts tied around their heads with blades of grass or pigeon feathers tucked into the back. They'd come pouring out of the archways like a pack of hyenas, hands going over their mouths like the clappers, making woo-woo noises. The new kids on the block would shit themselves and try to give it offmans, but the only safe place to jump was from the top of the wheels. The Milky Bar Kids didn't have a clue and many ended up in Ancoats Hospital, also known as The Butchers!

The Red Indians' bow and arrows would be all over us like darts. Made of bamboo from the Rag & Bone man, it was bad news if you copped one full on in the eye. Lots of us did get caught, mainly up the bugle, as we were like sitting ducks to the Apaches. Your conk was purple for days.

Another day out for us was spent on the River Irk, shooting air guns and catapults at the sewer rats, which we'd flush out with bangers, cannons and rip-raps. These rats were fat, ugly and slimy and we all had to stick close in case they'd have a go back at us. The older folk took house rats' tails to the Town Hall for a penny

INTRODUCTION

each but the biggest were the warehouse rats and the first time you came across one, you'd swear they were ugly cats. In the past, those warehouse rats were slung into pits for the dogs to attack and bets were placed on the outcome of how fast they'd be killed.

The River Irk led into a swimming pool-sized pond of toxic waste from the dye works, where the steam floating off the water was forever changing colour. One day, we were in full flow on our home made raft, along with Fred, the gang's dog, who we'd robbed from a big stately home. Fred was a Golden Labrador, so clean and full of life, and she became everyone's pet. There were loads of dogs from the flats, which we called Heinz's (something to do with them being mixed breeds). Fred was the only pedigree dog – she really was an awesome sight.

Now, the saying in Collyhurst was that, if you had a cat with a tail, you were posh! Cats were very rare and if we found one, it went straight over the wall into Willert Street's police dog compound. It was even better when the Dibble were in there, feeding the dogs - you could hear the screams and curses of Plod and the raging animals, which added to the nobble.

Back on the raft, suddenly Fred went mad after being stung by some kind of flying insect, which had us all flapping and tumbling about. Our friend Willie Dale fell overboard and came to the surface covered in huge leeches. We froze as the deadly weeds pulled him straight back under and it was perhaps the only time one of the parents ever came on the scene. It's still unreal to think how Jimmy Ford's old man saved Willie's life as we all abandoned ship.

Wilcox's Barrel Works had steel drums, which were stacked almost 70 feet high. We climbed these to gain entrance over the back fence, which was built into the side of the train embankment. It was only a six-foot climb over, but one day the drums could not take us and we found ourselves cascading down to where two howling guard dogs were waiting. The fire services had to come and burst through the gates to let us out. It was on top, the dogs had us and Fred scrambled back up, but there were hardly enough drums left to get distance between us and the dogs. As soon as the gates burst open, we all bolted out, but Fred, the poor fucker, fell straight down into the Irk and the rats ripped her to shreds. The RSPCA took Fred to the dogs' home and put her down. I hope the three years she'd had with our gang made up for the fact we'd given her an early shower.

Another big day came when the Tin School teamed up with St James's. They came charging down Rochdale Road shouting religious insults and baying for blood, and the fights on them there red hills were always mass mayhem. There was a huge red stone at the peak of the slag heap and whoever took it were the top dog gang until the next ding-dong. Once back in school, it took a whole afternoon for the nuns and teachers to administer the strap to all the cowboys present on the hill that day.

The area is known as the Sand Hills and it's totally different now, with green pastures and trees of all shapes and sizes. If you look closely, you'll see one long, cobbled street, threading its way from the top of Rochdale Road, down into the dip. It was common for it to be raining and cloudy in this area, while up above it would be bright sunshine. I remember once looking at the drop end of Eddington Street and there was rain bouncing off the cobbles and a huge rainbow forming above. Two of the O'Rourkes came running through the rain with their donkey and cart and, once above the drop, it looked as though they'd smashed through a glass pane as they were saturated to the skin whilst I was as dry as a bone.

I sat next to the O'Rourkes in school and I was looking forward to the following year when I'd change class. Even though they were sorted, they smelt bad and you dreaded copping a proper lung-full. They kept a donkey in their back yard, weather permitting, but if the weather got too bad, the donkey would be squeezed into the hallway. I remember the first time we saw the donkey, with its head above the door, snorting and ee-orring away. Many a time, the donkey's piss would almost flood their back yard and the smell was untrue, as it was right at the main entrance to our school.

We were known as the Collyhurst Cowboys but the tag didn't come from those days. Instead, it came a few years later when we stormed the football leagues for six years. We won every league –

INTRODUCTION

two doubles and a treble - and what a day it was when we won the treble. We had played up at Mellands, near Belle Vue, and bang on half time my mate Gagzy got the equaliser. During the second half we ran riot and seven or eight goals went in. We were given the Will Melland trophy to take home. It's still in Manchester now and I swear it's as big as the Charity Shield. We carted it back to the flats on the number 53 bus and it was a great feeling during assembly the following Monday morning, with 300 kids cheering us in.

Bus number 53 may well have the most famous route in Manchester. Setting off from Cheetham Hill, it winds its way around Manchester, through Collyhurst and across the Rochdale Canal and onto Hulme Hall Lane, where the evil Myra Hindley walked past us one day. She was wearing a black wig and was carrying a stack of Christmas parcels - one of which she dropped on purpose. Debate still continues as to whether or not Ian Brady led her astray. Bollocks! She was as guilty as sin! Young Lesley Anne Downing picked up the false present, which Hindley asked her to carry to the car. But more evil was waiting; in the car Brady had an ethol-covered rag, which he used to knock Lesley out. She became the couple's fourth victim.

From there, the 53 would continue, past Miles Platting, through Moss Side and Whalley Range and on to White City and its final destination, Old Trafford. The bus fare was cheap, although you'd pay a heavy price in travel sickness. And after watching the Reds in the Eighties, the return journey was dangerous.

The Guv'nors firm from Man City would wait, ready to ambush the bus with bricks and bottles as it came past Maine Road. They knew all the Collyhurst Devils were onboard, so up went the chant of the IRA song, "Duck boys, the bullets are coming," as the windows were peppered. The drivers would abandon the bus and fair dos to them. It was always the upper deck that copped for it, so Joe Public remained relatively safe downstairs.

When we'd get up to the big colleges, the teachers - never mind the kids - would be quaking in their boots. We looked a sight! We were dressed in hand-me-down togs and were all

MANCHESTER MAVERICKS

smoking woodbines. The boots we wore were like Billy's Boots and most were borrowed from older kids, so we had to pack newspaper inside the toe-caps to stop them from falling off.

After years playing on the flagstones and cobbles, playing on their lush, green pitch was some beano! Mr Keao would smirk, then tell us to get potting, as the pitches looked like snooker surfaces. The comments from the teachers in the home teams' dressing room were along the lines of, "They're just a bunch of cowboys," and so the name stuck.

Billy Bollard from Monsall was our captain in the main Senior League. The school had got his date of birth wrong so when the top year left, it turned out he'd have to stay for another half term. Billy was not only years ahead of us in the looks department, he was also a ten-pint-a-night kid, covered in tattoos by the famous cockney, Cash Cooper. Cash's dog Fang was tattooed (I think you'd get jail for that these days), but he wouldn't tattoo our hands until we were 16. Billy had "Cut here" tattooed across his Adam's apple, along with a dotted line, showing where to cut. Later, in his early Thirties, he went to the karzy in his local, The Queens, and passed away from the demon drink.

I will have to pop the question to the mavs - which football team do they support and for what reason? My own answer's obvious. My granddad and my mother never missed a game during the Fifties, this was when the whole nation took the Busby Babes to heart. All the stories I heard, about how their coffins were lined up inside Old Trafford following that fatal air crash were sad, even as a kid.

I first got into writing through the football fan clubs. While doing jail in a Swiss police holding block, the FA Cup Final fell on the same day as my son's 21st. I posted him my ticket and wrote to the Swiss Red Devils asking for a few souvenirs to send him and they printed my letter. Amazingly, it found its way to the lads from *Red Issue*, who then asked me to pen a few pages for their book, Red Army General. So it's no surprise my book, 'Grafters' was reviewed by all the football fanzines. But no matter what you write, it can never please everyone.

Newcastle's fanzine slagged it off, saying, "Blaney - what a

INTRODUCTION

wanker, not going to the Cup Final in Barcelona in 1999. Instead, he stayed at home watching it with his ma. What a plonker!" It's a fair enough comment from the Land of the Penguins. The fact is, I cherish being a plonker on that occasion. Having been to so many major sporting events, I felt the perfect place to watch that final was with my Mother, Syl. She's such a huge supporter, known by everyone at Old Trafford, where they treat her like the Queen.

I've had reviews in magazines like *The Big Issue,* in national and local papers, and even in sex mags. I think that even bad publicity is better than none at all. The worst review I had for 'Grafters' came from my own backyard, in *Red Issue.* They went into one about me be-moaning my working-class background. I knew 'Grafters' was never going to be everyone's cup of tea and I wasn't expecting many five-star comments, but all the lads agree that, coming from the same manor, so to speak, they should help to plug it. Priced at only £7.99, it's a fact it costs double that each Saturday to buy their fanzines and match programmes. It'll be interesting to hear what they've got to say about that.

One fella's comment on the Amazon website says how much he enjoyed reading 'Grafters' on his flight to the States. He said his wife read it on the journey home and was horrified! Footie mags are lost without our stories. Sure, the Man U roller coaster fills their pockets, but the fat cat soft-arses, writing their own cheques, are in a prime position to ask us what's needed at Old Trafford. But they never will.

A supporters' club is what's needed first. Next time you're in Barcelona, do as we did. Go into their supporters' club, smoke El Tel cigars (named after Terry Venables), drink beer and wine with the Catalans and eat their tapas. No doubt you'll end the night with their local hookers. I swear we got on like a house on fire and were always invited back.

The best thing about going to City's Maine Road was their supporters' club; eating a real Lancashire Hot Pot, washed down with a few pints while watching the build-up on the big screen.

Paddy Crerand's got it right, suggesting local lads under the age of 21 should get a section of their own, with membership cards allowing them a ticket to every other game. At the moment, the full right side is reserved for the media, and it doesn't take a rocket scientist to work out how much real passion they contribute. The Seventies are seen as the heyday, when the normal turnout was anything from 56,000 to over 60,000 supporters, even in the Second Division. Our away support was bigger than most teams' best home turnout. Fuck me, we only won one trophy in a whole decade and, back then, we could never match the Mickey's success. It was painfully hard at times, believe you me, but we stayed loyal to the core. Half the goals we scored were down to us sucking them in with all our chanting and the endless noise we made. Nowadays, we're all pushed and priced out and many now support FC United, an off-shoot team formed when the Glazers family took over United. At least there they can afford to take the family and buy a pie and programme.

But United will always be our religion, although the price of success has cost the working class our place in modern footie. We can no longer stand together and have a nobble or a singsong. As Eddie Beef says in Cass Pennant's best-selling book 'Top Boys', "It's one big fucking rip-off. They will be sorry when the Sky bubble goes pop. They will be coming around to our houses saying, 'Please come to the match, you can stand and swear as much as you want lads, we're fucking skint'."

When I passed for Manchester Federation Youth Club, Granddad treated me to a spend-up in Lewis's, the only store where you could buy football merchandise. I came away with a United tracksuit, which, in the Sixties, along with the shirts, never had a crest. But just the cherry red was enough, and there was a throw-over hood on the trackie top.

Later, when I was picked to join Oldham Youth, this trackie was a Godsend. I can honestly say that many a footballer has cried from the cold when they played on Little Wembley. It's still there today and it's a fact the only colder place for football training is Grimsby. My best mate, Carl Bailey, wasn't sure which sport to take up. Granada had just filmed him at school becoming the ABA Boxing Champion, but he'd also been asked to join Oldham on schoolboy terms. After his first training session, I had to carry

INTRODUCTION

him on my back because he was so stiff with cold and when he hit the first team's warm bath, the shock nearly killed him. On the bus home that night, he said, "Fuck that lark," and went back to boxing instead. He went on to fight on the same bill as Muhammad Ali in the Royal Albert Hall.

When we left school it was straight into the Smithfield Market with your brand new boot clogs - well the biz and so efficient at insulating your feet, we never had to wear Salfords (socks). Most of us had worked cash-in-hand during the summer holidays, but that was on the fruit, which was a totally different ball game in the foot department. Barrow boys wore Docs, the porters working the flower stalls wore army sandals and the salesmen wore black brogues. The salesmen's graft is a totally different world these days. You see, in our day, you had to be bent to work there. It was where the Quality Street gang were based and they used pubs like The Glue Pot, The Lower Turks Head and The George & Dragon (which later became The Band On The Wall). These pubs opened at 8am sharp and you had to be connected in order to gain entrance.

There was one stall for yoghurts, milk and eggs. It had a kind of curtain behind the salesman, which I took a good peek around one day. Behind were market coppers, waving in two wagons full of hookie gear, and this was the start of the mock auctions which were huge on Oldham Street in the Seventies. When the big companies shut down early, their forecourts were set up like mini cinemas, with hardcore porn, magazines and toys for sale and the market coppers ran this alongside the Quality Street gang – they were all were bent, but tough as fuck!

The coppers had to deal with the rowdy ruffians, as being a vibrant place with plenty of comings-and-goings, the market was a magnet for shady deals. In the early days, the Bully Boys gang would make their way up Rochdale Road, steaming into punters' carts and robbing them blind.

The Smithfield Market was like a college of crime and although most Collyhurst kids have done time in approved schools, detention centres and borstals, our experience on the market had put us in good stead. We had to learn the tricks. Our stall, Frank Coleman's, was situated at the far end next to the small toilet on Salmon Street. We had to get to the front entrance early, when the wagons from Aberdeen, Grimsby and Fleetwood came in, otherwise you might get swamped or trapped in the hectic traffic. It was a big no-no to try jibbing through the fruit and veg, as the fruit hawks would scan for any new faces to be had over. Your prize boxes of fish fillets were easy pickings for the clued-up Barrow Boys, who, sharp as Sheffield Stainless, would take them and replace them with a sack of turnips.

You had your work cut out at Christmas, as everyone on the fish and poultry had to graft each other's trades and even the professional fish porters dreaded the trip through the fruit. You'd tuck the turkeys into hiding places so, when you did get raided, there was a chance they'd rob all the shite, like boxes of offal and waste. We'd buy ice from Fred the Iceman (that's all he sold), either in huge kilo blocks, pineapple chunks, or dry flakes, which were the dearest. We went for the kilo blocks, which we'd sledgehammer and sprinkle over the rotten and filleted fish. It really kept you on your toes.

The mavericks' Whit Week tales will be tall, no doubt, as the Whitsuntide processions have been a tradition in Manchester since the days of George III. By the middle of the nineteenth century, there were more than 12,000 participants, rising to 23,000 in 1885. Not only were there Anglicans but Catholics too, who were just as keen to affirm their faith right up into the Seventies. However, the troubles in Northern Ireland brought the bombing campaign to the mainland, so the Whit Week processions had to be phased out due to the possibility of big trouble between the two faiths.

I must be one of very few that can recall marching with both the Catholics and Protestants during the Whitsun holidays. I was so intrigued by the Protestant bands that I couldn't help but get involved. One thing was for sure; it was the only time of year you were certain to get new clobber.

I joined the Cubs and had the hots for all the Brownies. As I looked older than my age, I was offered the great honour of carrying the Scouts flag, which had shoulder straps, attached to a

INTRODUCTION

navy belt. The belt had a small, leather container in which it held the base of the pole. I had to have a good pair of lungs that day, shouting, "Left! Left! Left, right, left!" when the bands had a short break.

It was hypnotising, rolling down Rochdale Road in a trance. I honestly thought this must be how they'd train people to fight wars, with military-style drums, bugles and sticks banging in time, which made your hair stand up. Sailor and Brownie girls were on the floats, holding Union Jacks, while the floats were led by a brass band and men in tall top hats.

This would all kick off at seven in the morning, and we'd arrive in Albert Square around the time of the nine bells. It took a few hours for the others to get in place, after which we'd head back home via Oldham Road. The local pubs got the okay to stay open all day and night, and consequently they got hammered. There was no room left for a fly and the heat soon had the older lot dancing and singing in the streets, sporting Kiss Me Quick and Dirty Dick hats. They were in fine voice, with red roses in abundance.

We were lucky to experience these walks at their peak. In the Eighties, the Catholics carried on the tradition, but in a very low-key way. They'd meet in Crown Square, where just a handful of people would walk the five minutes to the Town Hall for mass, then go home. It was shite. I took my old dear a few times, but we had a better time in the Cheshire Cheese pub with the locals from the Victoria Dwellings, all singing Collyhurst songs. This pub was once run by Collyhurst's champion boxer, Johnny King, whose Lonsdale belt took pride of place in a cabinet on the bar. Now Collyhurst Village has a walk named after him.

Bit by bit, over the last few years, Whit Week has begun to creep back in. The Irish now have a huge day out on St Pat's, and St George's Day sees the bands back on Oldham Road. If you call in Billy Green's, you'll get a blast from the past - the bulldog songs are still sung. Two years ago, Sky TV contacted me, asking where they could find an old-school pub to film for The UK's Toughest Pubs. It's no surprise I picked Billy Greens during Whitsuntide. The deal was that they'd interview world famous boxing trainer Brian Hughes and I, where we'd be credited as Brian Hughes, Author and MBE, and Colin Blaney, Author. The Cockney pundits, who contributed to the show, never even came up to the pub – they just talked for a few seconds in a safe studio about how you should never go into a pub on the Collyhurst estate. Their names, and the titles of the magazines they worked for, were splashed all over the screen, but there was fuck all about us.

It took me four weeks to put our part of that show together. I said to the head fella, "How many book sales do you think I've missed out on because of that?" as the show still gets shown world wide today.

I even sent the same television crew to Rhyl, where my son, Lee and his friends graft the fairground. They shot for three days, interviewing them for The UK's Toughest Seaside Resorts, with a promise to add "Thanks to Colin Blaney," to the credits. But there was fuck all again. When I finally asked Sky how it had happened, their excuse was that the main man had left a message on someone's desk to confirm names but in his rush to leave for the European Championship in Portugal the note got lost! Sky said they'd send me a compensation cheque for 130 pounds, which came weeks later.

The next time I was asked to film was for Bravo with Danny Dyer, who starred in the hit film, Football Factory, about football hooliganism. We copied it, street-style and the resulting show was named The Real Football Factories. I was promised I'd be credited as Colin Blaney, Author. Again, nothing. I got through to Bravo, who promised to fix it and when the show next aired, my name did appear, but with the tag 'Red Army Thug'!

Pubs and clubs play a part in the UK's new binging society. In our day, the drinking was under control. We all love a drink but the problem with booze seems to be its availability – 24-7, anywhere. I remember the first German motorway I travelled down in 1978, which had booze, wine and champagne on sale in the same section as your petrol. Then later, in the city of Köln, we got bottles of Becks in McDonald's. I spent between six and seven years grafting Deutschland, but I'm sure the UK's not ready for

INTRODUCTION

that kind of step up the ladder. Here in Collyhurst you can buy it at seven in the morning from the backdoor of the butcher's, so long as you know the tap and whistle.

We'll touch on stories of Manchester's pubs and clubs from the past, but drinking nowadays is dangerous. It seems you have to be mullered to blend in with the crowd and the amount of pissheads in need of a stay in The Priory is reaching its peak. In my day, there were no such places as detox units. Even counselling has reached its limit, but the only type of counselling you'd receive in my day was from your friends and neighbours.

To combat drinking, estate pubs these days make sure youths are over 21 and aren't wearing hoods or trackies. Most pubs keep the main room for the over-Forties, where you ring a bell to gain entrance. It's sad to say that I cannot stand most pubs nowadays; the culture of chatting has disappeared and the new, jet set ones treat you like scummy shite.

My all-time favourite fashion came from the skinhead era of 1969-1972, when we had working-class stamped all over us. Close-cropped hair, sheepskin jackets, crombies, Harrington and Levi jackets, Ben Sherman and Jaytex shirts with braces, stone-white Levis, Prince of Wales and Wrangler jeans and cords. Oxford and Royal brogues, worn during the week would be replaced on Saturdays by Bovver boots when I was a Stretford-Ender. So, with the mavs, we'll be going back over a few decades, hearing about their favourite and least favourite fashions.

My least favourite has to be the fashion worn by today's hoods. When break-dancing, the Buffalo Girls and Grand Master Flash came over from the States 20 years ago, hoods were well in vogue. They were worn, not only as fashion statements, available in all colours and fabrics, but were also worn for keeping fit. The only time the hoods came over our heads was when it rained. Today they're never worn off the head and bleak blacks and greys seem to be the favoured colours. The kids all look like the gang from the film, 'The Wanderers' who were called the Ducky Boys, they lived underground and were all full-time class A drug-users.

The thing is, in the mid-Eighties, we all wore Lacoste, Armani and Hugo Boss tops over our hoods, but the youth's clobber nowadays all looks like one brand: Market Tackle. Worse still is when they do wear the hood down – they look like death warmed up. I feel sorry for this generation, as they've got all this attitude, yet don't have a jar of glue (clue) as to where to take it, or what to do with it. Thank fuck in my day we had healthy heroes we could aspire to and in Collyhurst, the saying went, you were either a footballer, a boxer or a thief. Now any bod in bling takes the biscuit.

The funniest fashion I have ever seen has got to be the Pink Panthers on the Monsall estate, so called because, first thing in the morning at the shops, young girls and their mothers sport bare feet, or pink socks and flip-flops. They've got pink streaks in their hair, wear pink pyjamas with pink thongs hanging out, and many of them stay dressed this way for the whole day. Think pink.

I'll be asking about common Manchester sayings and their origins. My personal favourite comes from the mid-Seventies when my mates and I were learning the sneak. In Bognor Regis we teamed up with some street-smart Scouse zappers and Dublin dippers, who worked with the tough guys from Glasgow, who would say, "Hey, you think you're a tuff guy?" or "Tuff cookie". We loved the way everything they said was "tuff this" and "tuff that".

Hanging around with these bandits, we soon got a feel for the tricks of the trade and also began to pick up the Scouse lingo. An example is their way of calling the police "bizzies". We'd all grown up with Top Cat, who ran a firm of alley cats. His Achilles Heel was Officer Dibble, who was always on Top Cat's case. So the name Dibble caught on in Manchester after we all began using it. I was recently told the word "Dibble" had made it into the Street Dictionary.

Now, when interviewing the mavs, the following subject was without a doubt the one to strike a sour note. I asked what could be done to combat today's yob culture? Are they the monsters we bred? And should they be given the short, sharp shock treatment, as we were given when up in front of the juvenile courts?

The first time I had my collar felt I was cautioned for robbing teachers' purses. We all knew you were a cert to go down the

INTRODUCTION

third time you went to court, but many went down straight away. On my third appearance I was sent to Wythenshawe Rose Hill Detention Centre for 28 days and on release day I was back in school in time for dinner. I swear no one blinked an eyelid, it was so common.

It seems more like 13 times before offenders get sent away these days, where they're given computer games, Sky TV, tunes, phone cards and the like. Fuck me, the only perk we were given was on Sundays after scran, when we got 15 minutes of the BBC World News and the sports round-up. We were also allowed just 10 minutes in the library - three books max. I always came out with Edge stories, a bad-arse cowboy who carried a cut-throat blade in a pouch round the back of his neck for easy access, after his wife had been raped and killed by Red Indians. I read them all before moving on to stories about Adam Steele, who was another cowboy with a silver shotgun. Looking back, I treasure this treat, as from that point onwards I became a bookworm. A tip I received from a librarian was to choose a number and, whenever you reached that page in a book, make a crease. In jail you waste so much time reading and then thinking, "Bollocks, I've read this before". So whichever book you fancy, that certain page gets checked before you start reading. During my three months in the detention centre it never happened, but serving a three-year sentence in prison, it happened many a time, more so in German gaols, where there's not such a wide choice of books.

Personally, I feel sorry for the hoods, whose lives all revolve around their estate, which provides their only bit of safety. We used to travel all over Lancashire looking for cash-in-hand work on farms or in factories. We even used other youth clubs over in Ardwick or Ancoats. But these days, the hoods are all scared shitless to venture out. Not only are they lost, but they'd have to mix with strangers - a massive no-no to them. Their way of speaking is all mumble-tumble, with bits of Dread and Rasta, added to by the sucking of teeth. In our day, doing that would get you slagged off royal, like you were copying Skippy the Kangaroo.

One major headache I have with hoodies is the way they play their pods at full blast on the bus, so everyone can hear their tunes. I love all tunes myself, but the quality of these pods is so weak. OK, big deal, they hold thousands of tunes, but thousands of Mancs get their heads battered by these hoods on a daily basis. They buzz off the control they have over the older generation, but in our day, friends and neighbours were allowed to give you a firm clout if you were being a nause. When we were Boot Boys, aggro was on the menu daily, but no way did we ever give the public grief. Even when we bumped into rival gangs, most of the time the two cocks would just slug it out between them, and we only used weapons like our Levi belts, car aerials and steel combs when in trouble or overwhelmed.

Manchester's now the ASBO capital of Europe, but as to whether ASBOs are having any positive affect, I really doubt it. The hoods are as proud as peacocks, rolling up their trackie bottoms to expose their tags for all to see. They think it's even better to have their photos up, naming and shaming them, as it gives them notoriety in Shameless Land.

That hit TV show isn't a patch on how things really are on the north side estates. Here, we call it "Tameless". Last year, the head of the BBC visited Manchester and asked if I could get the cameras into the homes of the notorious families, to help them film a fly-on-the-wall documentary. The problem was, they wanted to film all day long, with joke wages. But these families earn more than that in just one day's graft.

An uncut version of Shameless would have been a monster hit, but maybe a programme like that could only be made when the BBC move their arses up here to Salford. They need to re-think the way they view us, instead of thinking of people from anywhere north of Watford Gap as thickos with flat caps with whippets. I've got news for the Cockneys, though - we view those from anywhere south of Stoke as Southern Softies!

When we all became football hooligans, we were forced by the courts to attend scrubs (attendance centres) every Saturday afternoon. So when the games kicked off at 3pm, we'd be stuck cleaning public halls. If you messed this up, the court would send you down for 30 days at Rose Hill young offenders' institute in Wythenshawe and after this stint, you'd return to court. If you'd

INTRODUCTION

been bad-arse or a smart-arse, a further 30 days awaited you, and for some kids this could happen up to three times. The older thugs and thieves would get a shock when the judge gave them the choice between an 18-month jail sentence and three years in the army. The smart ones chose the services and came out as citizens. Many went on to become chefs in top restaurants, others got driving licences for wagons and found good work.

I truly believe people like myself should be given the chance to work with the hoods, to help convince them a criminal career isn't the way to go. But you may as well be pissing in the wind. So I'll be asking the mavericks what they feel the future of yob culture will bring.

When we left the Smithfield Market in the early Seventies, its closure was sad for all the grafters and the new market on Ashton New Road was so small, it felt alien. Times were changing with the high street supermarkets becoming more common.

I went to work for the biggest stone-cleaning company in the UK, Clean Walls. My first job was sandblasting the Manchester University, which took over a year, and across the road is the Holy Name church, which we also sandblasted, both inside and out. We even cleaned the Smithfield Market, which has now been replaced by town apartments.

When I walk past these buildings and see them shining in the sun, I feel so proud and my work with Clean Walls led to my fascination with the local architecture. So it's no surprise I've asked the mavs which buildings are their favourites in Manchester, and why?

Manchester's music scene has also played a massive part in my love of the city. My favourite album has to be John Holt's 1,000 Volts of Holt, which got me right into reggae. I saw him play live at the PSV club in Hulme, which later became better known for its links with the punk scene when Tony Wilson took charge. Then there was 'The Clash' at the Electric Circus on Collyhurst Street during their White Riot Tour, when a coach-load of Cockneys turned up wearing pins and bin-liners. It got better inside the venue, where the Nazi punk women were getting gang-banged back stage.

MANCHESTER MAVERICKS

But topping them all was when Roxy Music played the Kings Hall in Belle Vue in 1975. While the Hall was being built in 1910, two kings - Edward VII and George V – reigned, hence the name. Also used for boxing, wrestling, demonstrations and exhibitions, it had a stage in the middle with the best acoustics in the land.

That night, when Brian Ferry walked out on stage singing The Bogus Man, dressed in a Lonsdale top, Levis and green Dunlop Flash trainers, I thought, "This fella's the King of Cool". The first time I heard Love is the Drug during the encore, it blew my mind and it still does today. That was a life-changing night, as from then on I copied Ferry and took to the casual look. I still adore Roxy Music and their recent show for Live Aid in Berlin spoke volumes.

My last visit to the Kings Hall, before it was demolished, was for the Bay City Rollers, with all the kids in tears, overcome and passing out. I worked selling strips of tartan for a pound a time, which the kids wore around their heads, necks and wrists. With the whole roll costing just a tenner, I came away with £250 profit – a fortune in the Seventies.

I'll be asking the mavs which music events in Manchester had an impact on their lives, and for what reason?

I'll also be asking the mavericks about their favourite people – those who achieved something, be it fame or whatever. Even if their heroes are not originally from Manchester, it doesn't matter. Look at someone like George Best – a real maverick who meant a lot to the people of Manchester.

My own top three – those who meant the most to me - happen to be Collyhurst Cowboys. When I was growing up, Busby Babe Carlo Sartori lived in the flats. As I was a tall kid, I was moved from the junior yard to play in goal for the seniors in the mid-Sixties, where I made the best save of my life in the dying minutes, denying Carlo the winner. Soon afterwards we saw him play for United at Old Trafford and he really stuck out with his carrot-top head. He wasn't the most skilful player, but he was a grafter and played out of his skin during the three FA Cup Semis versus Leeds. There were no goals until the third game at Bolton when, at the last moment, Billy Bremner forced one

INTRODUCTION

in for the sheep-shaggers. I was devastated as I wanted Carlo to play at Wembley so I could tell folk how I'd once had him under control. He left to play in Italy not long after, winning the cup with Bologna before returning to Manchester where he now runs a knife-sharpening biz.

Next is footballer Brian Kidd, who helped out the Colly kids in our local youth club. Brian Hughes helped with the boxing training, while Kiddo coached us at table tennis. At that time we had two teams: A and B, who won all the leagues. One year, when the B team won the cup final, Kiddo did his jacking jump, which later became a trademark in his Man U days. Kiddo and Carlo were always at our school, giving away signed footballs and joining in with the school presentations.

But my all-time favourite Manc has to be Norbert Stiles, the Toothless Tiger, who was given that nickname by Sister Veronica while playing football on the schoolyard. Years later, she also gave me my nickname; as I was full of energy, she said, "He's full of beans," so the name Beaner has stuck with me ever since.

When I went to see Nobby play, the first thing I noticed was the way he'd come running out of the tunnel and head straight over to the edge. He'd jump up and down to get a feel of the turf, then re-lace his boots. Only recently when I read his book did I twig there was a double reason for this. True, his laces may have needed tightening or loosening, but he also admitted it was a way of calming his nerves, a chance to get his breathing together before he turned into a Toothless Tiger and he was as blind as a bat. It was only when Busby saw him having problems, scanning the team sheet one day, that Sir Matt told him to sort himself out with some contact lenses. And that soon improved his game.

His passion to win influenced me throughout my own footballing days and I copied him, even down to the laces. If you look at the cover of his book, there he is, re-doing his laces with a huge grin. Quality.

The next question I asked the mavs was, do you respect the police? There was one giant local copper, Scarface, who won the utmost respect and in Collyhurst Library there's a photo of him. He really did rule the roost for more than 20 years in Willert

MANCHESTER MAVERICKS

Street and people were in awe of him, with his huge, thick scar. Rumour had it that a local villain had slashed him, but this isn't true - he got the scar during The Great War.

He was more than a dab-hand with his cosh, not only using it for cracking ribs and skulls, but like an expert darts player, he'd catch thieves around the legs with it when they tried to do a runner. Scarface wouldn't allow any street hawks on his patch selling swag, playing illegal cards, dice and pitch games, and he hated the drunks. He'd bang his cosh all over the cobbles and lampposts to gain attention when he needed help. And no one dared to refuse.

In our day, there was one copper who would jump in the taxi at Piccadilly with us, after he'd clocked on to us shoplifting. We always went for a sack-full of Levis, or Wranglers, and Officer Dibble would demand a cut. He was a pure pisshead who wouldn't give a toss about coming out on the lash with the grafters. But the next time you met him you could have been in the cells, where he'd give you no space or joy whatsoever!

I've had dealings with the Dibble all over the globe. I've done porridge in Strangeways, Walton, Wormwood Scrubs, Durham, Kirkham, Ashford, Lincoln, twice in Köln, twice in Oldenburg and twice in Kiel, plus Meppen, Amsterdam, Rotterdam, Zutphen, Leeuwarden, Luzern, Malmö, Bergen and Antwerp. I spent years in the cells. Once, after the Strangeways riot, we got shipped out to the Doncaster Police Secure Unit, which was built for all the Cockney armed robbers. We expected a hard time but the Dibble were nice as pie, arranging for us to see the United versus Palace final, letting us eat the same food as them, and the visits were relaxed.

I reckon the UK's Dibble are double sound. If you ever have the misfortune of getting banged up abroad, you'll soon wish you were back in Blighty. Just ask my mate Danny Healy who took a trip around the world after serving seven years for Post Office robberies. He called into Tokyo with a bag of weed, but unknown to him Japan have very strict policies on drugs, whereas in the UK now, if you're busted for a weed offence, it can be sorted out in customs without the courts even getting involved. Danny's

INTRODUCTION

now into his fifth year in a jail where you dare not even talk to a screw, or else you'll feel his bamboo. They have signs painted on the floor to show prisoners the way as they have to keep their heads down wherever they walk.

The UK police have to cope with the biggest drug intake in Europe and the gang and gun cultures aren't going away. To cap it all, we've also got the worst binge-drinkers and drivers in the world. Today, Booze Britain sees slappers wearing thongs up to their necks (women wear more on the beach than out on the binge) and the fellas are all spitting, swearing and cursing the Plod from the word go! Fuck me, in our day it was more likely you'd wind up in an ambulance following some treatment from the Dibble. The digs the Police gave out would be full on and even the Black Marias would be toppling over with the hidings they dished out. You'd be banged up for a full weekend and on the following Monday, the court would be 99 per cent likely to send you to grisly Risley Remand Centre. The fact is that the police had to charge you with assault in order to cover their own arses and I can hardly remember anyone getting a "not guilty" verdict.

At the end of today's TV police shows, you're told about the outcome of the court cases. Hardly any of the culprits get a sentence, just warnings or a fine at the most. I've felt shame watching English skinheads in bright yellow and pink Ben Sherman shirts, crying like pussycats when the cuffs go on. The fact is, skinheads these days are more likely to be seen down in the gay village on stag nights. It's only the Polish and German skinheads who are the real deal and it's always the English casuals who fight them, never the English skinheads.

I've asked the mavericks who they respect in life. For me, without a doubt it has to be the emergency services, who have saved my bacon so many times it's beyond belief. They're always getting stick about how late they are, but if all the dickheads who ring 999 for fuck-all reason would get a life, we'd have a better ambulance service. Just think of all the abuse they have to put up with, not only on the streets but back at the hospitals too.

The last question I asked was simple and the answer was a big "No!" from most mavericks: Have you any regrets?

MANCHESTER MAVERICKS

I have so many I dare not go into detail, but the main one concerns The Wide Awake Firm, of which I was the ringleader. The other grafters gave us that name at the concerts where we'd sell swag. It was down to our wired attitude and it summed us up perfectly. We went on to become Europe's most prolific gang of sneak thieves, banging Jacks (tills), pick-pocketing, robbing the tom (jewellery) shops and grafting with the elite from Yugoslavia, Italy, France, Algeria and even South America, where the grafters are trained in crime schools from an early age. Without a doubt, the South Americans are the best pickpockets in the world.

At the 1988 Olympics in Seoul we worked selling tickets with the American grafters, who call touting 'scalping'. Their ways of robbing were very carefully worked out, with their set-ups sometimes taking days to complete. They had all the best qualities for us to pick up our grafting methods from, and we were sneaking, snatching, dipping, conning, committing fraud and banging the Jacks within days.

They invited us over the pond to graft, but like a soft cunt I got to thinking, "What if I get nicked bang at it?" I do regret not having a bash, as just two or three jobs would have been enough to make a fortune. I would've hit the Jewish diamond markets, an idea I got from the film Marathon Man, where the fella sells his bling in Brooklyn. There's no doubt we would've scored, but reality bites for a grafter and no matter how good you are, on many occasions you'll end up locked up. Most of the time we sailed through the police pulls, even with the evidence stacked overwhelmingly against us. But we soon learnt that jail is an occupational hazard.

We once hit Taiwan's top tom shop, scoring a full tray of gold Cartiers. But at the airport the following day, the passport control's sly eyes were double-clocking everyone and I knew it was about to come on top. It was like the scene in Midnight Express, when Billy Hayes fronts the Turks. I said, "Let's have a change of clobber," as it was time for what we called The Bull Dog Mode. We'd used this tactic at customs all over Europe, where we'd dress in Union Jack shorts and t-shirts, showing our tattoos with our cameras clicking away like tourists. We'd even

INTRODUCTION

asked them for passport stamps as souvenirs, which we'd use to ghost onto the flights.

If it had come on top, we would've been looking at a sentence of between 20 and 25 years hard labour, where a bowl of rice with crushed cockroaches and bugs would've been our daily chow. The Tiddly-Winks are tough fuckers and no doubt a tough time would've awaited the Wide Awake lads if we'd got caught.

So why did the Land of Hot Dogs have me backing down? I can only put it down to the James Hadley Chase books I read in Stoke Heath borstal. As soon as I'd read the first, 'No Orchids For Miss Blandish' about a gang who were led by their mother, I was hooked on the cocktail of crime, sex, adventure and never-ending chases. Only when I was out on Civvy Strasse I missed one thing – the jail stories.

I switched to true crime mags, which contained 90 per cent Yank stories and one man's name kept coming up - Edward Bunker. Many years later I got to meet him at the launch of his biography: 'Mr Blue', the title of which he took from the small role he played in the film 'Reservoir Dogs'. Bunker tells it how it was; living on the mean streets of LA aged just five and stuck in reform schools from the age of seven to thirteen. He started his con life aged fifteen and, when he was just seventeen years old, he entered the notorious US jail, San Quentin, where he was the youngest ever con with a seven-year sentence. Many a time he'd had to use a tool (shank) and he joined in with the Chicano gangs, who were mainly Mexicans and were always at war with the Washington DC blacks. He describes how you're known as fresh fish when you first enter the holding tanks and many end up as punks (sex slaves). When confronted, the saying was, "It's blood on the blade or shit on my dick, cowboy," and I do wonder what I'd have done in that position. All I can say is, grafters have to create an edge because they live on the edge. I'd even say we're born on the edge. Peter Walsh, author of Gang War - The Inside Story of Manchester's Gangs, says it best: "Some people live for the day – a grafter lives for the minute".

BILLY HOPKINS

Billy Hopkins (better known to his family and friends as Wilfred Hopkins) was born in Collyhurst in 1928 and attended schools in Manchester. Before going into higher education, he worked as a copy boy for the Manchester Guardian. He later studied at the Universities of London, Manchester and Leeds and was involved in school-teaching and teacher-training in Liverpool, Manchester, Salford and Glasgow. He also worked in African universities in Kenya, Zimbabwe and Malawi.

He found fame in later life as the best-selling author of a series of novels profiling life in working class North Manchester before, during and just after the Second World War. Mr Hopkins, author, husband and father of six, died aged 83 in 2012.

I was born in 1928 only a stone's throw away from Les Dawson's stalking ground. It is also the birthplace of the actor John Thaw; there must be something in the water! I was brought up in the buildings on Collyhurst Road; these dwellings were built in the 1880's. The iron bridge that led you over the river Irk still remains there today as are the 77 steps which take you over the huge railway bridge onto Barry's rubbish tip which is still standing.

Memories of the smog and fog are still crystal clear in my mind, this part of Collyhurst was known as the dip (being down). It was without a doubt the worst area of Manchester - just check the health records and the death rates, they were appalling! Entire families were wiped out by the cholera outbreaks.

Besides the open flowing sewers that ran into the Irk, the river also carried all kinds of toxic shite; it was horrendous when it overflowed. All the houses and pubs used sand bags to keep it at bay yet still the sight was a grey cesspool of filth and garbage containing rusty bedsteads, decayed mattresses, twisted bicycles and decomposing dogs half eaten by the rats.

Recalling my time at Saint Wilfred's school, the beautiful Sister

BILL HOPKINS

Helen comes to mind whom I for sure looked up to as a Saint. She even resembled the statue of Saint Therese of Lisieux, the 'Little Flower of Jesus' which I won for answering the catechism questions.

One sad day she called a meeting to which all the school had to attend to announce that Teddy Smith had drowned in the Irk whilst throwing stones at the water rats, dangerous as it was, the swift current swept him away into the sewers.

The biggest day for me as a kid was at the 'Order of Rechabites' founded in 1835 in the Temperance Missionary Hall. It was common knowledge amongst the Catholics of Collyhurst that the Rechabites, despite the fame of their Kazoo with comb and paper band, were misguided heretics who were bound to go straight to hell for believing the right religion. On the other hand it was also common knowledge they held a Christmas party of breathtaking magnificence and I got a ticket from Dad. It was the equivalent to a Cup Final ticket for an adult. Perhaps he'd won it in a game of crib or found it outside Tubby Ainsworth's pub! I didn't care where it came from, the only thing on my mind was that I actually had a ticket.

Mam made sure I was in ship shape for six o'clock. I was shining like a polished red apple, and then on went my jersey; navy blue trousers with a striped elastic belt; long stockings with the colourful tops and finally my black leather boots which my Dad had buffed and buffed until they were gleaming. Mam said, "eat their cakes an' jelly son, but try not to join in their prayers and hymns if you can avoid it. That's a good boy." I recall to this day, ten tables had been laid out with patterned paper covers, serviettes, crackers and party hats. Seated at the tables were sixty boisterous kids almost wetting themselves with excitement, all waiting impatiently for the festivities to begin.

A tall bearded gentleman in a black suit (not unlike the pictures of Abraham Lincoln) appeared on stage, clapped his hands for attention and intoned his best church voice: "It does my heart good to see so many bright and shining little faces here before me. And this is what we are doing tonight, for the dear little children of Collyhurst have indeed come unto us to celebrate the birth of our Lord and saviour, Jesus Christ. But before we begin our feast, my dear children, let us stand, bow our heads and thank the great Lord above for his munificence."

For us lot the speech was not only incomprehensible but unbearably long, we were all eager to get on with the serious business at hand, namely the dispatch of all that seductive food sitting out there in the kitchen. The kids of Collyhurst however, had learned a pragmatism that John Dewey would have been proud of. They knew which side their bread was buttered on, and if to get all those lovely comestibles they had to take part in a few curious rituals, so be it.

All present we bowed our heads, surreptitiously I made a cross with my two index fingers like I'd seen in a Dracula picture, to ward off evil spirits. Then the nosh was brought in and what food! For some time the only sound in the hall were of kids chomping their way through mountains of food.

We'd never seen such a spread! Potted meat sandwiches quickly gobbled up followed by mince pies, chocolate cake and a choice of three kinds of jelly – the whole lot being washed down with copious quantities of sweet, milky tea served by the funereal Rechabites from large metal teapots.

When the repast had been devoured it became time to pay the piper and the price was the singing of hymns, Rechabite hymns were only just short of devil worship. The Kazoo band assembled on stage and began to tune up like the Hallé orchestra. The band struck up with its tiny zuzzing sound and they were off. With great gusto, the Rechabites and their followers sang out, their voices ringing to the rafters "Stand up for Jesus! Fight the good fight! Tell me the old, old story". None of these had ever been heard in Saint Patrick's church, I was convinced that my soul was turning blacker and blacker with every note I sang.

Next came the silent films - the memory of the hymn singing episode was soon lost in laughter at the antics of Charlie Chaplin and the deadpan face of Buster Keaton. Santa ho-hoed his way into the hall, the red robed figure must have been mad. With wild abandon he handed out boxed games of ludo, lotto, draughts, tiddlywinks and snakes and ladders. But like all the other delights that evening, they had to be paid for. This time with the prayers of this misguided religion. What would Father O'Brien say if he could see me now? I could hear the priests voice echoing in my head: "Prayers of a false religion… Grievous sin… Doomed to hell forever."

The most important event in the schools calendar were the Whit Weeks Walks. A few weeks before, all the Collyhurst kids were taken over to May's pawnbrokers to be kitted out: new shoes and stockings, grey breeches, a brightly coloured elastic belt with a hooked clasp, a new white shirt and a silk tie, a beautiful navy blue blazer with an embroidered emblem on the pocket and to crown it all off a new cap with the letters "SC" for Saint Chad's emblazoned on the front.

Whit Monday was for the Protestants. When it was sunny they all said "God knows his own" and if it rained "God waters his little flowers" we used the same expressions, it was one of the few things we had in common. Whit Friday was reserved for the Catholics. Churches all over the Salford diocese blew dust off the banners, statues, crucifixes and display floats bringing them out of storage. These were decked and covered in a profusion of beautiful flowers, ribbons and gaily coloured silks. I was open mouthed in awe and wonderment at the utter splendour and beauty of the people and pageantry of the occasion.

Seeing Stan White among the scrubbed faces of youth was a buzz. His Dad had run off with a younger woman the year before resulting in his Mam going on the game in order to support her young family. It was a surprise seeing him newly suited, hair gleaming and plastered flat with barber's hair oil with a bright red sash tied around his torso like an ambassador. The small girls looked fantastic in their bridesmaid dresses and long white gloves, the teachers with their unaccustomed well groomed, shining look and the parish priest in a black suit, gaiters, silk topper and a silver headed cane.

When the proud banners bearing the St Chad's legend and the silken streamers held by the beautiful maidens were raised, the stature of Our Lady of Lourdes was lifted on to the decorated carriage and the children of Mary took up their positions, when the school children were arranged in military order by the teachers. Then my heart swelled and overflowed with pride that I belonged and was a part of such an august body of people. The band struck up with "Colonel Bogey" and we were on our way!

Down Cheetham Hill, flowing like tributaries as other churches joined in and other bands struck up with rival tunes, the forward march of the glorious procession swelled to even greater lengths as church after church merged together: Corpus Christi; St Anne's; St Boniface's; St Malachy's and St Patrick's. There was no end. Down Corporation Street, along Market Street the thronging crowd cheered and shouted tumultuously: "Keep your 'ed up son!" From time to time a proud Mother would rush out to her son or daughter to give advice or thrust money or sweets into their hands.

Finally they reached Albert Square where a vast multitude beyond anything I had ever seen or imagined had assembled. Then the strains of "Faith of our Fathers" broke out and that massive crowd stopped it's excited gabble. Men and boys removed their hats and stood to attention, everyone joined in the hymn, many being moved to tears and sobbing at the sheer emotion of the scene.

> *Faith of our Fathers, living still,*
> *In spite of dungeon, fire, and sword,*
> *Oh how our hearts,*
> *Beat high with joy,*
> *When e'er we hear that glorious word,*
> *Faith of our Fathers, Holy Faith,*
> *We will be true to thee till death,*
> *We will be true to thee till death!*

At Saint Chad's there were many tough kids, remember these were tough times and none came tougher than Stan White. Not only was he cock-of-the-class he would fight many of the older boys in the two classes above. He was scared of no one and was incorrigible. At playtime he would, for ha'penny, let anyone have as many whacks at his hands as they wished with a strap that he had stolen. Only one punishment scared him: Miss McGurk's ladder! It was the equivalent of walking a pirate's plank. The classroom had a high ceiling with a trap door to the loft. Leading to this there was a ladder permanently in position.

"Up there in the roof" Miss McGurk had told the class, "it's very dark and there are hundreds and hundreds of rats ready to gnaw the very eyes out of any boy who's sent up there. If I find anyone in this class being sinful and wicked, up there he goes. I promise you!"

She was the most feared and hated teacher; Irish of old school-stern, unbending and often cruel as a disciplinarian. She was about forty years of age and wore flat, sensible shoes whilst carrying a massive leather handbag everywhere with her. On her lip (unlike Miss Gibbon) there was no hint of a moustache. No hint. It was a definite moustache. All the kids in the class, except the very tough ones like Stan White, lived in mortal fear of her, some of them being nervous wrecks biting down their fingernails to the quick. On her desk she had a brown strap which was always hot from use which she's used to hit out on the flimsiest pretext and sometimes when there was no pretext. It was rumoured that in the locked drawer of her desk she had a green strap which she had specially made for her in Ireland. When it came to straps, this it was said, was the jewel in the crown, the mother of all straps. Punishment with this piece of Irish leather was reserved for especially evil crimes such as: swearing; farting; playing with oneself or making too many blots or mistakes. Some of the kids were mental defectives or of very low intelligence. It didn't matter. She made no allowance for handicaps.

My next schooling was somewhat different. In 1939 I passed a 'scholarship' then moved on to the Xaverian Catholic College (a grammar school) it occupies a large campus in Victoria Park close to Saint Mary's Hospital right at the heart of Manchester's student quarters, providing excellent education for young people in and around Manchester from about 40 schools. Today it has 1,400 full time students and a new state of the art block entitled "Mayfield" with Business studies; Sociology; Psychology; IT; Computing; Economics and Media Studies.

In 1941 I was evacuated with the rest of the school to

MANCHESTER MAVERICKS

Blackpool where I had some pretty bizarre experiences, I can tell you. At the age of fifteen whilst I was still at school, I worked as a shoe shine boy at the American Red Cross in St Anne's Square. I earned fabulous amounts of money in tips from the American Doughboys who gave me my first detailed sex education. I left school in 1944 and went to work at the then *Manchester Guardian* as a copy boy. I had hope of becoming their star reporter but then I saw that without an Oxbridge education there were few prospects. I moved on to be a pen pushing clerk in the Inland Revenue. The hum-drum routine was driving me slowly mad and so before this could happen I decided to become a teacher and went to the college of St Mark and John, Chelsea (1945-47). I took up my first teaching post at a Secondary Modern in Manchester in 1947. I was put in charge of the top class, I was 19 at the time whilst my pupils were 14/15 and bitterly resenting having to stay an extra year. They gave me a hard time but my Collyhurst training had taught me a trick or two and I finally brought them round to their senses. I studied in the evenings at Manchester University and was awarded the degree of B.A (Admin) with Distinction 1955. I then attended Leeds University 1956/57 and was awarded a diploma in a boy's secondary school (I was 28!) I was later awarded the degree of M.E.D

During my career I wrote numerous academic articles (my field being Social Psychology of Education) and achieved my "Andy Warhol" fifteen minutes of fame when an article I wrote on General Culture hit every Monday morning newspaper in Britain whilst "Giles" did his morning cartoon on the subject! Thank God I was 7,000 miles away in Africa.

The Manchester folk I admired most are the head of St Chad's "Gus Travers" for his patience in running a school in a deprived district. Also Bill Bardsley of St Joseph's in Longsight, a great headmaster and scoutmaster who had liberal views on what constituted education. Bill allowed me to take my classes hiking in the Peak District under the pretext of studying map-reading and Geography, but it was a love of the countryside that the kids soon learnt (see *High Hopes*).

When it comes to my favourite music events it has to be at

BILL HOPKINS

Belle Vue in the Kings Hall. At the time I was courting my future wife and Sunday's Hallé Orchestra was conducted by Sir John Barbirolli. The Hallé is Britain's longest established professional symphony and was founded by the German pianist and conductor Charles Hallé. a refuge from the revolution in Paris in 1848. The first concert was at the Free Trade Hall on 30th January, 1858. In 1996 the Hallé moved to the Bridgewater Hall where it presents around eighty concerts a year.

My favourite buildings in Manchester are Sunlight House on Quay Street where I worked in the Inland Revenue as a lowly clerk. It's a fine art deco office building built in 1932 by Joseph Sunlight. At 14 stories and 135 feet it was reputed to be Northern England's first skyscraper and was for many years was the city's tallest building; constructed of steel and concrete clad in Portland stone. The original plans for forty stories were blocked by the city council. In the late 1990's it was renovated with shops and offices, it features a swimming pool which forms the centre of a commercial gym. The building is widely reputed to be haunted as it is a Grade II listed building.

The Central Library in Saint Peter's Square is another favourite in Manchester where I spent many hours studying for a degree (part time.) Without a doubt it's one of Manchester's most famous and well-loved landmarks, but perhaps it's not old as you think! The foundation stone was laid by the Prime Minister in 1930, the library was opened in 1934 by King George V.

In 1992, 58 years to the very same day, the King's granddaughter Queen Elizabeth formally opened the metro link at the library portico as it was used in the same ceremony. The library (and its neighbour, the Town Hall extension) was designed by the architect E. Vincent Harris and was influenced by the Roman Pantheon. The building is Grade II listed and much of the furniture is original from the architect's design. The library entrance, Shakespeare Hall, takes its name from the central stained glass window featuring the dramatist and some of his characters. Its ceiling features arms and crests from the city's illustrious heritage. The marble statue on the landing is the famous Reading Girl by G Ciniselli.

MANCHESTER MAVERICKS

You can't actually see the first floor dome from the street because it's lower than the surrounding walls. To see the top of the dome you need to go to the fourth floor. There are four tiers of steel book stacks underneath the Great Hall with shelves which would stretch over 35 miles if laid end to end. These are homes to the library's special collections and a vast number of first and early editions of major works are all stored in secure areas.

Manchester City Council is the only local authority to run a repertory theatre: the Library Theatre Company where you'll find a 300 seat theatre located in the basement.

Last but not least there was Finnigan's Dance Studio in Collyhurst on Queens Road. It was a wooden hut that recently burnt down where many couples made their dates here after bopping the nights away through the Rock and Roll era of the 50's. Very happy times.

I have no regrets in my life but I feel I have to touch on the youth yob culture that is a thorn in all society's sides. I feel so sorry for them as they are such an unhappy bunch. But I do wish they would throw their discarded chewing gum in the rubbish bins.

Although I do not have any regrets in life I am now faced with a dilemma: should I buy a Rolls or a Bentley?

Billy Hopkins, better known to his family and friends as Wilfred Hopkins.

SYLVIA BLANEY (ST. SYL)

My mother, Sylvia Blaney, is a saint and it's not only me who thinks she is! She acquired her (unofficial) canonisation firstly via the Catholic priest at Saint Malachy's in 1963 when on my first Holy Communion she changed from Protestant to Roman Catholic. Then later in the late 70's she was always posting me top letters to whatever jail I was serving time. They were always so neat, uplifting and cheerful but little did I know that until the mid 80's she had sent letters to lots of other Manchester lads doing time all over the world. By the time I realised and spoke to her about it she was even writing to prisoners on death row. She would post items to help while away the time such as paint brushes or glue kits but she had one golden rule; if they asked for cash they got sacked - simple!

My mum even asked me to help a few times. For example, a Moss Side woman, Tricia Hussain, got in proper trouble in Thailand. She had met an African con man who charmed the ladies and took them all on holidays, smoked the weed and convinced them all to carry a few ounces of the Herb through customs. Only thing was he switched it to heroin and many of the women ended up in jails with heavy sentences all over the globe. Trish was given 100 years and went under. Syl got me to post her letters and books via ship's mail which took 8 to 10 weeks to get there and they kept Tricia ticking over. Syl posted her many books about keeping faith and with my mum keeping on at her she became a born-again Christian and after 10 years got a King's Pardon.

Around that same time period the Pope had made a gypsy a saint and soon the chat went round Collyhurst that we should get in touch with Rome and make a case for Syl to be known as the Patron Saint of Prisoners. Sadly, we never did get round to it but the name stuck, hence her nickname.

My mum has written many books on local history and we jointly authored a book about Collyhurst and Smithfield Market that was distributed to North Manchester schools - how good's that!

I was born in Wythenshawe and spent most of my childhood days playing in Wythenshawe Park. In the heart of the park stands the famous Wythenshawe Hall which the Tatton family occupied for almost four hundred years. The hall was open to the general public to stroll around at their leisure picking up many interesting historical facts, with secret rooms including original wooden flooring and beams. Around the outside of the hall was a moat which is still visible today.

It was called 'The Garden City' when it was built; it was like the country, so I was very lucky. My father and his older brother Harold were both young men who'd joined the Territorial army in mid '39, then early in 1940 were upgraded into Manchester's finest fusiliers and together with around 6,000 they were ready for war. These men were the first from Lancashire to be shipped over to France. It was some sight seeing them all smartly march out of the White City gates behind a brass military band. All us Kitson's were waving union jacks and followed them over the swing bridge down to number one dock where ships awaited these brave men. I clearly remember families shouting up "do yourself proud son and give Jerry a bloody nose" and "There's VC heroes amongst you fellas". This was hard for me to understand, as I thought they had to die to receive a VC!

So then it became known as the phony war with no action, and you had the media for months printing funny pictures of Hitler all over the press. They usually consisted of him and his cronies all looking over at the British army, who were dug in the trenches with bulldog faces waiting for Fritz to make a move. The truth was that when the Krauts did mount their blitzkrieg attack they came at the Lancs seriously well equipped. Dad later said it was like trying to stop a runaway train, even after blowing up the bridges and retreating they could still see the Krauts building their own makeshift floating bridges and storm troopers steaming forward with a lucky mascot at the front, a fucking Sausage dog with a Kaiser tin helmet on, from that point on, it was on top! Days of retreating through barns and farm houses, losing men all the way as they couldn't carry the injured, then once on the beach at Dunkirk it was every man for himself; sleeping with dead bodies in blown out holes whilst the planes peppered the beach with another two days of hell trying to jump a boat back to Blighty. Harold was a nervous wreck when he finally got home. What gave him the horrors was seeing a Red Cross boat just 100

SYLVIA BLANEY

yards away take a direct hit, and then hearing all the screams from the wounded men as she sank.

Dad jumped on board a fishing boat with mostly French fellas who he said should have been left in France, I think he had them down as shit-houses and my god was he fuming the day he got home. You see the army had billeted fellas from all over the north closer to Manchester so as to ship them off to France, but first had them staying in families' spare rooms, and this poor soul from Leeds was just settling in when Dad literally threw him out on the street. His bags then came flying out of the upstairs window and he was told to sling his Yorkshire arse back to the barracks. I suppose after the defeat and humiliation from the Germans at Dunkirk no army top brass was going to call over and take him on, in fact he ended up in Lincolnshire barracks training for D-Day. I suppose that's when women started working, before that women never went to work. It was lovely; myself and my sister June looking after baby Roy, living in a country cottage for around six weeks, and Dad got us a German Sausage dog and called it Fritz!

My mum, Sylvia, on her wedding day

We were back in smoggy Manchester just in time for the Blitz. We had the Anderson shelter in the back yard, but my god it was so cold and damp it made us all ill just thinking about it. We used the shelter as a shed to store stuff, and used heavy blankets as hammocks tied up under the staircase, so whenever Hitler's bombs came down we were warm. For me the most terrifying part of the whole war was that so and so traitor Lord Haw-Haw, on the radio every night with his posh upper class voice, "Jairmany calling, Jairmany calling". The older folks all just took him as a clown but us kids hated it, more so when you heard him saying things like "Watch out if you're living near Ringway airport, our planes will use the Princess Parkway to guide them down to the south Manchester area" I even remember him saying the Forum Cinema and all the houses nearby were to be their targets. It was good to hear over the newsreels at the cinema that Mr Jairmany had been captured and was being brought back to England where Pierrepoint the hangman had the final say. It really cheered me up when he got hanged.

After the war, once the food rations stopped in the early 50's, we moved into The Locomotive pub in Collyhurst. Dad loved to chat to the locals about the war, only when I heard them all talking about Harry Kelly did I then understood that not all men awarded a VC have to die in action. Harry, born in 1887 in Collyhurst, joined up as soon as the war started, saving many lives on the Somme with outstanding bravery after getting wounded twice, four years later he was a Major. He later ran a shop and two pubs on Rochdale Road and as soon as the Spanish civil war started he yet again was in the thick of it fighting the fascists, soon being upped in rank to Commandente Generale, winning the Grand Cross of San Fernando, and even joined back up in 1939 living until 1960.

Wythenshawe Hall has just re-opened, so people can go in now. I know when I was kid they discovered a secret room in there. The hall goes back to about the sixteenth or seventeenth century. Past Wythenshawe there's some very old places, like Tatton Park, where I go every regularly and it's lovely inside and Dunham Massey, where I went for the Cheshire Fair. That's the wonderful thing about Manchester; it's a lively city nestled in amongst lots of countryside. From where I live now, you can drive ten minutes and be in the leafy Cheshire countryside, or drive an hour and be in Wales. All these opportunities for escape to the country were great when I was growing up, but there are some things only the city can offer, like the chance to see your favourite musicians and acts.

As a teenager I had my own pop idol, Gene Pitney. I think I knew every word to all the songs he wrote; he appeared at the

Golden Garter in Wythenshawe, which was my only chance to see him live in concert. I went with my husband, who never got a look in that night; it was my treat for Mothers' Day. I recall all the women, myself included, screaming and jumping around. Pitney never seemed to age. Prior to this concert I went to see Lena Horn at the Palace Theatre on Oxford Road. God was she fabulous! Shirley Bassey was another one I saw, it was so exciting! There will never be another like her. I admire her for getting so far from the depths of Tiger Bay.

The last concert I went to, only a couple of years ago, was the 'Lady Boys of Bangkok' at Salford Quays; they had figures any woman would die for, well worth every penny. The show was non-stop, the gowns were out of this world, and how they ever got in them is beyond me.

Growing up as a young, music-loving woman in Manchester, I was catered for and maybe even spoilt by the array of venues, all of them bringing the idols of my youth. It may have been Post-War Britain, but the acts that graced the stages of Manchester lit up the city with glamour, sex and a little bit of danger; all of the necessary ingredients needed for a young woman.

The time eventually came to experience a crucial part of being young; the first trip away without your parents. Mine was to the Isle of Man. I set off intending to have a good time on the one and only holiday camp on the island; it was situated high up on top of a mountain which had a lift to take you up, the only drawback was it had no bars. So every night, apart from Sunday when every pub was closed, we would go into town, bearing in mind drink in the forties was dirt cheap, we got sozzled, then back to camp to jive the night away into the early hours. The day we set sail back home to England I was in a terrible state having had too much to drink the night before. The sea was that rough and I knew I was going to throw up, so off I went below deck to the washrooms where I found every toilet and wash basin was occupied by people in the same position as myself. I dashed back up to the deck and hung myself over the rails. No sooner was I throwing up, the wind blew it back all over me; projectile vomit it was not! It never reached the water. When I finally got home my mother took one look at me and said "I don't know about a holiday, you had better go to bed." Needless to say I have never been back.

Those being the days of industry in Manchester, when I left school there were jobs waiting. I was a machinist for years and years. Many of the old churches in Manchester were turned into machine shops, but they've all closed down. We've lost all our trade now and have nothing to fill the gap. You were never out of work; if you left school on a Friday, you were in a job on Monday. There were machine shops all over Manchester, and everybody earned good money as well. I lived in Collyhurst flats, and my mum and dad ran a pub nearby. There used to be pubs on every corner and there's hardly any now. You could leave your front door open because you knew your neighbours and there was a sense of community, something I feel we've lost.

One particular place you could find this community gathered was Belle Vue, which for me during my teenage years was wonderful, it was the 'in place' to go and watch the dirt track racing. To get the best view you had to be near the front, as down the side you got covered in dirty cinders which went everywhere, you would go home looking like a chimney sweep. One of the most popular ballrooms was at Belle Vue. Then there were the animals; those poor elephants! One thing that stays in my mind is the elephants being chained up by the ankles to a stake in the ground, swaying from side to side. Many people took rides on them so at some point they were unchained, but Gorton hardly compares to the plains of Africa. There was also the scenic railway; I only went on once as when the car descended from the height of the track, I lurched forward and the poor man in front of me ended up with my lipstick all over his snow white mac. In later years when I lived in Miles Platting and had my eldest son, Colin, Belle Vue wasn't far away and became a regular day out for us. I have to laugh as I can still hear him say "Mam, can we go to Belle Vue?"

When fashion became more affordable and something everyone could follow, I was a young woman, and the timing could not have been better. My favourite fashion was the gabardine suit with a split at each side of the skirt. The split ended just above the knee. I thought it was the sexiest thing since sliced bread. When you sat down it revealed all your leg; nylons were very expensive then so most of us stuck transfers down the sides of our legs. When I compare this to some of the women's fashion today, ooh I don't like them. Some of how they dress is okay, but skirts twelve inches high and all that, no, no. And sex; if a girl got pregnant, they had to get married, whether they liked the bloke or not. That or you simply wouldn't see her, she'd go to relatives or anywhere, it was that bad. You didn't get women fighting then either, it just didn't happen. Nor did you get stabbings. I think parents were so strict then that kids were too frightened to do anything. And also you had to be in whether you liked it or not; if you were up for work for a certain hour, you had to be on that last bus, or you didn't get out again.

My thought on the youth of today is a very hard one for me. I find them very hard to judge having had two sons of my own in trouble over the past years. They have both stolen but had to pay the price the hard way by serving time in prison.

The biggest thing that really upsets me in today's world is the sheer senselessness of destruction. I recall having three young trees planted outside my house and within a month they had been uprooted by heartless yobs. Only a five minute walk from my house is a wooded area, to which the workmen in the height of winter over a period of around three months constructed a play area for the local children of the estate. It must have cost a fortune, yet as of today there is graffiti in every possible space, they have also ripped up the safety matting and burnt it, whilst setting fire to the wooden seating area and the tyre swings. I wish someone one day could explain to me what satisfaction they have gained from doing this. These children sure know that there will be a clip around the ear from us, yet it's us that end up in trouble; there is simply no justice any more. The only excuse they can give is that "we were bored", yet there is a youth club next door with great facilities which include Judo, Basketball, Football, Thai boxing and much more right on their doorstep.

When we were young, the opportunities for work meant we

didn't have the time to be bored. Paid work also allowed us to spend some of our hard-earned money, and some of that would undoubtedly be going in the till at Tommy Ducks.

Tommy Ducks on Oxford Road was one of the most famous and oldest pubs in Manchester. Sadly it was pulled down almost overnight. There was such an outcry from the public; this tiny "oldie worldie" pub was gone forever. It had a tiny bar and a vault, and the atmosphere was second to none, it was magic. All walks of life drank there. I recall one night sitting next to a chap and as soon as he opened his mouth I asked "are you the man in black?" He was the famous Valentine Dyall, off the radio, keeping in mind there wasn't television then. At the end of the nights out we would rush home to listen to his spooky tales. His opening line was 'this is your story teller, the man in black.' On Saturday night we would head on down to the Plaza on Oxford Road, then as famous as the Ritz. I lived all week for my night out on a Saturday in the Plaza. There were no bars in the dance halls during the fifties, so half way through the dancing we would go over to 'Tommy Ducks' for a few drinks.

The best buildings in Manchester aren't just the ones with barrels in the cellar. My favourite building in Manchester has got to be St Mary's -The Hidden Gem- on Mulberry Street; it's the oldest Catholic Church standing. It was built for the poor of the parish. During my years living in Collyhurst, every Friday without fail I headed into town to pay my rent of £1.05 to avoid getting into arrears and would never miss attending The Hidden Gem. I can honestly say I could never recall the church being empty. Scores of people would swarm in during their lunch hour. I don't know of any other churches that had its doors open all day so people could call in. I know that many old buildings need restoring in time but personally I loved that place before restoration took place a few years ago. It had original stone flagging that had been replaced with carpet and the Stations of the Cross were no longer there but had been replaced with paintings by a famous artist. All this modern art I can't make head nor tail of. The beautiful altar remains but unfortunately has been fitted with an alarm system to warn people not to go beyond a certain point; so much for being close to God!

Unfortunately, not all of Manchester's historic buildings have remained intact, Deansgate and the Arndale centre having of course been heavily damaged during the 1996 IRA bombing. It was a terrible shock; when you first saw it, it was unbelievable. It reminded me of The Blitz.

Another building in Manchester that's also had its time on the 10 o'clock news is Strangeway's Prison, home to the riots in 1990. The prisoners were out on the roof, their families stood below shouting up to them all day. I don't think anybody was frightened. I remember visiting, and even the visiting area where people have to sit with children was not nice, not clean. Compared to visiting in Holland, which is such a different system. The riots made people reconsider their ideas about the prison system and the police, something I find a bit of a tricky one to answer. Simply, if your home was burgled, the first person you contact would be the police. However, of course there are certainly a few corrupt ones out there, especially within the prison service. But in my opinion it will always be a world-wide problem. These people have to live with their conscience, and we all have one. Some folk get away with it while others don't, I am afraid that's life!

Just as every city has its villains, it also has its share of wonderful people admired by many. Mine was Billy Green, he was loved by all. He was a real genuine publican; so popular that he got a mention in "Coronation Street". To this day, the little pub off Rochdale Road is still called "Billy Greens." Another person would be Les Dawson, a truly humble, down to earth comedian, along with his friend Bernard Manning, who was so blue that you could cut the air with a knife. People travelled from all over to visit his Embassy Club. As famous as he was, he spared no airs or graces. Finally, L S Lowry; few have put Manchester on the map like he did with his fantastic paintings consisting of match stick men, cats and dogs, and the world of working people. He is well known all over the world, yet he lived a very sheltered life.

A city with as much character as Manchester would no doubt harvest some eccentric locals and some bizarre tales. Although I have to say the story that astounded me most happened when I didn't live here! I lived in Hong Kong for a couple of years, and there you didn't really live in houses or flats, you just rented a room, everybody lived like that. Opposite me lived a lady who every morning went out with a writing pad and a pen to teach English and she was as thick as a plank so I thought if she can do it, I can do it! My suspicions were proved right as one day she told me what she did; it turns out she was a prostitute! She was kidding me with the pad and pen. She said it was the first time there was someone from the building she could be friendly with; no one else would bother with her because she was a prostitute, but it didn't bother me. When she was having murder with her husband, I used to mind her money.

Having spent a few years in the East and seen my share of Europe, I would say I've travelled more than some. Despite this, one of the biggest regrets in my life is that I never learnt to drive, and now I'm too old and would not have the confidence. Being able to drive allows the world to become your oyster, and stops you having to depend on others to get you from A to B. When you have worked all your life to make ends meet and you retire, it's one long and very drawn out day to try and fill. With a car only, within an hour from Manchester you can be in Wales. Better still, an hour and a half allows you to take in the breathtaking scenery of the beautiful Lake District.

Both as a city and a home to millions, I think Manchester holds a special place in people's hearts, whether you come from here or not. I've been in taxis in Holland and Germany, and the minute you say you're from Manchester, they say 'Manchester United' and 'The Hidden Gem'. It is surprising what people really know about it. They think you come from somewhere if you come from Manchester. One image that will remain with me forever is of the children in Collyhurst playing out. Even though they had nothing, they were great people. Playing and having fun. They'd never known anything else, and they still got by. The people of Manchester I think are always themselves. It's not just the accent. If you stand at a bus-stop with somebody, you know their life-story in ten minutes. They get on with people; I think they're known for their friendliness. I went to London - I think

SYLVIA BLANEY

I've only ever been once - and I don't think anybody spoke, not the same people, not the same atmosphere.

ALAN HANCOCK "HANK"

When Punk hit our youth culture and the bands went on tour I tried my hand at selling T-shirts and Punk badges but truth was it was hard work getting a wage, then a good friend from Old Trafford said if I was to put up £500 his mate would print out a programme which would have no price on the cover so we'd just have to play it by ear so to speak. The next band touring was not really Punk but had like Punk roots, Adam and the Ants. Leeds was the start of the tour and we smashed it making good money charging a pound or two, it never mattered as the dosh came rolling in, it was the same at all the other venues.

After the shows back then the pubs on Chester Road all had lock ins, my God do I miss them, but pub culture has gone for ever but back then Malcolm's family would be on the lock ins and that was where I met Alan. Him being a Teddy Boy back in '56 till the 60's meant I was glued to all his conversions about that time period. Most enjoyable was the fact he was a proper red devil and followed the Busby Babes all over when they played away and he was there at the stadium when the coffins were all placed in United's Gymnasium and he was able to describe the peoples sadness and sorrow all over Manchester.

Alan has passed away now but his stories still live on whenever there's a Hancock meeting in the Toll Gate, the last pub that's local, I use this pub to see United games when I can't get a ticket and the spirit of Alan lives on, I just hope you readers get a taste of this top chap who was deffo a top Maverick from the Teddy Boy era!

I was born and bred in Barrack Street in Hulme with the Army Barracks opposite. All my family originated from an area in Salford famous for the hit book and film "Love on the Dole".

In 1939 my old man signed up for the Royal Artillery in the Cheshire pub in Hulme, it was run by Fred Buckley who later ran the famous Glue Pot pub in the Smithfield Market, my dad served in the war till 1945. Afterwards he worked in Salford at Greengates which back then was the rubber works. Dad had to cross over a bridge every day to get there; it was named after Mark Addy who was one of Salford's most legendary sons. During his life time Mr Addy gained fame for rescuing no fewer than 50 people from drowning in the Irwell. As a young lad he assisted his father in the running of the family business of his boat hire company. Although he was unable to swim he was no stranger to water. He was awarded many medals from the Royal Humane Society; his last rescue resulted in a fatal illness that saw him off and was brought on by swallowing the heavily polluted waters of the Irwell. A pub bearing his name still exists today on the Salford bank of the River Irwell. So come on you guys and dolls go and have a drink on him, in his memory. He was a saviour.

Alan, on the right at Yates's in Blackpool in 1956.

My Gran Barmister was always down the Old Cart road in her shawl; bonnet and clogs yelling out "Get Your Umpire" as she had a wicked lisp and said that instead of "Get your Empire" the biggest newspaper around at that time! After this she would hit the slaughterhouse for lips and lugs which were bits from the pig that didn't taste too bad when she'd worked her magic on them. I can remember jumping over the brown paving stones that she had cleaned at the front and believe you me, she cleaned the back alley too, what a Gran! She was so clean and proud! Even our bit of a window sill next to the front door got her treatment, in the Spring her eye-catching planters were a sight to see in full bloom.

I attended Saint Wilfred's R C School in Hulme, the same school as Albert Scanlon who went on to become a Busby Babe. But as for my education - zilch, although my older brother Brian done okay as he was picked out for Saint Margaret's and played alongside Dennis Viollet, the first United player to score a goal for an English team in Europe when we beat Anderlecht in 1956. Brian also went onto a scholarship! In 1948, the best day of our lives was the cup final against Blackpool, it was like the war was now really over, as all Manchester residents had street parties to send off the older folks down to Wembley and bring back the cup. It was akin to 1977 Jubilee day with all the streets decked out with Union Jacks from lamp post to lamp post! Rule Britannia.

As kids we played out till all hours of the night, our back doors could be kept unlocked as we had fuck all to rob really. But we all felt safe in every street in them days. I liked playing a homemade version of street cricket, played next to any alley, the target was a few sticks and a slime pole going over the tops which the other team had three chances to strike it out with some dodgy ball. If you hit the target the other team all had to run like fuck, it was a bit like Rally-Vo! or kick the can.

Our favourite toffees were Uncle Joe's mint balls (they were the best) and huge slabs of toffee broken up with a hammer, it made a cracking noise when it split. Then we got stuck into that hard sticky toffee with a Banana flavour now and then, Sherbet dips for the girls better known as Kay-Ly and we all loved Spanish liquorice, which was black and chewy.

I recall the first day of May, when all the girls would be singing and dancing, we would all dress up in either our older sister's or our mother's clothes worn inside out. We all had huge women's hats on, crawl under the fire entrance to the chimney and soot ourselves until we were jet black. We'd then go out steaming all the pubs on the old Cart Road. We called this "Nigger Storming", the girls changed their minds! I don't blame 'em.

The big day out shopping was monthly at the Co-op facing Hulme church, at Christmas we'd go into Deansgate window shopping then up to Oldham Street to the real world. This is where my Old Dear could relax with the prices being within her range; the big store, Kendall's, was like the Harrods of Manchester in those days. Our local swimming place was the Pomona canal "cut". It was a health risk to say the least, full of bikes and prams. I also left a terrible toxic taste, we always skimmed into the cut but never dived as you'd get cut by something for sure, I always thought that's why it was called the cut! The black oily parts were always the warmest so that's the place I always dove into. I'd then swim through the first clearest water in that area, this would wash off the oily shite. Another day out swimming was Sale Lido it was an Art Deco building with a 15 ft diving board and a spring board nearby. The upstairs had wrought iron barriers all the way around with cafés, in the back was a huge glass dome that let the sun rays beam onto the tiled walls. It felt like you were in the tropics.

The big event was Easter up in Hale Barns, Cheshire: camping and swimming in the River Bollin over the whole weekend! We had our own Whit Week, the Stretford pageant. The fair would arrive en masse in Hullard Park, Old Trafford. All the local floats and wagons would be displaying huge adverts; Duerr's Jam donated £1,000 to the local charity! I firmly believe that Charity begins at home. How many big names raise money for charities then see it all get shanked by the big boys? Why not give it to the likes of inner city youth clubs? It would help the yobs and hoodies who need mini vans for sporting events and the odd break to the coast, like the Black cabs in Manchester and Salford who taxi all the kids free to the jam buttie holiday campsite in Rhyl.

The big fairground that came twice a year was exciting. It parked up right on our doorstep; this huge black croft was some sight at night with flashing lights. The fella on the microphone from the waltzers was always giving it plenty: "The Louder you scream the faster you go!" That always got "woo's" galore from the girls. At Christmas we'd sometimes get snow and that would brighten up our days and Silcocks of Warrington with their boxing booth came to the same site. It was the sure place to be when the gloves were thrown out to the challengers, remember in them days the boxers were like our local Gangsters; that's who we all aspired to be. What a great feeling when we would sneak under the thick canopy to see a few brutal encounters. My number one pub was on the Old Cart road called 'The Star'. It was the only pub in the whole of Manchester that was a McEwan's. During the mid 70's they joined up with a Scottish and Newcastle Brewery, situated just behind Saint Georges Church which is at the end of the Mancunian fly-over tucked away in the side street near the

MANCHESTER MAVERICKS

"The Manchester Regiment".

In 1956 I turned into a Teddy boy after seeing the hit film "Rock around the Clock" at the Gaiety theatre. All the Teds took over the aisles dancing and bopping away, then it went sour as the mob started to rip out the seats and the staff and police came bowling in and turned the hosepipes on the mob. We soon backed off, making our way out of the nearest exit.

I bought my whistle and flute (suit) from Walter Smith on Stretford Road, his brother had a tailors in All Saints Square, the jacket lapels were blue velvet, the rainbow spots were also blue, with half moon pockets like the ones cowboys had back then. Like most Teds I got my footwear from Timpson's; they cost two quid with thick creep soles, most had a crocodile or cow skin pattern woven into the front and sides. They all had a chain across the front, mine was shiny blue to match my collar and raindrops. My Dickie Dirt (shirt) had cut off collars, I was also wearing a blue tie with a Windsor knot as thin as possible. All this with my drain piped trousers! Other Teds sported Winkle Pickers which were sharp pointed shoes which were very handy in gang fights.

For my barnet I copied the Tony Curtis look. The huge quiff that you ran your fingers through which then made a neat line down the back to the base: the famous Duck's Arse! The first time I saw the Teddy boys from Manchester it was in the newspapers after a mob came out of the Cumberland Suite at Belle Vue. All the fighting was in the Gardens, it was reported about seventy Teds all going for it big time, you can read the article in the "History of Belle Vue." It's definitely worth a look.

The Teds would go all to the Locarno (which was the Lido baths) it had a huge wooden cover over the pool that created the dance floor, the upstairs cafés were turned into bars, Thursday night was like the Lonnie Donegan Skiffle night, cheap entrance and the tunes came from a washboard with some kind of metal thing round players' hands that ran up and down the board with a wicked echo effect.

Saturday night was the big Rock and Roll night, once we were in we'd all get passes then nip out to the Bulls Head boozer still there on the corner of School Road, there were no Rocker or Biker gangs to fight with so it was mainly local lads, one of my mates was a fucker. He carried a huge blade around for slashing seats and bursting balloons which would always go down like a pile of bile with the local ladies.

The Wythenshawe Warriors always brought a hefty crew so you had to be on your toes, Sundays was a cracking night up the road in Broadheath at the Ice Skating rink. This was a better place to cop for women, if you had a few bob then you would move on to the Palace, later in the 7Q's it re-opened as the Blue Rooms, a Northern Soul club and is now a Mecca Bingo!

Another big day out was when the Star pub had their Easter trip to Blackpool, but being as we were Teddy Boy's we all got launched out of the Winter Gardens, our lot went to a huge pub on the front called The Huntsman after that. I remember us all bouncing and bopping our way down to the fair ground when the War of the Roses with Yorkshire kicked off, Teddy boy's jumping into the open air swimming pool to get away from the fighting. To this day it makes me chuckle, truth is I still hate Yorkshire. My favourite number one song ever inside Old Trafford was "Can you hear them Yorkshire sing? I can't hear a fucking thing!" and we never did!

Brian Hinley from Hulme nicknamed me "Duke" around this time, maybe something to do with living on Duke Street. I've still never really found out if that was why.

I remember working early shifts at Stretford Gas and one day jumping on the bus. My mucker from Saint Wilfred's, Albert Scanlon, was sprawled out on the long seat stretched out like he needed a good kip with his bag under the staircase ready for the trip to Belgrade for the quarter final in February 1958, he was on his way to Old Trafford to meet the team bus, then on to Ringway Airport. The next day after working late I was in the showers when a Yorkie shouted over to me sarcastically that the Busby Babes had crashed, I threw my best shot right onto his conk and still in the raw chased him out into the yard. As I said, I have no time for Yorkies.

I then jumped the bus back to Chester Road and there was the sign outside the newsagents telling about the disaster, that's when it really sank in. Only a few months ago there was a TV documentary about the crash with Albert Scanlon being one of the main characters. I know he and his family never approved of it along with a few others, feelings were strong as I could not bring myself to watch it.

My personal favourite United player was 'Snake Hips' Eddie Colman. When he was out on the razzle in the Ritz Eddie always told the young women his job was on the docks as back then they earned more money than footballers! Another United player from Salford who died in the crash was Geoffrey Bent, his old man worked with my uncle Bert on the railway trucks at Sandhole Colliery for over 40 years.

One night two mates and I were all on early shifts after a heavy drinking session in the Star we decided to break into the local Nursery thinking we'd get our heads down for a few hours but as you'd expect we all got caught snoring our heads off. I remember saying to the judge, "What the fuck can you nick from a Nursery! We only wanted to sleep your honour." He was called Judge Steel. I remembered that fucker's name all my life as he sentenced me to do Borstal Training.

The first night in Strangeways soon got me thinking "well let's face the facts. I will have to just get on and accept this stupid sentence", knowing that I wasn't going to taste a pint of the Star's best bitter for a year or two. I got a homemade tattoo on my chest of a pint of foaming beer spilling out of a pint pot, with two scrolls and the words saying 'The Star' in the top scroll and 'McEwans' in the other.

I went here, there and everywhere before I eventually got to Borstal, it took me about six months to reach that barren coast line in Ipswich. The Borstal had 6 large houses, mine was Saint Georges the oldest wing, nowadays it's an agricultural college. St David's house was just a corrugated iron hut almost touching the cliffs. The rest of the houses St Michaels, St Andrews, St Johns and St Pats were all made from shitty old red bricks. The first week, coming up to the weekend, I knew I would have to assert myself with a cockney kid who was right on my case. Even the toughest lads had to go through some kind of ritual, so me and this cockney went at it in the kit room for a good five minutes before the screws got a grip and believe you me it felt like I'd done 12 rounds in the ring, most of the boys were supporting the cockney.

The borstal had a north-south divide - all Cockneys and home counties stuck together and they had around 70 per cent of the population, We soon had to learn how to walk the walk and never back down even if it meant a hiding, remember I was 5 foot nothing but was soon mixing it and getting noticed, I soon got picked out to play right wing on the footie team, then a kid called Tich, a flyweight from Bethnal Green, convinced me that if I joined the boxing team I would be a cert for a pint after the fights. Captain of the Borstals boxing team was Johnny Tottoh, I knew his brother Alan who went on to box for the GB team at the Olympics in Mexico 1968. He turned professional but Johnny never did, in Manchester's boxing circles they always talk about why he never turned pro.

Tottoh started by winning the British ABA schoolboy Championship at the age of 13, from Cavendish School his record of 3 titles in 3 years on the bounce took 39 years to equal. He lost his first two fights then went on a roll of winning over 50 in a row, he's still as strong as an Ox to this day. With the utmost respect, he ruled the roost when in charge on the door of the worst fighting club throughout the whole of the 70's and 80's; "Papa's", better known as Snappers, on Newton Street. Johnny was well known for his very clever style carrying the clout of a mule. Being Mancs, he soon took me under his wing and my time at borstal from that point became quite easy.

The daddy of my wing was a Watford lad who wasn't a bully, he wouldn't even call himself the Daddy but if he ever got the piss took out of his accent then you saw the other side of him, he was very nasty.

My best mate all the way through my sentence was from Glasgow, Willy McCarthy, nicknamed "tough guy" or "tuffie" which he fucking hated and got him into all kinds of shite. To this day I still call Glaswegians tough guys, "See you there tough guy"; "alright there tough cookie!" It tickles me pink. Willy was on the boxing team and was the Daddy of St Andrew's house. After a year the big Summer Fete came round and the PTI Brooksie was really up for the chance of taking the "Bird Trophy" away from last year's winners, Suffolk. It was fantastic to fight under the huge canopy with such a loud and happy crowd. Everyone, even the losers, got a prize - mine was in a huge cardboard box and still to this day I can't work out why it was so big as it only had a small Fruit bowl in it, I gave it to my sister who's now living down under with that same bowl.

Now you can picture the PTI's face with the Trophy, he's over the moon to say the least, and said there's fifty bob for doing the job and the lads share it! That amount in them days was bucket loads to go bananas in a huge marquee tent which was full of hot food and beer stalls, three hours later we all turned up hammered for the bus back to Borstal, not one kid tried to do a bunk or a runner as we called it.

Even though it was an open jail, it had a huge river going round it with a seven mile bridge that somehow helped the screws, and you have to think in them days getting away from that kind of remote area meant you stuck out like Blackpool tower to local farmers. There was a US base nearby which is still there today called Bent Waters, trying to escape was on par with escaping from Colditz, the journey home was so fucking barren.

The good times didn't last long, the riot started first thing Friday morning in the drill yard (this was where the whole borstal would have to be accounted for) then everyone marched military style to the workshops. Then on the return to the dining halls into the main kitchen it kicked off good style. This mass brawl soon became very ugly, all the screws were ex-military and they soon had the upper hand, my own hands were being thrown about like swinging hammers and I chuckle to myself now when I recall never being so happy as to have a Yorkie alongside me to save my bacon. He came from Barnsley and he had the Barnsley Chop alright. In them days the main place for all the bad seeds who got Shanghaied was out to Reading jail. My mate Tich went, he wasn't a fighter just a real nice lad and a boxer. He was even nicknamed Break-Legs saying went "Off to break a leg" as that's what you'd expect in Reading, the beatings whilst en route down the Block were shocking. It was great to hear about Tich via a screw one Sunday morning a few months later when he had won a fight over in Holland which had been on BBC radio.

My opinion on the 18 months I served inside? It was better than any schooling I ever did and moulded me into the man I am today, maybe today's snotty yobs could do with a dose of Borstal - your release date all depended on how quick you learnt to toe the line and that alone makes sense.

Once I was back into the swing of life I moved over the canal into the Ordsall area of Salford and got myself sorted with a job on the Docks. My house cost £1,200 on Higson Street, I sold that house and moved nearer to the Docks on Soho Street costing me £2,000 from Nana Mills who moved on to Railway Road over the Swing bridge. The Dockers all stuck together when we were out on strike it was Yea or Ney, yes I do admit I wished many a time it was Ney! The group were ten strong and would unload all kinds of cargos, when the dinner time break came it was straight into The Trafford public house for every one. I would like to get a small point over at this point, the original Grid was Salford Pete. He would down at least 8 pints every dinner then go straight back to some gruelling graft pounding around them 140 pound bags (Dead Pigs), Pete would wrap up his work kit in a military manner, slip on his Green Beret and march home singing war tunes.

The best fights I ever saw were the one to ones under the sheds mainly on the weekends, some of them great fights ended up carrying on for weeks. The main one that sticks out in my mind is of my mate from Hulme Johnny Clinton v Albert Ginger - both were gaffers as well, it took the best part of a full winter for Johnny to finally do Ginger.

After work (stamping off) on the Fridays we'd all visit two clubs just off Cannon Street, the Chanteclair and The Rooster, which had Jackie Brown the boxer working the door as he was going through hard times. He once got a jail sentence for an ugly fight on the way back from Blackpool and ended up with three months hard labour. The entrance was a huge steel door that had a coded bell and a slit for the doormen to check you out, then Les Harper would give you all the nod to get down these huge slab stairs. Les was from Salford and one of the most respected bouncers in his day, the owner was a good fella, an ex-steel constructor called Tommy Harold, all the "townies" liked them both! Other pubs I frequently visited were the Blob shops on Oldham Street, and the 'Band on the Wall' where I loved singing "The Bird Dog" by the Everly brothers! Now unfortunately this famous pub is a yuppie club.

One Yuppie bar which back in the 50's and 60's was the place to be seen in was the famous Long Bar, it was underneath the old Odeon cinema. One night in there I met The Rochdale Thunderbolt, Jock McAvoy. He was having to use crutches and got angry waiting at the bar which led to a confrontation with a local bouncer and I swear McAvoy left his crutches with one almighty effort and still sparkled the doorman out cold and landed back into his crutches - Bang! And within a split sec hobbled away to his corner - it's all in Brian Hughes' book about him. Also not long after I met Johnny King, another Collyhurst boxer, who had a pub in Hulme. He was a very nice quiet guy but looked very ill.

The best concerts for me were in 1957; Tommy Steele, then Frankie Lymon (an African American) and the teenagers sang "why must I be a teenager in love" and lastly Johnny Mathis a few years later - both gigs were at the Palace!

I loved gambling and my favourite venue was Belle Vue dogs. On Saturday nights we'd all get Steamboats and then tuck into the huge Hash and Red Cabbage, it was in here one bank holiday that I heard the plane Rocky Marciano was on had crashed into a mountain, "it'd take a fucking mountain to kill that cunt" I remember saying.

My best memories of Belle Vue were going to the Circus and seeing the midget Little Billy and the ringmaster who was the famous George Lockhart who went on into the 70's and retired at 90! I took my own kids and put them all on the huge Elephant "Mary" that fitted four or five on each side. She was used as a taxi from the zoo over to the fairground by a fella called Phil Fernandez who wore a turban and those turned up shoes. He was

ALAN HANCOCK

the first 'Paki' I'd ever seen in drag!

In 1972 the Star pub took me on my first holiday abroad to Lloret de Mar, they had raffles and collections so all in all it cost me six bob! It was all men and only a few spuds a pint, we had daily sessions in the pool. It was a nightmare at night, the wine was flowing down spick style, Dick Hetersley, a huge steel erector, had it mastered until the last night he jumped or belly flopped into the pool straight to the bottom and stuck like glue. Being a huge fella it took us all a few minutes to dive down and scrape him up, to this day he can't remember a thing!

My new nickname around this time period from the woman I am still with today was, "a rebel without a clue". The first time I came home steaming drunk I'd lost my keys. One day in 1972 walking down Oxford Road I noticed all the sandblasting fellas working on Manchester University and the Holy Name Church both on Oxford Road, these two iconic buildings are my favourites even today and whenever I pass by I always take a look inside the church. It took two years to finish and was well worth it, anyone unfamiliar with Manchester, next time you pass have a proper look.

Of today's Yob Culture I say that boot camps, borstals and the birch should all come back! I would gladly do it myself; putting gobshites like Pete Docherty up for six of the best would be a nice start, them cunts won't want to come back again, ain't no S and M pleasure here, we're talking pain - a bucket of salt rubbed into the cuts!

As for the booze, most get hammered on that white-shite cider. Just ban the fucking horrible stuff. In my days the beer was that clear you could read your newspaper though the glass and mild was like looking at a Guinness it was that dark and smooth. I think there's too many chemicals in today's alcohol. Fuck me look at the work force on a Monday morning these days, that's if they even make it, their heads are up their arse holes.

Manchester sayings that were around in my youth were: a Blood Stain was a ten bob note, a "clod" was an old penny, a Joey was a 3 bob bit, and in the early 60's a Tanner was called an Elsie after Elise Tanner from Coronation Street. The star from

MANCHESTER MAVERICKS

Ancoats, we called her the Stout Queen. I love local sayings like Newton Heaths are your Teeth, but we Mancs just say Newtons like Salford's for socks (Salford Docks).

The fashions I disliked with hatred were the huge platform boots, penny rounds and pointed tip concord collars. I also hated the brummie bags that had pockets on the side as big as wardrobes that were worn over the platform shoes. Big clod hopping efforts they were, the waistline was 3 to 5 buttons. Huge mops of long curly hair with tashes and beards. It was in the mid 70's when glam rock took over and men dressed to shock.

Other Mancs I rate are Bill Tarmey who played Jack Duckworth - he's a fine singer and comedian, I saw him many times when he toured the working men's circuit. Robert Powell from Stretford is up there, a mad Stretford Ender himself. Then there's Tony Wilson Mr Manchester they call him (my arse) I detested him soon as I saw him on the TV show called "Scene" at 6:30pm Granada years ago I wanted to bump into him. My old dear used to cut and blow his Grandmother's hair and even she said he was a gob shite!

Being the only person in my Borstal that played for the football team and the boxing team I can honestly say boxing gives me just as much a thrill as any footie game, I suppose it all started as a kid hearing stories about Johnny Cusick (Nipper) from Hulme they say his only downfall was to burst onto the scene when Jackie Brown and Johnny King were top dogs, he finally got to beat them both and go on to win British and Empire tiles, but then served in the armed forces from 1940-46 so never had the right chance to make his mark.

My favourite boxer of all time is Ken Buchanan who held two world titles in 1971. He got stripped of the WBC for failing to fight Pedro Carrasco in June 1972 and defended his WBA belt against the undefeated Roberto Duran at boxing's Mecca - Madison Square Gardens in New York. This fight was toe to toe all the way until the end of that 13th round when Duran landed a low blow into the mid-section, an illegal area of the body. It's been shown on TV countless times but it put Buchanan in hospital and even though he lost that title I rate him up there with the very best.

I respect my parents greatly and also the rest of my family. As for respecting the Police, I believe they are an evil necessity. I don't have any regrets in life apart from wishing I went for the other bypass operation which would mean I'd still be able to have the odd pint.

KATH RILEY

I can't help but admire the modern day Northern Quarter. Right at the heart of it is the original stonework of the Fish market. It stands proud and back in the day when they demolished the Smithfield Market, the sandblasting company my old man ran offered to clean the fish market stonework for free. All around this area nowadays are upmarket Bistros, bars and restaurants all serving top of the range grub and booze. A lot of the filming you see on TV shows is done round there and even big budget Hollywood films have used the area as a backdrop. It says a lot about Manchester's progress that the area has been transformed. Sadly, one thing that's almost gone are the old school pubs but if you are local and in the know there are still a few tucked away and one that sticks out is "The Hare and Hound".

Back when I worked at Smithfield this pub opened at 8am and there was a back entrance where you had to knock on. A market copper would open it as the first table inside was used by the coppers who had their own uniform very similar to a normal policeman's. Everyone who used the pub at that early time knew to be on their best behaviour, the barmaids were first class characters - talk about being on the ball! I was lucky to get to sell knock off stuff to them and even ended up doing a small trade in fish. That was back in 1972 before the market closed down. It was a sad time and every Crimbo I always call in for old time's sake so I'm sure you can imagine how chuffed I was this year to bump into Kath Riley She was with all her family doing the same as myself going down memory lane, what a top opportunity to get a few pages from her about herself and her time as a barmaid. I just hope it paints a picture of the 1970's when we were both in our prime.

I was born 1935 so grew up as a war baby. My memories of the 5 years of hardship of the war years were not so bad - in fact even though everyone was struggling with the cold, damp, fear of the Nazis and terrible diets, I have many happy memories of lots of love and warmth for the people who were part of my everyday life. During the air raids, most people in Moss Side had the small Anderson tin shelters in their back yards to take cover. We lived on Acomb Street, the area was a mass of Coronation

Street style two up, two down black brick snug as a bug houses. A lot of our neighbours were Irish and Polish and they were all very strong Catholics and we got along really well. Most locals worked in the nearby Dunlop rubber factory, doing all kinds of shift work 24/7. We had a useless tin shelter in our back yard so would rather use the huge communal underground shelter just off Princess Parkway near Alexander Park. We all seemed safe down there and all the people seemed happy. I suppose with me being so young I was able to feel that way without worrying about the bombers above.

In the early 1950's many West Indians started to move into Moss Side. Next door to us came the Williams family. The dad was a merchant seaman and would always nip in for a chit chat about his travels and pass over some food, that went down well. The Yams he gave us were like a root vegetable, a bit like a potato and we'd par boil them then put them over the coal fire and have them like you'd have spuds over the bonfire; nice and crisp outside and soft inside - what a treat they were! Soon after I remember the first Indian family moving in our street, The Singhs. Their old man wore one of them huge head scarfs and, having never seen one before, it came as a shock really. My mother used to say "Poor soul look at the size of that tea towel he has wrapped around his head, it must be really sore".

I was educated at The Holy Name RC school on Greenheys Lane in Chorlton-on-Medlock. It was the best time as a kid with so much going on. My mother was always busy as she ran a lodging house nearby as well so I would enjoy helping her out with a lot of this and that cleaning up. I got married in 1956 to a southern Irish man with the same surname as myself – Riley. He liked a drink at weekends and we'd go to The Mersey Bank on Princess Road and they had a fantastic band on run by Reg Coats. For almost 20 years it was rammed every weekend. I took a job as a chartered accountant in Withington and that lasted a few years until I had four children, then after few years I took part time work behind the bar in the little Robin Hood opposite Whitworth Park. I say this as from that point on I totally immersed myself into the lifestyle of a barmaid who loved every part of her job. The interacting with drunks always made things enjoyable as I loved the craic.

Right up till the 21st century local pubs were really social places to trade chat and let your hair down without having to looking over your shoulder in case there was trouble brewing. Saying that I don't blame anyone as its got to be hard work with all the easy money and drugs that play such a big part in today's lifestyle. I must mention other pubs that mean a lot to me; The Glue Pot, one of the many old market pubs, The Yew Tree on Wythenshawe Road, The Heaton Park Hotel run by Edna Stroner, such a lovely women, who always gave out a little bonus in the wage packet when the pub made a extra few bob. Nowadays I'm sure that's a thing of the past!

I worked a few years for local Ancoats legend Foo Foo Lammar. He had a club off Shudehill called The Picador. On the First floor there were drag acts and Frank would compère with lots of gay and lesbian jokes. Frank was openly gay but no one messed with him, he could handle all the drunks and knocked quite a few out cold. Upstairs was a trendy disco with lots of good music. I remember they would play the full album Around Midnight by John Holt. In the late 70's he opened up a class club called Foo-Foo's Palace near Piccadilly train Station. Next door he ran a small punk club that was really rough called The Ranch. No way would I work there but it made Frank a good few pennies. In the 80's he did tours of quite big venues like the Apollo in Ardwick, in the 90's he was asked to move to London and work with the BBC but being so close to Manchester's night life and the people he turned it down and Paul O'Grady did it instead. Fair enough he did a good job. I suppose really we were all glad Frank stayed in Manchester. If you get chance to read his book you won't be disappointed, I promise.

As for this pub were in now; it's got to be one of the last old school market pubs still with its original décor. It was a nice surprise to run into Colin after all these years, Other pubs in the Northern Quarter still serving locals that are from our era include The Unicorn, Wheatsheaf, Burton Arms, Millstone, and The City. When I'm in the city centre I like to chill out in churches before

KATH RILEY

I visit a pub hoping it'll be a chatty day. The Cathedral and The Hidden Gem are brill, but my favourite has to be the Holy Name on Oxford Road. If you go in, checkout the size of the shells that hold the holy water. I had my Holy Communion there and my parents got married there, it's such a wonderful building and one of the oldest in Manchester, it really means a lot to me. I always light a candle for the youth of today, hoping they can avoid the spice and smelly skunk they have problems with. See in Moss Side it was always natural bush weed that was smoked and seemed to chill out whoever was having a spliff. Nowadays they're wired to the moon!

As a kid I now realise how lucky our lot were to be so happy. The Whit-week Walks were bigger events than Halloween, Christmas and New Year back then. In the procession to Albert Square we passed The Brunswick ale house, a well-known prostitute from the next street to us would be stood up on a bar stool with a woodbine dangling out of her mouth supping from a Bottle of pale-ale shouting out "Kathleen Riley, hold yer Lilly up, Gal" I swear I went purple every time. But soon the huge crowds would cheer us all and it was all well again.

In the early 70's my friend's husband won big on the Littlewood's pools so took us all to Lloret de Mar, it was all in two weeks for £120. How good was that! We had a ball! I've been all over the world since but nothing could ever top that holiday, I even came home bronze and kept the tan all summer.

I'm a massive United fan and still get to see a few games every season. I'm very good friends with Sir Matt's daughter Sheenagh. Also my other two friends married players; Dennis Viollet and Shay Brennan; both Busby Babes. I think it's not a bad thing about all the tourists we have at Old Trafford these days, it's just the way football is in the 21st century.

As for seeing bands back in the day, the in place was The Ritz, dancing to Phil Moss's band, he was my favourite at the time. I liked the Charlie Basset band that played on a revolving stage till 11 then it was the mad dash for the last bus home. I went to Liverpool to see The Beatles in the Cavern and it was so hot down there. I also saw my favourite artist, Shirley Bassey, at the Apollo and again at the live club. I'm still a big fan and have booked tickets to see her soon.

As a young lady I wore the straight skirts with the splits, and box jackets we got on credit from Joan Barrie's on Market Street while we got our high heels from the Science shop. I went a lot to the Kings Hall at Belle Vue quite often. I remember my sister took me to see Johnny Ray. Part of his act was when he sang the big hit "Crying" and he had his head at end in a wet hanky which he always threw into the crowd. Well she caught it that night and still has it in a frame at home.

What I miss most is small talk in pubs as back in my day you'd educate each other. I once meet Gerald Kaufman, the Labour MP for Gorton and I said to him "Any chance he could help me getting a bath, I know its only a small problem". He replied "It may be a little thing to me but a big thing for yourself, I will see to it" and true to his word he sorted me out! What a top chap! I also met and had a few drinks with Ena Sharples, the battle axe queen from Corrie, she was proper Ancoats!

What's pleased me recently was passing the old Fish market building that's now called Manchester craft and design centre that's just round the corner off Tib Street. It's been there for years and for decades it was basically the only thing in the area. Now it's surrounded by trendy bars and restaurants and doesn't look out of place.

As for regrets, well I've got a few… I suppose I should have tried running a pub full time, no matter what size, as for me it was all about being social and getting along with folk who wanted to get along. Never in a million years would I wish any lady to run a pub nowadays, it's very rare that you find a good crowd willing to just chat away without any malice. Mind you saying that there's hardly any traditional pubs left, as most seem to have been turned into Gastropubs or Bistros. Good luck to them but I preferred the old fashioned boozers I grew up working in and they are very thin on the ground nowadays.

BILL KEETH

It's a great feeling when a writing project is done and dusted being able to add the acknowledgements and mention a person who helped you - even better when it's a close friend or family but over the 20 years I've been writing it seems most of my thank yous go to Library's and certain members as they're so on the ball with help in all kinds of ways.

Fact is Central Library is almost like my own office and it was here where I met Bill Keeth. He was arranging a book launch for his novel 'Manchester Kiss'. I'd read his book 'Every Street in Manchester' so we soon got chatting away. It seemed he was doing a mini tour of libraries and invited me along as I had just got Grafters reprinted with The Undesirables,, It was so easy to ask Bill a few questions on the road and get few pages in order. I'm sure you'll agree he's a Maverick who's got a sweet way of putting over his thoughts about our great city and its people.

Nowadays I am Bill Keeth, the author of 'Every Street in Manchester' and (as of September, 2006) it's sequel, 'Manchester Kiss'. But my real name is as Irish as the Bog of Allen. Bill Keeth is my pen-name. Why use a pen-name, you ask?

Well, my books are about North Manchester, and I don't want anyone thinking otherwise. Because I'm about as far removed from Ireland as is the Potato Blight of the 1840's. It's not that I don't have any understanding or any empathy with Irish history. Far from it! But, unlike my Dad – who labelled every one of his seven kids with an Irish Christian name – I don't think of myself as an Irishman. Not that there's anything wrong in thinking you're an Irishman. I don't see the point of it if you are in essence and in truth a North Manchester man. Which is what my Dad was – and a better one than he (or I) ever realised, despite his painting the house green, wearing tweedy things, vamping 'diddley-diddley' tunes on the piano keyboard and keeping shamrock in the bath on occasion – the occasion being St Patrick's Day (17th March) and the vigil thereof.

"Not for me, Dad. I'll go the Breastplate though!"

Mind you, it could have been a lot worse, I suppose. Because this was his 1930s' mind-set, the leisure hours of his youth having been spent at the Gaelic League on Dickenson Street off St Peter's Square, Manchester. Had he been a different sort of person entirely (thankfully, a person he never could have been), he might have embarrassed me irredeemably by parading (this was the 1930s, remember) in a Black shirt or a Brown.

From age 5 to age 11 I attended Mount Carmel school in Blackley. Not the new school opposite the church on Wilson Road but the old building (now demolished) adjacent to Harpurhey Baths, and known to one and all as 'Shepherd Street University'. This, in fact, is a lie because the kids that went to Holy Trinity called it "Mount Caramel", as we in turn, called their school "Holy Tripeshop."

Then, from age 11 to 18 (free pass in hand) I bussed it across town to Xaverian College in Rusholme. Later, after a stint in the Civil Service for my sins (1962-65), I attended De La Salle Teacher Training College, Hopwood Hall in Middleton. It wasn't much more than a cowboy town at the time but I found the place much improved in the mid to late 1970s when I studied for a degree there, writing a (long since binned) first novel during that same sabbatical year. Women had been admitted to the campus by then and, when they've a mind to do so, they will invariably civilise an establishment.

Chapter 18 of 'Every Street in Manchester' depicts a parish procession in North Manchester during the 1950s. The Whit Walks in Manchester city centre were essentially the same, except for the fact that a whole crowd of C of E parishes walked on the Monday of Whit Week, whilst we left-footers turned out en masse on the Friday. Each contingent took great pride in actually getting into town in the first place, with many buses not running, or running along unaccustomed routes (e.g. via Collyhurst Road and Dantzic Street) in order for them not to collide with the walkers or "scholars", as the old folk lining the "cart road" referred to the school kids in the procession.

Other features of the Whit Walks, I remember, were the discarded fruit boxes that were picked up from Smithfield Market on Shudehill (they were used for sitting on whilst watching the walks: luxury!) and 'eggy butties' that were made at home (for breakfast and elevenses: a gourmet's dream!).

One Whit Friday, aged 19 and stupid, I remember gaining access with a gang of similarly stupid pals to one of the pubs on Kennedy Street, as the front door opened to admit the Holland's pie man. It may have been The Vine or the City Arms - it was, at any rate, a pub where the resident landlord wasn't also a city councillor. We found there was already a full house in there, as well as the Kerry Pipers' big drum. It wasn't yet 9.00am, and not one of us had had breakfast! "Yuk! Pass the Alka-Seltzer!"

Of Mancunian landmarks, I thought Belle Vue the mankiest. And I don't mean that in any Mancunian sense of the word. At Belle Vue I'd clock the peeling paintwork and lacklustre animals rather than the Bobs and other esteemed amusements. What spoiled it for me, I think, was a trip to Belle Vue circus from Mount Carmel school. During the course of which a cheeky-chappie type called Billy Sullivan, aged around 9 years old, cheerfully hailed a clown who two minutes before had been gleefully entertaining us in the circus ring. However the clown treated Billy Sullivan and the rest of us kids to the choicest mouthful I have ever heard this side of Bernard Manning's effluently-worded microphone. I have never felt quite the same about circuses since. Fair's fair, though, because Belle Vue's Top Ten Club with Jimmy Savile on Sunday nights circa 1963 was fine. I can remember hearing 'The Beatles - I Saw Her Standing There' for the very first time at the Top Ten Club, and realising, though I was otherwise occupied (boogying on down) at the time, that I was witnessing musical history in the making. The Terminal Teenager Jimmy Savile used to leave his Rolls Royce at the entrance to the dance hall, showing off – and it was never once scratched to my knowledge. How's about that for law and order, guys 'n' gals? (See Chapter 6 of Every Street in Manchester.)

MANCHESTER MAVERICKS

I frequently visited the Alliance Inn in my formative years, by which I mean the old Alliance on Rochdale Road, next to Kate Street (as was). The old Alliance was a beer house, pure and simple – not having a licence to retail spirits. But talk about quality of life! My dad could recall being in the Alliance with his dad on a mid-week afternoon during WWII with waiter service readily available, the waiter simply being summoned by the pressing of a bell.

Mid-week in the mid-1960s I used the Greens Arms on Ashton New Road, Clayton (Wilson's Mild being like nectar at that time) and the Folkestone Hotel only occasionally (Swales! "Pass me those Alka-Seltzer again!"), then a bit more frequently when it went over to Boddingtons. The Haddon Hall in Droylsden also featured on this bibulous itinerary. I still get in the Haddon for a mid-week beef steak at under a fiver a throw! Come Summer, I'd maybe spend Friday nights suited up in the cocktail bar of the Lord Nelson, up at the junction of Hulmes Road/Lord Lane, Failsworth. I was on Shank's Pony at the time, of course, which is why the Nelson seemed welcoming only in Summer. I didn't drive or have access to a car until 1966 – a 3-litre Wolseley 699, which was just as thirsty as I was. It did 15 mpg around the town and 25 mpg on a run. Thank God for cheap, lead-loaded petrol at the ICI service station on Church Lane, Harpurhey, at 3/6d a gallon. (That's 17.5p a gallon to you!)

Friday night and Sunday night in my teenage years were spent (like good coin of the realm) at Ada Street Club at the back of the Alliance. And what I wouldn't give nowadays to hear Larry Williams singing 'Boney Moronie' on that stonking great record player with the metal stylus they had up on stage! Especially if it was followed by 'The Olympics' with 'Western Movies'; both records were 10" shellac 78s, by the way. So, if you got lucky with a girl at Ada Street, you risked smashing your favourite record taking her home. 78s were less of a problem for the pure of heart!

Then, from 1960 onwards, the World Famous Embassy Club proved to be a convenient stomping-ground. (What ever happened to my Life Membership that I paid a quid for, Bernard?)

Thereafter, the Domino Club on Grey Mare Lane beckoned.

BILL KEETH

At the Domino I remember seeing 'Joe Brown & the Bruvvers', Peter & Gordon (public schoolboys from the Home Counties, who were given a rough ride there), and 'Johnny Duncan & the Blue Grass Boys'. I couldn't be bothered turning out to see The Big O. (Can you believe that?)

Also, at St Bernadette's Club, Withington, I remember seeing 'The Merseybeats' and (very nearly) 'The Beatles' – except that St Bernadette's resolutely refused to pay those greedy Scousers the £80 they were asking for. (Oh, we knew what value for money was when we saw it!)

Work-wise, I suppose I'd better begin at the beginning. Over the years I've been a Paper boy; Grocer's boy; Window cleaner; Topper and Tailer of onions at Pixie Pickles (12/6d for 4 hundredweight of shallots – a wage to bring tears to already watering eyes!); Postman (at Christmas); Bar man; Waiter; Civil servant; Salesman in a Tailor's shop; Warehouseman; a member of the Navy; Football pools and insurance collector; Play centre supervisor; Newspaper haulier; Shellfish salesman; Cabbie – black cabs & private hire; DJ; Art dealer; Retailer (of TVs, typewriters, in-car stereos, 7" vinyl singles) – and finally a teacher.

For a time in the late Sixties I worked as a waiter at the Whitegate, Chadderton, and the Thatched House, Moston, saving up to get married in the first instance. And then keeping my wife in the style to which she'd quickly become accustomed to in the second – that is, housebound out in the sticks (one bus Royton, as it then was) with two bread snatchers we'd accumulated within two years of getting wed. (Pity we didn't know what was causing it...)

Then for twelve years from 1977 last orders were quaffed in the Waggon and Horses, a Boddingtons' house in Rhodes Village, Middleton, where the long-serving landlord was ex-Royal Marine Roy Barry – a tough guy with incomparable patience and a weird sense of humour. One Winter's night some Herbert broke up a bar stool and put it on the fire. 'Just for that,' said Roy, 'you're getting no more coal from me.' If you got yourself barred by Roy Barry, you stayed barred. Fair play to him too! He barred 'The Bear' once upon a time, though who 'The Bear' was,

MANCHESTER MAVERICKS

I couldn't possibly comment. Best leave that to Brian Hughes MBE – backed up by his stable of world class boxers.

Here's a little vignette that sticks in my mind concerning the wide cross section of humanity that boozed in The Waggon. Where there might be Vespa scooters parked up beside Daimlers and scramblers outside. I was in the Vault one day, looking across to the hatch letting on to the pool room where one player inclines himself across the pool table to address the cue ball. A punk rocker, complete with Mohican haircut, tattoos, earrings, Doc Martens and denims (the lot!) takes his shot, whereupon his opponent appears, cue at the ready; NHS specs, trilby, suit and tie, Columbo's raincoat – and bicycle clips. (Bicycle clips, I swear it!)

If you ever catch me crying, it'll be about people, not things. So my five favourite buildings in Manchester are in each instance places where I have been made to feel welcome and consequently happy.

So first off I fully intend to re-visit that house on Grange Drive, Blackley, where my Auntie Sue lived until 1966 with my maternal grandmother, a much younger aunt who was a great cook, whilst her husband (a veteran of El Alamein, Tobruk and the Italian Campaign, a keen cricketer. *Daily Herald* reader and Christian gentleman). For twenty-four years of my life and hers, my Auntie Sue spoiled me rotten. In actual fact, she was my great-aunt. (Everybody seemed to have an unmarried great-aunt when I was a kid, the direct result, I suspect, of the country losing so many marriageable males in WWI.) What follows here hardly scratches the surface of my undying indebtedness to her. It was she who bought me stacks of American comics which detailed the amazing exploits of Superboy, Superman, Batman and Robin, Blackhawk and Green Lantern, thereby initiating my induction into the noble art of comic-swapping. Which in my day was played on the smallest playing field known to man – that is, a donkey-stoned doorstep, with two piles of comics and an equal number of pre-adolescent backsides athwart it.

Then, from age 20 onwards, what assumed even greater importance in my life was a little palace of a council house on Vale Street, Clayton, Manchester 11, this being the setting for two pearls of great price. (Actually, there were four in residence, though I speak only of two, not to risk depressing the market.) One of these I've already mentioned (She Who Nevermore Shall Windswept Be), the other being the best mother-in-law known to mortal man. (Ergo, more correctly, Mother-of-pearl, I suppose – though to my certain knowledge, she is and was infinitely more valuable than mother-of-pearl can ever be.)

Next, the former County Court on Quay Street, diagonally across from the Opera House (cater-cornered, as the Americans say). It looms large on the skyline, its eastern elevation facing Lower Byrom Street because this is where I met She Who Nevermore Shall Windswept Be. It's a listed building, complete with Adams' staircase and blue-plaque, though not for my particular reason as yet, though certainly on two other counts. First of all, this building is the original site of Owens College, the educational embryo that would become the Victoria University of Manchester. But before that time it had been the home of the philanthropist Richard Cobden, who with his fellow MPs – Bury's Robert Peel and Rochdale's John Bright – paid the Corn Laws that had fostered starvation, not only amongst their own countrymen, but away to the West where my own forbears on the Galway-Mayo border, in Longford and Kilkenny. And also thousands like them that had been constrained to uproot themselves from their Irish heath and ship out of Dun Laoghaire in search of bread and unblighted potatoes.

Number 4 on my list of favourite buildings is St John Vianney's Church, Moston, where you'll find me on high days and holidays among a congregation of sterling Mancunian worth. Many of the descendants of the "poor and huddled masses" mentioned above, a force in world affairs they are now. Not the least of it's being that, in addition to their countless works of charity throughout the year, they lend much-needed financial support to a village on the Indian subcontinent.

And last but no means least, I rate the old Blackley Library (now demolished, the new North City Library having recently taking its place) and Central Library, too – and these buildings in tandem for the simple reason that, with 7 kids, a dog and a cat marauding free range round my parental home on Wilson Road, Blackley, I would not have been able to study for my O Levels or A Levels without them. And, without studying for my O Levels and A Levels, I might never have learnt about, or been able to discuss with conviction politicians like Cobden and Bright and Peel whose proud careers are proof that politics in the UK wasn't always the dirty word it has become, I feel, in too many instances latterly become.

I've mentioned seeing 'The Merseybeats' at St Bernadette's, Withington, where they did a cracking rock 'n' roll set one Friday night in the mid-1960s. In the 1960s too I saw Little Richard at the Odeon, Oxford Street, where he delivered a truly impressive full-throated lap of honour around the auditorium, twice in one night. But to my mind, the very best concert I've ever attended in my life was given by 10cc at the Apollo, Ardwick, circa 1982.

The auditorium was packed, the atmosphere electric. Eric Stewart is socking it to us on lead guitar whilst Graham Gouldman, generous to a fault, is treating the audience to unnecessarily profligate and consummately complicated bass lines. For shame, subsequent to this event, I left my own Gibson jumbo acoustic untouched for a full twelve months.

What a star he is, the boy Gouldman! A genius, no less! Penning (years before 10cc was even a twinkle) 'For Your Love' and 'Evil-Hearted You' for 'The Yardbirds', and 'Bus Stop' for 'The Hollies'. And what a very special song 'Bus Stop' is, only meeting its equal, I think in, 'Love Hurts'. The Bryants wrote 'Love Hurts' for the 'Everly Brothers' – with lyrics spare and the storyline graphic!

My favourite Mancunians? Oof! And only five in number! Well, that's a real toughie! But here goes, for what it's worth:

One – She Who Nevermore Shall Windswept Be. Because we had 5 kids between 1968 and 1984, and she just got on with it. Rather than having anybody and everybody looking after the kids for her.

Two – Fr Brian Seale of St John Vianney's church, Moston. He's a priest, and that suits me, though maybe not you. (Neither do all priests suit me, I can tell you, though, as luck would have it, you only need one at a time.) But as with any true professional, Fr Brian's message is invariably warm, cerebral, clearly-stated and inviting.

I cannot and will not tolerate so-called 'experts' or 'professionals' in whatever field of human (or superhuman) endeavour. People who use their expertise to brow beat people, to berate, to show off and ultimately, of course – to keep people at bay and even drive them away. To behave like that is to make too much of oneself when the nobler course of action (the proper course of action) is to indicate the discipline itself as being deserving of any accolade or potential adherence that's up for grabs.

Three – the totally unassuming Wilf McGuinness who is still at Man United: as affable in his maturity as he was as a (very talented) lad at school. (Mount Carmel school, naturally!)

Four – Brian Kidd, who is justly renowned for the welcome he extends to younger fans. Treat a child with a bit of respect, I say, and you've a fair chance he'll turn out to be both respectful and respectable. (Mind you, Jack Connolly, my old teacher from Xaverian, now retired, would be an eminently suitable candidate for acclaim of similar ilk.)

Five – the eminently approachable Billy Hopkins of 'Our Kid' fame. I reckon it will be quite an achievement if I'm even half as decent as he is when I'm a million-seller – as, indeed, it will be quite an achievement if I ever become a million seller!

Six (Oh, I've overdone it, you say? So who's counting?) – Voila! Adolphe Valette, L. S. Lowry's teacher, whose paintings may be viewed at Manchester Art Gallery every day of the week apart from Monday. (Incidentally, those same paintings were at Queen's Park Art Gallery when I was a kid, before Manchester Art Gallery happened to re-discover them.) Adolphe Valette painted a Manchester (much of it was still there when I was growing up: horses and carts, horses with nosebags, horses nodding their heads so as to set up a pace as they went uphill.) Adolphe Valette painted a damp, smoggy, foggy, rainswept, almost dreamily businesslike Manchester that existed in the first quarter of the twentieth century. Which nourished on my behalf so many of the people and places whose names and worth I would eventually come to cherish.

I don't bother with Football. I decked off that particular Blue bus, aged 12, in defiance of my Blue-blooded Dad. (See Chapter 2 of Every Street in Manchester.) And it's probably just as well too, because my wife's family are season ticket-sporting Reds. In fact, Football saved her Dad's life during WWII. He played for the King's Own battalion team, so they wouldn't hear of him volunteering for the Chindits! He got away with his life plus a life pension for breaking his wrist in a bad tackle on a Sikh goalkeeper at Simla! With regard to my own lack of interest in Football, though, you know the old joke about Gene Autry being asked to sing a song: having just heard about the burned-out ranch house, the poisoned well, the dead cattle, the kidnapped kids and scalped wife? Well, even today, to see Man City's goalmouth under threat from the opposing team is to feel like Gene Autry must have felt. And you'll be getting no song from me either! (Tribalism is a terrible thing.)

Aged 14, I positively yearned for a finger-length, velvet-collared, violently-coloured Teddy Boy jacket. (Thank God, my Mother wouldn't permit it!) So that's the all-time sartorial low of my career. Mind you, I did succeed in procuring a thumb-length, link-buttoned, Donegal tweed, fleck jacket of happy memory. And I liked wearing my crepe-soled brothel creepers and yellow socks too! And also a raincoat worn with the collar up – even at the height of summer under a blazing sun! But the thought of the Windsor-knotted ties I rejoiced in during the late 1950s nowadays makes me cringe.

If you fancy a closer look at my early 1960s'/post-Ted wardrobe, you might care to check out Albert Finney's gear in 'Saturday Night and Sunday Morning'. That's me up and dressed. Literally! (It's a good film too.)

Come Beatlemania, I loved being suited up after working mucky all week (Gas Board: see Chapter 1 of Every Street in Manchester.) Giraffe collar (do you remember them?); knitted tie with minuscule knot; "winklepickers" and a "bum freezer" Italian jacket with one-and-a-quarter inch lapels. Great gear. Mind you, I was in better shape then than I am now. The last time I tried a reefer jacket on at ASDA, Harpurhey, I looked like Tate & Lyle's Mr Cube.

Looking back clothes-wise, I suppose I was a Mod, though I never thought of it in those terms, but I was always suited up due to having a Saturday job at Burton's in Piccadilly and having access to good suits at a discount. At Burton's, Piccadilly (Branch 364), which was managed at the time by the ever affable Jack Riley, my oppo Paul Grainger, youngest scion of a north Manchester Irish Dancing family (though, no Michael Flatley himself except on Broadhurst Fields with a size-5 case ball at his feet.) Paul Grainger and I, being part-timers, were barred by company rules from earning commission, though we were allowed to claim an extra ten bob (50p to you) for any window model or left-on-hand bargain we might succeed in foisting on to an unsuspecting public.

Window model suits combined Schwarzenegger shoulders with waists no wider than waspish, whilst left-on-hand items were similar oddments, often startlingly styled and coloured, which never had been claimed by the drunks, jokesters, and aesthetically-challenged mutants who had originally commissioned them.

Still, ten bob represented a full 20% of our take home pay in those days, so perhaps Paul Grainger and I may be forgiven for concentrating our weekly efforts, come Saturday, on this section of the stock. For it was by no means unusual for us to double our take home pay in this way. Nor, incidentally, was it in any way unusual for the genial Jack Riley to be besieged mid-week with complaints about these same items from a phalanx of female relatives of our Saturday customers who could invariably lay claim to superior fashion sense prior to demanding the master's money back!

Time fogs the memory forty years on, and though I will cheerfully admit to being responsible for selling the electric blue zoot suit to – well, Gabby Hayes, I suppose you could call him, I am no longer certain whether it was Paul or I who sent the circus midget off home with a half dozen waistcoats ranging from size 32" to 48" chest. Similarly, I simply cannot remember which of us it was who sold the George Melly stage suit to the man from

MANCHESTER MAVERICKS

the Prudential.

You'll never believe this. But it was as late as November, 1993 before I ventured overseas because with five kids in tow by 1984, we also had a touring caravan too! But come 1993 my wife delivered an ultimatum: "No!" She declared and henceforth, she was never ever going to shelter behind wind-swept rocks in Tenby or Torquay! So we flew out to Sorrento on her behalf. What a dream! Sitting outside in shirt sleeve order as late as the first week in November! (The Italians had their thermals on!) And, with Pompeii being nearby via the Transvesuviana rail link, I was personally a three-time visitor in a fortnight.

My attitude to regret is ambivalent at best. On the one hand, I do deeply resent the fact that I was not best treated at work. But it's not something I dwell upon because I'm a great believer in Providence.

"Life is what happens to you while you're busy making other plans," said John Lennon. (The only time he was divinely inspired, it seems to me.) Because it occurs to me that, if I had been treated better at work, then maybe I wouldn't have written 'Every Street in Manchester' and 'Manchester Kiss'. Therefore I feel pain is a vital creative force, contentment probably is not.

Even so, I cannot help but regret that things were harder for a time than perhaps they should have been. However we managed, as we have always managed. And so one thing I do regret more than anything in the world is if She Who Nevermore Shall Windswept Be has ever for a moment had cause to doubt that she is the air I breathe, the rain that cools me, the ground that holds me upright, the vision that delights my waking hours, the voice that's music to my ears, the warmth that reminds me I am alive and the thought of whom now causes the truth of things to be stated plainly thus:

'How slender the thread whereby my dreams are hung!'
'You serious?'
'That's for me to know and you to find out.'
'That's what I'm tranner do.'
'Tranner do?
'Trying to do.'

'That's more like it. Didn't hurt too much, did it?

I regret not having given up smoking many years before I did. I chucked it in February, 1987. I was smoking 60 cigarettes a day when I came across a quiet time in my life, recognised it for what it was, and made sure I grasped the nettle. It was like scaling the Berlin Wall and getting away free. I walked the Pennine Way that same year in celebration of the fact.

Finally, I regret to say that, with regard to Bill Keeth (author nowadays, non-smoker too), to eat one chocolate biscuit is – whimper! – to eat a packet of chocolate biscuits, and to wonder too whether She Who Nevermore Shall Windswept Be has got anything else in the cupboard while I'm at it. (I don't suppose there's any of that Alka-Seltzer left, is there?)

On a more serious note, I truly detest the thought that we live in an age and country where women and children, the old and the infirm are not safe on the streets even in broad daylight. A society where I have to watch my back at night, walking home from a quiz night at the pub. But what we do need to guard against, I believe, is running away with the idea that the whole country's like that. Because there are no yobs in the hills, believe me! (See Chapter 32 of Manchester Kiss.) I'm positive that the far majority of the population are decent folk.

However unfortunately – at least in respect of 'Yob Culture' – the yobs of which we speak of are to be found in the city, where work dictates where most of us also must live. Worse still, no government (either Tory or new Labour) have the least intention of sorting the problem out. Because our "governments" merely twiddle with things they have neither the imagination nor the guts to employ any radical solution. And I really do feel that nothing short of a radical solution is required where 'Yob Culture' is concerned.

Teachers in New Zealand (where there is a dearth of teachers in country areas) are required to serve time in "country service", so to speak. That is, they must commit themselves to doing a stint of teaching away from home. So, in the UK, where there is obviously a need for the yobs amongst the teenage population to learn civil responsibility, I believe they should be taught the way of things by means of compulsory national service. By which I mean national service in a very much wider sense than simply being recruited into the Army, Navy, or the Air Force and leaving it at that.

To tell the truth, I don't think there will ever be peace on earth until the British Armed Forces are disbanded, and their complements being transferred to a United Nations' network of forces. (Was it James Cameron in the FT who estimated that, with the sole exception of 1967, the British Army has been on active service somewhere in the world in every year since the end of WWII?) Because it is far too easy for military minds to decide: "Okay, let's go to war. Because we'll only have to spend the same money on war games, if we don't go to war, don't-cha know?" (And be damned to all the lives that will be lost in the process!)

What I envisage is compulsory national service that would have older teenagers helping in schools, in old folks' homes – in Manchester Dogs' Home, for that matter – in multifarious social services' establishments, and being allocated under benevolent supervision to various civic duties from school dinners to dustbins. Perhaps serving abroad with organisations such as Unicef amongst many others, and the UN armed forces too, should they show an aptitude for that. Meanwhile, we, as a nation, would learn not to regard such service as something to be looked down upon or sneered at. Rather would we come to see it as service that is honourable indeed, service attracting all due praise and reward.

There are certainly ways of doing these things, provided there's a will to do them. Take the Duke of Edinburgh's Award Scheme and the Prince's Trust, for example – though personally I would prefer to see the initiative taken away from the sniffy Royals.

Hey, let's get our own heads straight about things while we're about it too. I mean, why couldn't there be a parallel scheme? Say, whereby adults who are in employment would be encouraged to take individual unemployed teenagers to work for a spell. And, if that doesn't suit for whatever reason (I mean, I don't envisage kids down the sewers or doing brain surgery – or riding out a Force 10 gale in a fishing smack in mid-Atlantic), then why not have people volunteer instead to supervise youth clubs and other socialising ventures? There's no good reason why a High Court judge couldn't lead a party along the Pennine Way. (We're all on the same team, aren't we? Or are we?)

But it's never going to happen, is it? Well, not under the self-serving Thatcherite/Blairite regimes that has masqueraded a good government in the last thirty years or so. As with so many other things the Government ought to be fettling, it's up to Joe Public to sort things out for themselves, beginning by asking themselves whether it really is the case that 'Yob Culture' has neither excuse, explanation, nor cure because 'monkey see, monkey do' is the rule in this particular jungle. And maybe what the Joe Public need to do is take a closer look at their own attitudes, opinions and perceptions – that is, at the way in which they are seen to behave in public.

Do the Joe Public party have any 'Yob Culture' tendencies of their own, by any chance? Do they spit in the street, or otherwise void themselves in public, effin' and jeffin' while they're about it? What's their attitude to getting personally rat-legged every Saturday night of their life? Do they perhaps go along with the tabloid newspapers' sleazy perception of the females of our species? Is the English flag they flew during the World Cup really about football? Or is it a discreet nod in the direction of NF fascism? Is Joe Public concerned about issues like these? Because, if not, they should be. And maybe what 'Yob Culture' really needs is for the physician to heal himself before starting in on prescribing remedies to cure the patient.

See Chapter 5, of 'Manchester Kiss' where I quote the things that are important to me: 'Freedom and Fair-Dealing, Honesty, Fraternity, Social Justice, and Truth.' I respect anybody and everybody who personifies or espouses any or all of these ideals.

I respect people who know their own minds, especially if they are maybe having to struggle upstream against the general trend of opinion in society – against the zeitgeist, if you like. Because wrongheadedness usually has a majority vote, it seems to me – e.g. Nazi Germany, the Spanish Inquisition, Soviet Russia, the financial pundits (their name is Legion!) who, during the

Eighties and early Nineties had nothing but good to say about Equitable Life.

And so, I respect David, Lord Alton of Liverpool, who speaks out for the unborn, who can't speak for themselves. And I rate Bono Vox and Cliff Richard, who know that much is expected of those to whom much is given. I'm not sure Bob Geldof knows as much – but he'll do for me, whatever he knows, though it beats me why an Irishman (and a great one, begob!) would need, require or settle for an English knighthood.

I also rate Max Clifford, the publicist – not as a publicist, but as a father who cares for his disabled daughter. I respect the actor, Paul Nicholas – not the greatest Thespian of our generation, I'm sure he'd privately agree. But what I like about Paul Nicholas is that he works at treading the boards. He's not the sort of name who swans in for a cameo role, pocketing in the process an undeserved bundle for minimum effort. He's a working actor – a trouper. And to my mind, he will always be a better actor because of it. (Mind you, I might just as easily have picked Bruce Alexander for this same role – he who is perhaps better known as Inspector Frost's undeservedly underrated Mullet.)

Hey, lighten up! Because life's not only about respect, is it? It's about liking things too. In which case, let me state quite categorically that I like: rock 'n' roll music; beat music; reggae; soul; country and western too. I like books a lot – though far too many books for me to go into here. So, I'll mention just three – my current must-read: 'The Curious Incident of the Dog in the Night-Time' by Mark Haddon; and (just so you don't think I'm a fan of Whitbread prize winners in general, which I'm not), an old favourite of mine: 'Walking Wounded' by William McIllvanney, lest we forget the abomination of desolation that was Thatcherism, Mother of Blairism. (Incidentally, William McIllvanney is a former Whitbread prize winner, though, happily not with this book.) I'll leave you to unearth this treasure trove for yourselves, 'Sawn-Off Tales' by David Gaffney which is a veritable Mancunian masterpiece.

I like paintings and painters. I like anything to do with the Pennine Way. I like a good laugh. (Tommy Cooper, Ken Dodd –

where is your like today?) I like kids that can behave themselves – and adults too. I like holidays in Italy and on the Costa del Sol. (I like holidays in Torbay, too, though nowadays they are forbidden by She Who Nevermore Shall Windswept Be.) I like to read a book a day on holiday. I like the Roman antiquities. I like that first dive into the swimming baths. I like a cooked breakfast, and pepper on my tomatoes, I like black coffee and whisky drowned with ice and soda. I love estate cars.

With regard to law and order, individual policemen can be okay – or not, as the case may be. If an old lady with Alzheimer's or a kiddy goes missing – well, yes, the police are the bee's knees. But certainly a visit to the police station for whatever reason, innocent or otherwise, continues to be an unpleasant experience due to the off-hand, even arrogant manner of a few officers who need to be pensioned off before there are no Asians or Argentinians left to shoot. And I really do have serious misgivings about the way in which the police deal (or, rather, fail to deal) with most of the petty crime that blights the city streets. (Noticing another plate glass window smashed in north Manchester this morning, I realised it was the car showroom's turn this week.) The public perception (with which I'm inclined to agree) is that the police prefer to prosecute motorists, because motorists are essentially law-abiding at heart and are also easier to catch.

In any case, there aren't enough police to begin with, because I really don't think there is the will (at government, county, city, and local level) to sort things out. And why ever should there be when the local magistrates, the constituency MP, the Prime Minister – all these people who lead cosily closeted lives far removed from the city streets?

Consider this. If the police in North Manchester were, policing downtown Baghdad instead, is the standard of policing North Manchester gets really the best shot the police would give it under the scrutiny of the world's media? Somehow I don't think so.

Manchester itself, like any other city in the country, has to like it or lump it – especially on a Saturday night. From what I'm told by a serving GMP officer, Manchester A Division it is hell on earth on a Saturday night, when the city centre serves as an ambulance station, so to speak, for A&E at the MRI.

The trouble is, I think that despite the knee-jerk legislation that invariably makes the headlines, the real message that is being sent out from Chequers about law and order is this: "Insulate yourself with money. Because it's every man for himself out there, and I have no idea what to do about it. Make sure you live in a district far removed from the inner city. Oh, and always travel – if you really must travel – in a locked car, preferably chauffeur-driven, vacating the whole shebang as often and for as long as you possibly can, adjourning to your villa on the Costa, though I can tell you Lombardy is very nice. Because for my part, I am, as I say, damned if I know what to do about it all – and neither do I care, having had the foresight to insulate myself in the financial sense I would unhesitatingly recommend to the rest of you."

It is almost as if successive "governments" in the UK have actually caved in to 'Yob Culture'. They are effectively permitting it to impose its own curfew on a civilian population that has every right to expect instead the full protection of the law. It is to be hoped that the same civilian population will continue to eschew vigilantism as a means of redress.

GEORGE SMITH

I first met George in a pub called "The Sea Hawk" that was built in 1971 to serve the seven Tower blocks in Hulme - these became known as the Seven Sisters. Four of the blocks have since been taken down which is a shame as I'm a great lover of tower blocks, more so nowadays as most have had extras such as winter gardens with glass panels closing in the old balconies. Many of the old tower blocks have been massively improved over the years, it's great to see. Back then there would be a crowd of us leaning on the verandahs and having a good old chin-wag. After the pub one night I got chatting with a guy called Judda, which was George's nickname. He always reminded me of Robert Powell who played Jesus Christ on the telly at the time - he had a really easy going Manchester accent. When you meet someone who's open and chats away it's a real buzz, the funny stories come over better if the accent's rolling as smoothly as his does.

I had a good friend in the same tower block as Judda who let me hire out his flat at times, in fact his flat was directly underneath Judda's, and soon we started to drink in a small wine bar just off Deansgate called "The Gallery" - when it first opened it was a small cellar with the beer barrels being used as tables, then the next door office space created room for a pool table with a few more tables and about a year later the car showroom next door was put up for sale and it became the best place down the southside of Manchester city centre. I'd say for a good ten years we had it boxed off and never had any hassle. Roufy was the DJ and they sold bottles of Grolsch which was strong, cheap Dutch lager.

The owner, Jimmy, would sort us out at the end of the night with taxis and a few crates to take back to Judda's and very soon the craic would begin back at his with plenty of supping and he'd get the guitars and mouth organ out. Above Judda's was a Pirate Radio station that played reggae and they would get involved and before long it was a bit of a party. They were proper good times when I think back. So I'm over the moon he's given me some pages towards Mavericks, hope you yourself think the same.

MANCHESTER MAVERICKS

My name is George Smith, at school I was called "Smile" whilst now it's "Judda". I was educated at Stretford Juniors and from our entire year only one person went on to Grammar school. We all went 100 yards down the road to Old Trafford Boys C of E. It had plenty of Catholics, Cypriots, Turks, Africans and Asians, it was like the League of Nations. There were also lots of kids who were expelled from their school that came to ours, it was like a mad house.

My parents were from Salford, my grandparents were from Hulme. My Granddad was in the first war and on his way out with the transport to the front when there was a stop off for a brew and a ciggie and right there on the other side of the road was his brother Pete who shouted over "you'll soon be earning your fucking kings shilling, our kid!" as plenty of Manchester Fusiliers took the piss, they had it rough back then. Fact here you can check the Manchesters got 26 VCs, more than any other battalion in that war and it says something that the VCs were all won before breakfast.

When the war was over they finally met back up in 1920 and that was when Pete was up in court. A 6ft 3in Irish copper hobbled in who Pete had mixed it with on the cobbles. He lifted his leg onto the dock showing the state it was in, he also told the court that Pete had ripped his tunic, split his lip, broke his nose and jumped up and down on his helmet!

The judge asked "What have you got to say for yourself?"

Pete said "I'm 5ft 8ins and if I can do all that to him how about making me a boxer!" He got an extra three months on top for contempt and in them days 6 months hard labour in Strangeways was no joke.

When I was 5 I went to live over in Canada with my uncle and my Dad and they took me to a huge department store in Toronto at Christmas. I thought I was going to see Father Christmas but it turned out to be an appearance by William Boyd the actor who played Hopalong Cassidy, he was huge in them days, even his horse "Tonto" was. I had my photo taken with him, what a buzz! I had a massive problem when I got back to Manny though. I got picked on because I'd picked up a Yank accent, I was glad when the mixed races came into ours to take the heat away from me, even today old mates still call out "alright Hopalong!"

I used to love helping Uncle Pete out on his Rag and Bone cart, we'd give the young kids balloons and a dangerous bow and arrow made out of bamboo, and our main blag was a gold fish. We'd shout "Rags for Fish, everyone's a swimmer!" Our house was full of gold fish, at first my Mam went bonkers as they were in all mad places so in the end, as all my family were Man City fans, they had twelve fish all named after the City team and manager, I can only remember the name of Bert Trautmann captain of City and the German national team, he was also a German prisoner of war whose job it was to clear away all the unexploded bombs up at Liverpool docks. He liked England so much that much he stayed over here for years, a true legend.

George 'Rudda' Smith (centre) in his 70s finery

I even had to wear my City shirt out on the horse and cart, and was taken to see city at Maine Road for years. Then after getting beat on the street by bagful of goals every other day, I felt enough was enough - see all the other lads were united so I finally became the first red devil in our family.

We'd moved from the Old Cart Road, which is the stretch of Chester Road from 'The Star' pub next to the Mancunian flyover and the Manchester Regiment pubs up to the Northumberland pub. Fact was my name alongside "MUFC" was on this pub wall for over twenty years, I'm gutted it isn't there now. The rest of

MANCHESTER MAVERICKS

Chester Road is sad to see nowadays, not one pub to have a natter over a pint with the locals in but it's the same all over Manchester I suppose, still with most pubs losing money who's to blame?

The toughest pubs were in the centre of Hulme, '3 Legs of Man' and 'The Platford' were a massive no-no! We then went to live on Railway Road right next to the bridge that leads you over to the Stretford End, I swear it was that close when Man U scored all the ornaments would shake and fall over.

This was my plot as a kid for selling the *Manchester Evening News* after games, then later in every pub along Chester Road the famous football 'Pinks'. I've only ever seen away fans at this end when Everton played Liverpool in 1971 in the FA cup Semi, imagine 60,000 Scouse Scabs on my fucking doorstep, everyone of them a smelly cunt.

In those days the Stretford End was known as one of the hardest for any other mob to even think about coming in to have a rumble with the Red Army, we all had our own patches, like Swinton, Salford, Gorton and Wythenshawe had the left side of the Tunnel, Collyhurst, Ancoats, Middleton, Monsall and Miles Platting had the right side whereas our mob from OT, Hulme, Stretford and Urmston always hung a massive union jack over the tunnel top tier – we always stood in the top area above the tunnel. Cock of the Stretford end was never really straightforward as there was a good few big hitters like big Dave from Warrington, Gibbo, Jeff Lewis, Crusher, Mad Eyes, Gaftney and Nutty Norman who, even though I hated him, was the cock in my books.

Norman just vanished overnight around 1970 (thank fuck) I've seen him run down the tunnel at half time fuming if our team was losing and he'd be kicking shins and arses with his Toe-Tackers which were them Commando Steel toe capped boots, he was a bad arse bully in my books, but I have to give him one huge credit, he would lead a mob wherever the Bovverboys went for aggro.

Our best days as Scally kids were spent robbing the trucks that parked up for the weekends on a huge truckers gaff near ours. They even had truckers Molls, like gangsters have loose women who want it full on and don't even want paying. So they'd be out for the count after knobbing the Molls, when we'd slash the canvas and crack away for over an hour at least to and fro with industrial bin liners and old prams which would be loaded up at the bottom of the railway line then we'd walk the half mile praying like fuck no trains came back up the embankment and stash the loot next to the old railway sheds in the sand wagons attached to the trains until the next day. We had the lot, we even called them 'Lucky bags' like the ones you'd get as kids which had all different kinds of toffees inside. We'd get all kinds of booze and cigs. I remember the next day once we sacked school and filled the sink with Baby chams, Q C Wine and Gin. Fact was in the early days the Manchester saying was the only way out of Manchester is with a bottle of Gin. They meant get pissed and forget the place it was so rough, but as a kid I always thought it meant you'd be checked by customs like in war time and you had to bribe them with Gin! Well never mind Mother's Ruin, my very own Mother made a mad appearance. Whilst we were all blowing ginger biscuits into the drinks, we all got her high heels hammered on our nappers, then always found this one strange after she'd booted everyone out. She then just put her feet up and demanded I make her a cup of tea like nothing had happened!

A few weeks later a kid got nicked, cunt went too far robbing a wallet. We all got turned over and down to Talbot Road police station and charged, then we had to appear in Strangeways court. Built into the back next to the car park the crown court got blitzed by Hilter's bombs. Old Dear says to me "see as were going into court, see that window up there across the yard, well your Uncle Brian's in there and that's where you're gonna end up soon if you don't calm down".

Soon after we committed what we thought was the Crime of the Century at Belle Vue one hot day. I'm not sure how it first came about but as we got near the fairground there must have been a massive accident or the Queen was visiting as everyone came running out of their Kiosks. It just turned into a ghost town, we looked through the glass front of the nearest cabin and there was a wedge waiting to be liberated, whoff! Off like Goff I'm telling you, a bumper £300 we'd copped for. I went weak at the knees, I was even smelling them notes! Anyway it took us fucking hours to get home through all the back alleyways with us not even able to talk with excitement.

What excites me most in life is gambling, it all came about when I placed my first ever bet on for my Granddad in Hulme. He lived within a maze of two up, two down houses that all looked the same to me but his back yard stuck out as it was always freshly white-washed. There weren't any betting shops and the way it worked was Granddad wrote his thing on normal slip paper with his little sign and gave me the 10 bob note which went straight down my Salford's. When you entered the yard itself you passed the Scullery where all the fellas were supping Bottles of Brown Ale with smoke thick as smog seeping out the cracks. Tap the top part of the main window to the front room and it came up a touch. The fella always wore one of those gambler's visors they wear in the old films during card games, I told him I was George's Grandson, he took the slip and spoke, nodded or winked!

He never gave me any slip back but said "okay then young George" by the time I got back he'd just heard his horse win on the radio so took me with him to pick up his winnings. He said to me with a huge grin "what football boots do you want" it seems as a kid all I had to do was hand a slip in and for years I'd get another present.

Then I remember when the bookies went legal, I bowled in with North West Malc and did what I've always done, put 2 Shillings right on the nose, I never go for each ways. Bond Boy brought me in a bumper result, £18! My biggest win is £23,000 but I soon spent half of it back in the same bookies that same week, so opted out and treated me and the missus to a holiday in the Caribbean.

Another gamble was over in Toronto with my old man at the track. There was a bet where all the punters at that meeting would have to pick 3 numbers and put them in a bucket back to the bookie. Whoever got the same three shared the pot which was 2 dollars.

So on the way home he had the radio on for the last race and the fucker came up, he pulled over this huge Cadi looked at me for what seemed like forever. Me not having a clue what the evil stares for, then he said "I've been coming here for five fucking years and you turn up turnips first time" it was a $150 win! Then he hugged me in a bear grip and gave it "Hot Dam you Bwoy"

When I left school my first job was a five-year apprentice job as a motor mechanic for the council, I took it just to please the family as Granddad worked there and had gone out of his way to get me in. I lasted four weeks, I still can't even drive today.

I went working with Malc on Oldham Street for a Jewish fella in a clothing warehouse, this was a top perk which didn't last long as the missing stock could only be down to us.

We were then into the Mod fashion big time. The way of life meant the world to us, I went over to Ardwick where I bought a Lambretta. The fella asked "are you okay to drive?" I just paid him the hackers and went straight over the flower bed on the roundabout, all the traffic had to stop whilst I finally got to grips with the fucker. I'd never even been on a scooter never mind drive one.

Our haircuts were cool classic cuts like 'suedeheads'. Later in the early 70's it was even better if you had the slim lamb chop sideburns or boards to show the rest you were an older teen. Our main club then was the first Twisted Wheel on Brazennose Street. We were total Mods, what a life style! Long leather coats had the edge on parkas but not really on the long trips to Rhyl if you get the drift weather wise! Our hair collars were separate then the shirt with gold studs with a very small knotted tie. Our hair cuts were class, we took blueys till they were coming out of our ears well before Wigan came around - the speed pills that came via the "Chemist Crackers". This was the term used for them lads who only robbed chemists for that box on the wall which had all the top tackle, the main shop for Mods was Henrys, not the one on Market Street but Stretford Road. I always wore a black velvet pork pie hat that had a very neat small rim like the old school black guys down the Moss. You'd top it off with a dot on your shirt like a stud pin with a Lancs rose.

We hated Rockers, yet they did pull a lot of women. The film

MANCHESTER MAVERICKS

'The Wild Ones' was still big at that time, also they were clean cut even their hairstyles were more akin to the Teddy boys. Greasers came a touch later, they were minging with beards and big ugly pork chop side burns which were all bushy and messy. Fucking stinking to high heaven. Mean like their Levis which were called originals as they shit, pissed and spewed up all over them and they never ever got washed. I must admit I was jealous of their girl gang bangs though.

The main place for the kick off was Rhyl. Bank holidays would be spent in a massive pub next to the fairground, it's still there today called 'The Schooner'. We used to take a decent crew over up to twenty handed, all the lads took the piss out of the Vespa Scooters. We called them pregnant panels, thing was you couldn't chrome them up to look cool with all the mirrors and the ferret's tail top of the huge aerial. Fact was Vespas were very speedy just never looked the business and some scooters that did look the bollix had piss poor engines that got slagged off by the rockers as being akin to a hair dryer.

Their favourite weapons were chains with locks attached; us Mods most times would need to have the better numbers to get a result. I remember us all throwing stupid things like deckchairs and ice cream carts at the Bikers whilst dogging their flying pint pots. Next we all got into being smart Hippies big time, me and Dink hired a stall out that was underneath Kendall's on the underground passage from Kendall's through to Deansgate, the top jolly end of town.

We sold Afghan coats; candles with scents and velvet shoulder bags. Truth was we never really counted up our takings; which were okay. We just got stoned on African weed all day, then get hammered on Wilson's Bitter every night, after wrapping up the stall we'd then have to pass George Best's Boutique which was the number one gaff in Manchester's city centre. Yet you should have seen the look on his and Mike Summerbee's kippers when we passed by in our top clobber, we had the edge in those days.

Dink and I went doing at bit of summer graft robbing all the old public phone boxes down in Cornwall. It was simple really, we'd just had a perfect size piece of strong plastic which went right into the top part of the change slot and all being out of town tourists who used them phones meant it was pennies from heaven for us. The money was decent as we'd relive the lot around 7ish - we were the only ones on that scam but of course it came on top in the end in St. Ives down to us both being too cocky and pissed robbing the boxes on the same camp site where we'd parked our caravan.

The main fella who ran the camp phoned up and Dinks prints came up, then our doors came off. We got barred from all of Cornwall. Dink went to DCI and got two years' probation in 1968. Then I moved to Plymouth with John Dod (Doddie) from Stretford we had a ball, lots of sex sessions, selling dope to tourists and Yank sailors who were all in charge of this high tech ship that was always docking up over most weekends. They all got busted and the local police were mad as fuck about it.

We moved digs but like a real goon I took my bed with me as it looked like it cost a lot and the ugly plug head landlord was a cunt. It was clean and the perfect size for me so I had it off. Twat head went all over town and finally nailed me to the Police, as luck would have it being the end of the season I'd slipped the net but a week later got my doors booted in at a shitty bed sit in Whalley Range. Me and Doddie spent three long nights in Talbot Street Dibble shop.

I got handcuffed first thing on the fourth morning by two Plymouth plods who put us in our own carriage which had a sign up saying "Prisoners under escort". Another three nights in Plymouth, then three weeks down the block in Exeter jail which was a very old Victorian jail. At court they told us how lucky we were not to be going back to jail as they gave us £20 fines for a fucking stinking bed!

We used the Belle Vue Bowling Alley as a good meeting point and hangout, then into the two main pubs in the town. 'The Old Wellington Inn' better known by Mancs as 'The Shambles', it was first built onto Market Street then when Manchester got blitzed (1940-41) the entire surroundings were destroyed. In the 60's the whole pub got moved down towards Saint Ann's Square, then the IRA blast ripped half the city centre apart, and yes it survived again! It then got moved next to Sinclair's Oyster Bar which has a wicked Oyster and beef pie which is still going strong today.

Corn Exchange is next door to them and it's and facing it is our own big wheel just like the one on the river Thames in London. There's a huge video screen showing top sporting events live or news events for the public, another favourite Manchester building of mine is Manchester Cathedral built in the 15th century, it's been changed many times it even got hit in the blitz. Its roots go back to the Doomsday book as the 'Angel of Stone' that was dug up there came from Collyhurst Quarry. Inside the red stones that were used as the base came from Red Bank next to the River Irk.

By 1968 I'd had enough of England so I fucked off to the desert in Israel, I thought it would be like camping and thought I was certain to get a nice tan, which did happen for a couple of weeks, not worth going into the details about the disasters that happened but I was lucky in the end to get out alive. It's a fact lots of Europeans would try and get work on the Kibbutz via agencies, I landed in the first bar and I clicked with the owner after a few mints chatting about politics, he was born on a Kibbutz and gave me a note to take down that got me a top job straight away.

It would of helped if he told me it was up in the Golan Heights where there was no official war but believe you me they let each other know they were active as the shelling was always snapping away at your nerves. I was selling draw to all the yanks around the swimming pools, they always bought at least 50 grammes, I lasted a full year then came home to work selling swag for Dinks. The fashion I hated the most was all them New Romantic cunts who carved out hair on one full side, they could see fuck all. It was done up with white paste like makeup, biggest arse-hole from that time period was that faggot face Mark Almond. Maybe if the truth was to be known: I'd just lost my youth and was jealous of him and the youth around that time.

The most brutal fights I've ever seen were definitely in Moss Side, every now and then a load of Tinker Gypos would pull off the open back wagon and get stuck into all the black guys with working tools. Even the women would get involved with the heavy stuff, there was no 'Gunchester' in the area in them days, mainly machetes and ambulances galore for both sides.

The best fight I've ever seen on the box has to be when Barry McGuigan fought Pedrosa and Barry took the world title, amazingly he lost it trying to beat a Texan in Texas in an open air car park. It was bound to get to him and it said it all in the last round when he made the sign of the cross. Defeat was definitely on the cards.

I miss the frontline in Moss Side. It had a taxi rank with a shebeen above it and around the corner was the Reno and just up a few doorways the old school Nile attracted mainly the over 30's and Babes cooked the Jerk and rice, next corner was Dougie's - a famous barber who afro celebs and gangsters all used.

Longford Park when the fair came was always a definite venue for fights, mainly down to mobs from other areas. The Rockers were never daft enough to turn up. The roughest club in our day was at the back of Chorlton Street Bus Station called "Heaven and Hell" People came from all over the North, you got a free ticket if you were still alive around seven in the morning you'd get a milky coffee with two rounds of Holy Ghost (toast).

My best concert ever in Manchester was 1964; I went down to the Palace on Oxford Road really just to get a feel and maybe a glimpse at the band getting of their coach. Meet a few of the lads and had a good few pints in the crown pub then made our way back to the gig when a genuine gent came up to me and said, "Do you want to see the Stones?" Does a bear shit in the woods? Fact was his sister had not turned up, what a result!

Well how good's this I thought, only two rows away from Jagger up on stage doing his funky jives. I stood there with my gob open catching flies, my mates just wouldn't believe me the next day.

My first holiday abroad came via a best mate at school whose family had a Ford Pop or Anglia. It took us three days to get to Lloret De Mar, we'd used camp sites in Belgium and France getting through them was a deadly nightmare. We were over the moon to get into a hired Spanish Villa, it was a mega buzz all week in really hot sunshine swimming and eating well, though I

MANCHESTER MAVERICKS

never got a shag, it still had grown in my mind that it would be here where I'd lose my cherry, so the next year I went back with my cousin on a plane for the first time ever, I was flapping a bit after a few days I had the top tan, just needed to shoot my duff in the right place not in my hand again if you get my drift. And what a result I had copped off with a scouser on the daft photo shoot with a silly Donkey, she even had the kiss me quick hat on. It was a mad policy in them days with young women having to be back in their rooms, I had to hide her a few times in the wardrobe but the main Spic fella finally caught her after a few nights and slung her out in shame with the family all downstairs looking for her, he told me any more pussy and I'd be out of the hotel on my arse.

I think it took me a couple days before I'd realised that girls enjoy sex as well as men, as the next night she took me for a blow job on the rocks! And I don't mean crushed ice in her mouth.

When I was in my late 20's I thought it was time to stay with my cousin over in Canada, now I have other cousins over there but this one unknown to me was running with the main biker gang and was in the police's top ten files. So one night he came into the bar shaking with anger and going a touch mental, see he'd woke up in the night and his direct neighbour had jumped over his balcony, slid the glass door open into his bedroom wanked and shot his duff all over him and his Mrs whilst they were both asleep. As you can imagine Dave woke up and soon got onto the shady neighbour's antics and asked me to help out, like you do.

I banged his door with my best Brit accent clear as a whistle "I'm a salesman can you give us five minutes of your time", this was just to gain entrance as it had a TV intercom.

As he opened up his own front door I've give him a Hulme Hammerhead, and put the cunt right on his arse then kicked him back inside his flat, where events soon went pear-shaped. My cousin had crept in behind me, I heard loud clicking noises from his Pump-action shotgun, Dave's now ready to do serious damage. Thinking fast I picked up the fella's Banjo and walloped him right over his bonce, I even remember saying "Don't ever go near his Gaff again!" Thing was the neighbours had seen Dave with the gun and were thirteen floors up and can see all these black and whites (Dibble cars) screeching around our block, it was a full on siege. It hadn't clicked in the heavy shite that was going down as we'd even sent his missus down for 6 packs of cold beers. Next thing the doors got busted down and we both had guns to our heads. Only then did I hear the sirens blaring away well in the background of my brain.

After a few hours locked up in the craziest and scariest place I've ever had to deal with, the police finally heard me out, they went round to the stalker who had kilos of weed stashed and was really off his head with the affects so he was now banged up. After three bad arse days in a pod (cell) we all went to court, I said as I had family and had lived there for five years I wanted to emigrate, I was on the next plane home to Blighty and told by the customs to just fuck off home then apply for another visa after a year, which I did and got the knock back as they'd now put me down as one of the up and coming tearaways wanting to join Dave's new biker gang.

Dave, unknown to me at that time, had spent just over two years in jail, then got a life ban and deported, he soon set up business in Rhyl with the very first pizza take away with his old man from Partington who had good contacts which reaped rewards as they started to serve up all the clubs in North Wales. When he did go back over the pond it was to chill out on his own small island where he'd spend quality time hunting and shooting. Then the Police soon had him brought in for a turn over, they nailed the skin of his Balls to the table, and he got a real good hiding before finally they got rid of him for good.

Yob culture in Manchester is sickening really – it's time for the government to bring back the short sharp shock when young offenders take the piss on the streets and in the courts, it doesn't matter what the crime is they commit, the courts need to learn how to sentence the youth with what fits that crime, not the person, most police don't give a shit about anyone anymore. The hoods and yobs need to be given sentences in boot camps or bring back the borstals no fucking frills, gone are there rights to Sky TV, PlayStation games. Fuck me in our days it took weeks just to get a radio and even then it had to have ear plugs.

MANCHESTER MAVERICKS

We were all fuckers in our day but at least we knew the street rules. They need to know them as well, this would give us all space to breath, look at them after a bottle of night rider with their late night raids wanting just to damage people's gardens, cars and property; this has to stop, in our days the older generation had the right of the parents to keep us all in check which they did. Not saying don't be a scally if that's what they aspire to be, just ask the cunts to remember us locals don't want their shite. As for national service, it's debatable as long as they could clean the youth up in detox centres that would have to be run just like army camps themselves.

Remember the guys we all looked up to were one-on-one fighters in car parks yet they'd shake hands and then get leathered together no matter what back in the pub afterwards. Always shaking hands: respect! There was even a time when a fella would walk into 'The Vault' drink his pint sharpest then put the pint pot upside down for everyone to see, it was a silent but deadly way to offer out the hardest fella in that pub. Then it was out on the cobbles.

What you have now are total average kids who need a bad rep to stay coolio, it's a shame and a sham or whatever? If a person goes out with evil in their mind and commit evil crimes they give up their life, simple as that.

Top 5 Mancs in my book are Les Dawson a real Comedy class act; Bernard Manning even though he's a blue nose or conk? (City); Ian McShane who was a Stretford Ender even his Dad played for Man U in his day! Robert Powell from the hit TV show 'The Detectives' funny as fuck, and finally Jack Smethurst who was tops in the massive hit TV show that would never be seen again "Love Thy Neighbour" he was also Eddie Yates' cousin in 'The Street', always on the tap in the Rovers, a funny pair of piss heads.

Top places I admire are the Manchester Library built in 1934 love the "Central Ref" as it's known with the domed reading room. It looks like the Royal Albert Hall in London the only difference being it's all white. I love the way the town hall extension was built by Vincent Harris, said by the experts to be his finest work.

It has a unique 200 foot wall that's curved to parallel the shape of the library, it was opened by King George VI in the thirties. I saw the play "Angels with Manky Faces" all about the Scuttler gangs back in the late 19th century in the theatre there a couple of years ago, I'm hoping it becomes a film. I love going over to Salford Quays, it took fifteen years to sort out that vast wasteland, they even pumped oxygen into the waters and canals which now are clear for fishing or water sport events.

The Lowry's a real winner for me, I believe it's built for the people. It has a triangular shape the size of five football pitches. From the outside it has a ship-like look as it was built on pier eight, even the porthole windows in the tower, stairways and landings gives it a maritime feeling. The colour scheme in the karzys (toilets) use the funnel colours of the Manchester liners, and at night the whole building glows.

The White City entrance still looks cool, it was great to have a gamble on Friday afternoons when they had the dogs running, won a few bob but always blew it by midnight, never regretted any of my blow outs, they seemed a good time to let steam off. Any regrets in life? Yes, a big one in fact. When all our lot got really into music I soon realised without a doubt we had the talent to make a band out of ourselves - just a shame we never went down that road.

BRIAN HUGHES MBE

Brian Hughes is a legend in Collyhurst. An example of his role in the community comes from a famous incident not long after he'd started Collyhurst & Moston Lads Club. He saw two lads going at it hammer and tongs under Lilly Lamb's arch off Collyhurst Street which was the main entrance into the flats themselves. Intervening, Brian split the lads up and invited them to the Lads club later that day to finish their beef "properly" in the ring with gloves on.

When we joined the club in 1967 Jimmy Kidd (brother of the United player, Brian) was Brian's assistant and by that time they had a few black Moss Side lads who were good boxers. There was a good gel between everyone at the club and the number one heavyweight was Kenny Webber, it was brill watching him in action. Brian always wanted to train a world heavyweight champion but unfortunately it never happened.

Brian also ran the senior football team which had Len Cantello as captain - he turned out to be a top player at West Bromwich Albion and later on another local lad Remi Moses joined WBA before coming to United. Locally we called Remi 'the new Nobby Stiles'.

So once I read Brian's first book about Manchester's very first world boxing champion, Jackie Brown, who went to the same school (Saint Pat's) as Brain, I had to ask him how the hell he went about such a task as it's no secret Brian left school with the same qualifications as myself - ie. zero. Nothing had really lodged upstairs with me from formal learning at any decent level in any of the lessons. He replied to my letters and gave me a bit of advice that got me into writing and I was surprised at the ease with which the stories came out. Just the act of writing a good story made my day. I suppose the one tip I'd love to pass on to any reader who fancies a go at writing from Brian is simply what he drummed into myself; just write a page every day and by the end of the year there's enough for a book!

Brian Hughes worked at the gym on Oscar Street for over 50 years until his retirement in 2011 by which time he'd trained several world champions and umpteen British and Commonwealth champions. Suffice to say he'd built the club up from humble beginnings to become one of the best boxing stables in the world with its own particular style.

BRIAN HUGHES MBE

Recently a new street in Collyhurst was named after Brian and just round the corner there's Nobby Stiles Drive and nearby a Johnny King Avenue. Johnny also went to Saint Pats and took the boxing crown away from Jackie Brown in two top fights so again Brian wrote a book about him called "For King and Country".

Brian's also wrote a few books about his beloved Manchester United as well as boxing - they are well worth a read!

I started school at St Pat's from the age of three just when the Second World War started. My mother was unmarried, which in those days was seen as a huge sin especially with the community being predominantly Catholic back then. It was one down from being a homosexual which would get you run out of town after a good lynching. Sister Veronica sticks out in my mind whenever I think about the good side of Collyhurst. She's known down our end as the Mother Teresa of Manchester. I tell you what, if there were people around like her today you wouldn't have any trouble, you wouldn't need these 'Super Nannies' on the television. Discipline was always top at St Pat's. You were frightened to death of even having a limb out of place never mind the stuff kids get away with today. The discipline was really severe, it was that fear which kept you in line. I remember talking to some kids in the club about what discipline they have now and they don't have anything from older respected heads like we did. There were a few tough kids at our school that got in trouble. I remember two of them coming back to school after being in Juvenile court in the morning and they'd both been birched, they told everyone how the pain was enough to knock a person out. The other two kids were sent to approved school for at least a year.

St. Pat's was separated between boys and girls. The girls had their playground on the roof whilst the boys were packed in downstairs. I remember the build up to when I was due to leave school; it was about three weeks before we left. A priest was talking to me, Billy and Kevin and he said: "Now boys, you're going out into the big wide world. It's a wicked world out there, lads. You're going to meet lovely ladies. And alls you need to remember is to stick with your own kind - those lovely

MANCHESTER MAVERICKS

Catholic girls, the children of our Holy Mary." Kevin snickered and he got a right crack. It always stayed with you, the fear that the discipline provoked. I think it's a good kind of fear though. It's what's lacking today, you were frightened to go home and tell your parents because you would get another beating. When I left Pat's the only thing I knew was religion, I was a total dunce.

One frosty day me and Sausage Flannigan were collecting milk bottle tops for the blind and somehow we both went into the convent, the girl's part, even though we weren't supposed to. Nobody told us to go in. The teachers, as you can imagine, were a bit surprised to see two boys from the other school coming over. We got to the top and all of a sudden we heard this fluttering like a flock of birds coming down and it was the headmistress. "Right, you two!" and she pushed us into her office, she locked the door with a giant ring of keys and Sausage started laughing. She turned around with this giant bunch of keys and whacked him across the face. He was bleeding like mad. "What are you two wicked boys doing in here!" she then told Sausage to get a wash and gave him some plasters. These days you'd get a stretch in jail for just backhanding lippy kids.

We'd never seen any vegetation like grass as kids but within St Pat's they had this patch where they'd grow vegetables. We'd never seen anything like it, We didn't even know what it was. As a kid in the six weeks holidays we all use to get on a number 17 bus for a penny all the way up to Rochdale taking our jam butties and a bottle of water, then we looked for work on the farms, we all had to stay out all day because everyone's parents would be working. That was the only holiday that you had unless you got a doctor's note to say you were run down and needed a break in North Wales. These were known in Collyhurst as Convalescence Holidays. Around 50 kids every week had the pleasure of bunking down in huge stately homes near the wide open windy beaches.

People often say, "You could leave your back door open", I swear that isn't just a saying, it's the truth! We'd go through my Auntie's yard door everyday and make ourselves jam or sugar butties and just shut the door leaving it on its latch, most families only had the one key which the old man would use every blue

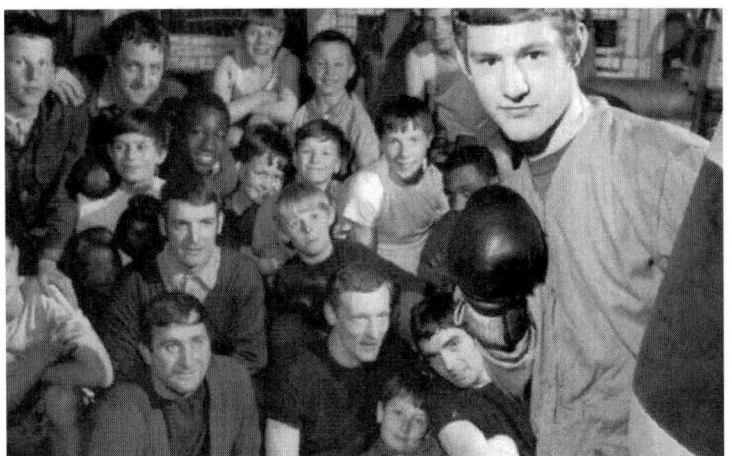

Two Collyhurst legends in one here as Manchester United striker Brian Kidd poses for a newspaper picture in front of the kids from the gym and Chief Coach Brian Hughes (bottom left).

moon as it never made sense to fork out money for keys. Suppose there was nothing to steal in any of the houses unless you were desperate and on the run from the law.

George Stanley was the leader of the lads club I went to next to Saint Pat's; he was a major in the Armed forces and stood around 6 foot 4, a fine fella he was. He had the air and grace of a film star in those days, a very cool dude. If he found you messing about in the club he'd make you run up and down Osbourne Road at least twenty times. Saying that I learnt a lot from him and have to thank him for instilling some discipline into me when I was almost ready to leave school. He used to go and watch Jimmy Murphy train the Busby Babes over at The Cliff in Salford; Soon I was tagging along and it stood me in good stead in terms of learning about coaching. I was amazed by the way Murphy could adjust his voice. His tone could go from that of a deafening demon to something akin to a gentle whisper in a fraction of a second, he'd get a grip of someone with a hot head like Billy Whelan, take him over to the touchline, put his arm round him and then he'd be whispering, "now Billy, don't you take any of these people seriously on the pitch here today my sunshine, just remember that me and Matt are very impressed." He was incredibly adaptable and firm with his football lessons and I would try my best to copy his gift of the gab with my boxers at the same time.

Being a Catholic school back in them days we were the under dogs, although we all believed we were the most charismatic. For Whit Week walks Pat's had the bagpipers and a women's flute band. We also had the Mac Sweeney pipe band, they once led half of Collyhurst over to Belle Vue just so they could hear the crowd's reaction inside the King's Hall to Jackie Brown's fight when he became Manchester's first world champ.

I remember one year the priest and the nuns told us that a famous bishop was going to be in Albert Square, they were treating him like he was Elvis Presley. And when we got there we all got an ice cream each and the teacher just said "right everybody get in line" and we marched straight back up towards Piccadilly Gardens where the Bishop would stand on the corner. The Head of the Church or certain Nuns would go and kiss his ring, just like they do in all the old style Mafia films. Whit Monday would be the Church of England and they'd have lots of bugles and drums we called them the "Der-Der- bands", the noise they made was powerful, you would think they were off to fight Napoleon at Waterloo.

Later on you'd see all the prods going into the pubs drinking and signing away and sounding fine and I remember thinking, I hope when I get older surely we could all go together? They all say that there's only one God. Nowadays they'd love to do that because of the Muslims. Especially with parties like the BNP raising its ugly head again. I used to live on Sand Street near to the "Orange River" which is also known as the River Irk and you'd see all the fights. Lots of 'Orange Men' from Liverpool used to come to Manchester on Prod day and march together from the old dwellings on Collyhurst Road. Living across from us was a woman who was a part of the 'Orange' and on the Monday the 'Orange Men' would all stand outside our house with union jacks around them and would dance outside ours mainly because they knew we were Catholic. My Mam would be saying, "don't go near the door, son, them bulldogs get uglier as the day gets longer."

On the night before the Catholics march my Gran and Mother would always put candles outside in the back yard and then pray that it wouldn't rain. The protestant women would shout over, "I hope it pisses it down all day and night tomorrow!" And the next morning us Catholics would shout back, "God knows the righteous!" It was a fantastic time because you'd get such huge crowds in town, it was such a brilliant occasion and I think it's very sad that the tradition died out. There was a St George's parade last year in Miles Platting to the city and I thought it was a brilliant day for the Protestants and the tourists as we still have Catholic parades on Paddy's day and when the Italians march around Ancoats. It's also good now to see different nationalities and religions joining in, we all need to stick together or the country's going to be too divided. Years ago everyone was behind the British troops whereas now they are being treated like mugs, I think it's diabolical.

The conditions of the bleak black crofts we played football on made our performances flawless when it was time to play for the school on the flat red shale pitches. My dream was to play football for Manchester United. I soon found out I was nowhere near good enough during one of the matches where we all knew football scouts were on the touchline. I was moved up to centre forward and as the ball came down on the goal keeper, he jumped up to grab the ball I knocked him flying and nodded the ball into the back of their net; it was the only goal I've ever scored. The Priest from the other school Saint Clare's came running on and announced it as a foul shouting, "you can't give him that Ref" but the referee said "Don't you argue with me Father!" and my goal won us the game. I was told after I was 'too clumsy'. Those words knocked the stuffing out of me.

It was guaranteed that in almost every game on Monsall's Red Rec you'd have some poor kid having to go over the road to Monsall Hospital and get an injection after getting carried away sliding into tackles, as the dirty shale embedded itself into the cut and it would soon get infected. Soon after that game it dawned on me that I was no Eddie Colman and I decided a life on the open waves would be a good move for my future, so I joined the merchant navy after leaving school. I came back home on my first leave and was passing through the huge arch way on Collyhurst Street that led you inside the flats. I remember the Lamb family lived next to this entrance and so just for that reason alone it became known as Lilly Lamb's arch, named after the mother. Inside on this day there was two lads fighting and really getting nowhere so I separated them and invited them to put on the gloves upstairs in Collyhurst Lads club and finish the fight and then have the bottle to shake hands and move on, this was my introduction into the boxing world that took me all the way to meeting HM Queen in Buckingham Palace to receive an MBE. There I was proud as a peacock, suited and booted with my old school mate Norbert Stiles alongside me who was also up for an MBE!

We've become obsessed with political correctness. There was a woman on the television the other day talking about forced marriages. She was a very well educated Muslim woman and at fourteen she was told that she was going into a marriage. She ran away because she'd seen her elder sister go into one at the same age. The custom is that nobody within the family would ever bother with you again. She ran away and was taken into a children's home where she'd gone to school and went onto university where she'd become a Doctor. One of the things she said was: "When you go on holiday to Spain or wherever you go, you know you must obey the rules of that society." What she was saying is, why does this country and government allow these arranged marriages. They can bring new wives over into the country. How can the English tax payer allow this to go on, in truth the English tax payer doesn't have a clue! When she asked a Labour MP he replied, "It's a part of your culture" to which she responded, "we're in Great Britain, why should this be allowed?" I believe it's time to wake up.

Looking back, as a kid the only day out you'd get during the six week summer holiday was up in Sunny Gorton at Belle Vue. We spent many sunny days in there just walking around the zoo, it was fantastic with all the animals in their cages, the noises from the exotic birds and chimps always cheered us up but now when you look back in hindsight you realise it must have been cruel keeping the big cats and monkeys enclosed. Going to the King's Hall was the highlight of the week, more so if you were lucky enough to see any of the local boxers such as Jimmy Swords, Kenny Webber and co fight on a Saturday night.

If an outside boxer came from far away and won there wasn't any of this booing or rioting you're certain to get nowadays, back then the crowd always applauded the opposition. They were true sporting gentlemen. Another big treat back then was going to Daisy Nook over the Easter holiday period, there would be always be lots going on with massive fairground in the centre of it all.

I remember as a kid that Boggart Hole Clough fairground was a top day out, also when Billy Smart's Circus landed there, it was very popular with the boxing booths. I used to go to the 'Rainbow Gym' on Rochdale Road; it was at the back of the big Queen's pub. "Anyone who'll last a round with him, you'll get three quid." I was only about thirteen or fourteen and volunteered myself. This fella was a pro, I remember him putting his hand on my shoulder and saying "you're not going in there son, you're staying right here." My biggest buzz back then as a spectator was seeing a local boxer called Matt Jacobs boxing Johnny Pritchard - it might have been for a title in the sixties. It was a full house, the atmosphere was tremendous, it's very hard to get them days back but saying that Manchester is once again the Capital of Boxing in Europe and known throughout the world as having the very best talent fight here in our city with packed out venues.

After the big fights everyone headed for the best pub in North Manchester called 'The Salvage' now it was a rumour for many years the name Salvage came from when Collyhurst Flats were bombed and all the bricks were used to build the pub, that's nonsense; the pub was serving pints well before the war, but them bricks did get salvaged and pigeon courts in the flats were built on the verandas. There used to be top quality singing competitions in 'The Salvage' always a snare drum with a piano in the background so it was always full of happy singing men and women.

The club I liked best was the Northern Sporting Club; a

fella that lived there was called Dougie who used to own it. It was just past Queen's Park on the left hand side. Carl Douglas would knock out some belters there as well as Matt Monroe. Jackie Charlton was on there in the early days too, he was a lovely looking fella, immaculately dressed, he was also a puff which back then was kept well in the dark. Suppose fair to say people termed puffs all as 'queer' which itself was the worst word you could call them. But you'd have to go to London's West End to get that kind of entertainment. Then there was the Embassy club and Delmont's. I saw Billy Fury there; he was big in rock and roll back then, I remember it costing me ten bob for the ticket.

Because we couldn't afford a wireless or a television in them days, going to the pictures was a huge deal. The *Manchester Evening News* and *Evening Chronicle* would have three or four pages dedicated to what was on at the flicks because it was so popular. When a special occasion took place like a cup final or something like that it would be promoted in a special box, separate from the rest of the information and picture houses. All the fellas would go.

My favourite picture house was one on Butler Street called 'The Wrecks' but we always called it 'The Cini'. When there was a picture on twelve to twenty of us would all meet and go. One of us would go to the toilet whilst everyone else waited outside. They'd boot the door and we'd all scurry in climbing under seats and everything.

Fashion in the sixties was the best for me, I wore suits. I wore mallard suits made by Peart. He was famous for how he did the shoulders on them; they used to have lovely padded shoulders. You'd be saving up for a while to get a suit off him, you'd get them right near the Playhouse. The fifties were the worst in terms of fashion for me because we were that poor we just lived on hand-me-downs. At St Pat's until you were fourteen they didn't like you wearing long pants and then they were just grey slacks. I never bothered to learn, I just went to work on Smithfield Market but in them days you had to have a leaving certificate. Just before we left some of the lads came down and said that I had to go to the leaving party. The day that you left school you'd have to take part in a ritual, you'd attend mass in the morning and the teacher

[AFFILIATED TO N.A.B.C.]
...ghtbowne Road, Moston, Manchester - Telephone: 061-683 4693

CHIEF COACH   TREASURER   PRESIDENT
Brian Hughes   Mr. A. Clark   Mr. T. Jones
                                     Grovers Solicitors
                                     Hobins Chambers
                                     64 A Bridge Street
                                     Manchester
                                     Phone: 061-832 5144
                                     Fax: 061-833 1337

Tel: 061-620 2916

December 1997.

Dear Colin,

Many thanks for your recent and, always welcome letter. Once again I must apologise for the delay in replying but I am quite busy training Robbie Reid for his world championship match against Sugar Boy Malinga on 13 December. Hopefully, afterwards I can have a well earned rest.

You sound as if you have a really good story to tell of the years in Collyhurst where we grew up. Look, take it from me and I am as thick as the proverbial short plank. You can write your story. How do you start? Well quite simply write your story down in a large note pad, or if you have access to a computer or word processor, simply use one finger as I am doing now writing this letter to you. Like I say if you haven't got anything then write it by hand. I swear that is how I wrote the two books I have written.

Once you feel you have covered all the story. And remember, start from where you were born; what school you attended; mention schoolboy friends, teachers; how you spent your leisure time. Then go on to what you did after leaving school etc. Always remember to mention any funny incidents. Your marriage and other important events you need to relate to. Once this has been done. Get somebody to type it out for you and get at least two people to proof read it for you. Asking them to correct or delete whatever they believe needs doing. Then if your satisfied, get it published.

I am going to get the tapes done for you before your mother goes over to Germany. Colin, I would love to put other tapes on this one but I am so tied up I just have not got the time to look in the attic for them.

Incidently, last Friday I was filmed for Granada, for a one hour Munich special out next year. Duncan Edwards mother was there, she's 88, marvellous woman.

Well I must close for now Colin. May myself and my family wish you and yours everything good for Christmas and every success and good health for 1998! God Bless you all.

Yours faithfully.

COLLYHURST & MOSTON
LADS CLUB

CHIEF COACH   COACHES   PRESIDENT
Brian Hughes   Patrick Burnell   Tom Jones
                   Kenny Webber   13 Plantree Ave,
                   ...   Hale,
                                        Cheshire.
(061) 620 2916   (0161)980-2651

27 October 1997.

Dear Colin,

Please forgive me for taking so long to reply to your very welcome letter. It was sent to me by the printer of the Tommy Taylor book. What a lovely surprise to hear from you. Glad to hear you are doing well. Don't apologise for your spelling, mine is wicked. Mind you I only want to St. Patricks.

I hope you liked the Jackie Brown book. I have another book out shortly about Willie Pep an American world champion who I first saw on the old Collyhurst cinema Pathe newsreels. Happy memories.

Time has changed and its a different world to the one I grew up in and even from the many years I spent at Willert street. They say times I can never forget. Lads like yourself and the lads you mention in your letter will always be fondly remembered by myself. It was me who started the football teams back at the old Colly lads Club. George Myte was among my first players along with Len Cantello. We won the league and cup, but more important we gave lads a little bit of glory and happiness.

It is wonderful when I travel to various pubs or clubs or functions and meet lads like yourself, past members. Old Noel Sykes was a scream. Do you remember him? he looked like Jimmy Edwards the comedian. I was born and bred in Sand street, near Wilcox Barrel works. I am proud to tell people I come from Collyhurst. My books will be proof as well. Next year I am bringing a book out about Johnny King, another Collyhurst boxing champion.

If you still need the second part of 'Reds In Europe' I would be only to pleased to get it videoed for you. Let me know. Granada are doing another programme for next year. The 40th anniversary of Munich. As for myself, well I am struggling a little. I am suffering with diabetes and kidney problems, mind you there are people far more serious than me. I enjoy doing these books it

keeps me alert, tomorrow, I am doing a tribute to Wilf McGuiness who is 60 next week.

Well I must close for now Colin. Once again please forgive my bad manners in not replying much sooner. I wish you and your family everything that is good and healthy. God Bless you all.

Two letters that changed my life from Brian Hughes. A great coach in the ring and an inspiration to everyone who met him out of it!

would put a breakfast on for you. After that you'd call on all the teachers, but I didn't want to do that.

In the early 1950's a woman was murdered off Collyhurst Road, it was unusual at that time because murder wasn't as common place as it is today. I never left this country until 1963, I went to Dublin for a wedding staying in a hotel. Everything was different, even the food. I even drank Guinness!

Nowadays with the yob culture that's got a grip on the nation, where time after time some kids are finally sent to young offender's institution for either six weeks or six months, but when I was a lad a few mates got sent for Borstal Training and that would be a minimum of nine months up to three years, the first thing the screws would do was shave your hair off with clippers in the main hall in front of 300 lads. In those days your entire family was shamed because of it. The next level up was Borstal Recall for the lads who never learnt the first time round, they'd get whipped with a cane; there wasn't any of this answering back. In all honesty I wouldn't want punishment and discipline to go back to how it used to be, I don't want that at all. I hear people say, "Put them in the Army! Make them do National Service!" They wouldn't get them in the Army! Do you think these Muslim people would allow one of their children to join the Army? We can't afford to bring National Service back because they would be spending more time in the courts trying to get out of it than serving for their country, it would cost a fortune!

I think good discipline lies with the families. I have four children and I didn't marry until I was in my thirties. I vowed when I got married that my wife would never hear me swear and that I'd never hit her, I vowed that I'd spend as much time as possible with my kids. Family is the main thing. A family has to make clear what is right and what is wrong.

ROUFY

I first came across Roufy while working for Clean Walls in 1973, we were the biggest sandblasting and acid washing company in the UK. Steve and his best mate Andy Chips, who was Greek, worked with a Cockney family, The Risbies, who came up from the big Smoke to live and work in Manchester; reason being all the best work was here. Steve took me to the curry mile well before it became known and him being half Indian looked after me food wise. I left Manchester in 1975 and didn't see him again till 1978 when I had joined a group of grafters who had all been invited by two brothers, The Dinks from Stretford, to sell merchandise for Status Quo legally on their "Rocking All Over the World" tour. We first worked loads of concert halls around the north of England, then over to Scandi and into Germany, Holland, Belgium and finished in France. Then back to work all the concert halls in the south of England and the summer festivals.

Now, fact was I'd go down to graft to London back then mainly robbing Marks and Spencer tills as the cash was unreal that we got from them around that time. Many times we'd stay overnight and bump into the Dinks in Camden Lock, Dingwalls, Eltro or the Pali club, most times they'd invite us back to their top class apartment in Ladbroke Grove, they both loved sniffing the Charlie and fuck me after an hour or so they would waffle on and on about the upcoming tour with Quo over in Asia then over to Australia. I knew they'd put away at least 50k to invest in swag so it was a done deal and we were all told we'd be their grafters. The deal was we had to pay our own way over to Japan and get to work the full tour knowing the chances were good to change all our lifestyles for a better future.

So the last gig was Reading Festival in September and about 10 of us had all passed our earnings over to the Dinks inside the caravan back stage, the money went as always into the Dinks briefcase which was then just put under a table. I knew there were also the takings from the Dinks themselves in that case and I worked out that there was about 15-20 grand just sitting there. When they started to explain to us all about getting over to Tokyo to meet up I knew it was all bollocks having heard

MANCHESTER MAVERICKS

quite a few different versions of the same story from the nights when they were on the coke. I thought 'that case needs to be had offmans and fuck the Dinks' and I made a move but all the lads were on me with crazy stares and mouth movements saying not to with a few of them saying "Don't you dare fuck this up Blaney!" I told them "don't worry I'll give you all a decent drink out of it" but it was a massive no-no so I had to abandon the idea.

Anyway no surprise that two weeks later they just fucked off to Asia and hired local workers to sell the merchandise with a small wage and a packed lunch, then over to Australia where they done the same and never looked back. From that point on they just took over the swag game and the only time we'd see them was getting out of limos at the biggest gigs in Europe with that fucking suitcase and bodyguards looking after them as they knew how much we hated them, by that time we just worked for ourselves and without a doubt missed out. I always say to Steve when Reading comes round "the case that got away eh!" Last time I heard about them they had made a few million from the One Direction tours all over the globe. As they say 'you win some you lose some'.

To get back to the point, Roufy was one of my closest mates and he's got a few tales to tell…

In the 60s, when I was 10 or 11 growing up in Old Trafford, I had a band with a young group of lads, but only one of us could actually play guitar. The local cinema on a Saturday afternoon used to put us on as a band. We'd go on stage, and my drum kit was made out of cardboard, so I'd just stand there with sticks pretending to play drums like Ringo. I remember we used to walk in with all the kids queuing up on a Saturday afternoon for the matinee. We'd walk in with cardboard guitars and my drum kit and bits of wood, set it up with mikes made out of cardboard and perform along to The Rolling Stones, or "She Loves You", and we'd do that for about half an hour before the film started. We used to get all the local press down going "Yeah these kids are great and that" but none of us were actually played anything, it was all mimed. We had loads of pictures in the *Evening News*, the local *Stretford Journal* and the like, my fifteen minutes of fame.

A few years later I took up work as a sandblaster, working on things like the Town Hall. At first that building was black, in the

ROUFY

60s, and when I say black I mean black. At that time Manchester was full of fog and smog, so they brought smokeless fuel in, because everyone was burning coal in them days and that's why every building in Manchester turned black, because every household had a chimney belting out smoke. In the early '70s they made it what they called a 'Smokeless City' and that changed the whole atmosphere in Manchester because after that we never got any fog. We always got fog that was so thick you couldn't see your hand in front of you, especially right after Bonfire Night in November. Before they brought in smokeless for months and months you'd get foggy days and sometimes it was so you couldn't go into school, that's how thick it was. You couldn't make your way there. The new fuel was called coke, and it was like a sponge. You bought bags of coke, and had it delivered. Outside your house, especially where we were in Old Trafford, there'd be a hole at the front door where the coal man would lift it off and pour the coal down. You'd have to go through the kitchen into the cellar with your shovel to get a bucket of coke for the fire.

Sandblasting is where I first met Colin, he was doing that and I was a paint washer at the hospital. Certain hospitals and NHS trusts couldn't afford to paint their buildings, so they brought in paint washers, who in other words just washed the walls with a bucket and sponge with this chemical in it. You'd run your sponge down the wall, and then it was black and white, it'd just strip it but not take the paint off, Christ knows what was in that stuff. We were all supposed to wear gloves and all our hands were red raw through using this bloody chemical. It was called Pickle.

So that's where I met Colin. I remember there's a bit in his book where I was stood on the scaffolding in five-inch platform boots, that's how me and my mate used to go to work, dressed as if we've come straight off the stage. Platform boots, dungarees

MANCHESTER MAVERICKS

with all diamond stars going down them, this being like 1968-69 up to 1970. That's how we used to work because all these nurses would say "Oh my god who are all these guys on the scaffolding" wearing heels with five different platforms and golden stars in the middle. We used to go to London and buy them from Freddie Mercury. In the very early '70s Freddie Mercury had a clothes stall on Kensington High Street. This must have been just a few years before Queen made it because they were a sort of heavy rock band then, before they got more progressive rock, operas and all that. Freddie Mercury was very flamboyant even then, but when they got big nobody at the time knew he was gay, I remember my gran saying "Is he a man or a woman?" because he wore make up. He was the very first glam rock star in my opinion, before Marc Bolan even. We used to see T-Rex, just round the corner from here down the road from Manchester Polytechnic there was a building called Cavendish House. It's still there today but it is offices now. At the time it was a student union bar and had a stage where all the bands used to play, and from '68-69 up to '73-74 I saw everyone there. Cream played there. Vinegar Joe, which had Robert Palmer in it. The girl singing with him was a Salford girl called Elkie Brooks, she had a massive hit called 'Pearl's a Singer' in the early '70s.

It'd take a whole book to name all the bands I saw there, I don't know where to begin because there was just so many bands that used to play round that corner. Then as they got bigger they'd play further down the road next to the academy. Before the academy was built you had the students' union next door, and upstairs there was a concert hall with a big stage and people like Traffic played. Every major band of the day played there and because I was still at school, but not a student, I used to go to the Stretford Technical College and blag I was a student just to get the card. You could never get in unless you had a student card, so you'd go in the offices of the student union on Stretford Road here and you'd say "Yeah I'm a student", they took your name and took your photograph and gave you the card. They never checked out what course you were on, it was never asked in those days, and it always got you in because it was free on a Saturday night.

Marc Bolan and Micky Finn, back in those days, were called Tyrannosaurus Rex. They were all folky and Marc Bolan would sit cross-legged on a cushion with ballet shoes on, singing about hobbits and Lord of the Rings stuff, fairies and elves. There was none of this glitter and shiny gear at the time, no Top of the Pops, just acoustic guitars, Tolkien and John Peel, who put them on the map. Because Marc Bolan looked so fucking weird, like nothing we'd seen before, you'd think 'Is he an elf?' I used to have all the posters from the gigs in my room; The Edgar Broughton Band, Tyrannosaurus Rex. So many massive bands, like Steppenwolf and people like that from America, all played there on Oxford Road. I don't know if I should say this but coming out one night I went down the back stairs and saw all of Traffic's equipment was there, so I nicked a guitar and I had it for years, later swapping it for a suede coat, Steve Winwood's probably still looking for it.

In '68–69, when I was still at school, there was an all-night place in Manchester called The Magic Village where they had people like Pink Floyd and Jethro Tull, neither of which were massive at the time, but they were getting bigger. I remember one night me and my mate were walking around there tripping off our nuts, and we were only 14 at the time, just kids, but we hung out with older lads. It was being around older lads that got me going to see bands, smoking dope, doing LSD, growing up fast! The film 'Easy Rider' came out at that time, and then the film 'Woodstock' came out, along with the introduction of stereo sound in the cinema. I remember being at the Cinema Royal next to The Midland Hotel, going outside one night and there was a huge 'Woodstock' poster of the crowd all wrapped in blankets in a field, and I thought 'I've got to have that for my bedroom', so I ripped it off the wall and carried it home, it was my pride and joy. The Cinema Royal used to be a theatre, I haven't a clue what it is now but you can still see a bust of William Shakespeare in an alcove above the door. That part of Manchester, Peter Street, was the original Theatre part of Manchester, it was where all the show and music halls were. To add to that, Oxford Road, when I was a child, had nine cinemas! I think there's only

MANCHESTER MAVERICKS

The Cornerhouse now.

My parents met there actually; it was called The Tatler then and my mum was a torch-lady, or an usher. As you came into the cinema you were greeted by torch-ladies, who'd give you your ticket and show you to your seat. Then at the interval or the end of the film she'd be there selling ice-creams and Kia-Ora Orange, choc-ices and peanuts. She met my dad in there, who was a merchant seaman from Bangladesh. He settled in Manchester and set up a curry house on Stretford Road with his mates. That's how takeaways started, in the late '50s, as little cafés for migrant workers from India, Pakistan and Bangladesh, and they owned and ran them for their mates serving chapattis and curry and rice, there was none of that chicken tikka. In the early days of the curry houses most people couldn't stand the smell. Where I was brought up in Old Trafford it was the early days of the immigrants arriving from India and Jamaica, when a lot of people arrived on that ship called The Windrush, and on Alexandra Road in Moss Side there's a centre called 'The Windrush Centre'. A lot of the kids that live in Moss Side, all the grandchildren of those early people, don't know what the Windrush was, they know the centre but not the reason for its name. There's a mural by Hulme Library of the ship, a great big fresco. It's important I think to mark your community buildings and roads with its history.

For example the first Rolls Royce came out of Hulme, and you've got street names all over the place in tribute; Royce Road, Rolls Crescent. The pair, Henry Royce and Charles Rolls, met in the Midland Hotel, in the French Restaurant, where they discussed making a car together, and in a garage they made the first model of what is the most famous British car two hundred yards from where I'm sat writing this. In tribute there used to be a pub on that spot called The Sir Henry Royce. Also if you look up at the wall of The Junction pub there's a picture of a Rolls-Royce, and unless you know the connection you'd be non-plussed, but directly across the road is where the first Rolls-Royce was made.

Unless you're from Manchester or know the history of this city, a lot of people don't realise the sheer amount of what has come out of Manchester. They split the atom here back in the day, and to this day the University is breaking ground, winning the Nobel Prize for experiments with graphene. Only in recent times is Alan Turing and his great work here getting the recognition it deserves, I've been telling people about Alan Turing for twenty years! Not only did he break the enigma code, but he pioneered the first computer at the university. Thankfully he got pardoned a few years ago, but the poor man did so much and got punished for something that was no one's business. There's a bronze statue in Sackville Street park in commemoration to him, obviously along with a million and one buildings and institutes. It's fantastic that now everyone knows who he was and the crucial work he did, because in my eyes he's a real Manchester maverick.

<u>808 STATE</u>

In 1997 808-State went on tour, it was part of the 'MegaDog' tour. 'MegaDog', in the 90's, was the best night in Manchester, but it was only on every two or three months. It was a sound-system from London, ran by two brothers, one was the DJ and the other did the rigging. They used to set up all these ultra-violet banners, it looked fantastic, and the music was sort of Trance-Techno, although we didn't really have a name for it at the time. This was the time when a lot of white guys with dreads were turning up all over the place, 'Crustys' I think we called them. It was bands like E-Static, Transglobal Underground, Dreadzone, and 808 State were always on the bill, either live or DJing. That went on for years, and finally right near the death of it all, they decided to do a tour of America, called the American Electronic Tour. 1997 in America was a time where no one understood what was going on in terms of dance music. So they were on the bill with people like Moby and Grooverider. I remember him because he was on late one night in Florida, and Big Lucy shouted down to me, 'Go and get the records!', so I ran to the tour bus to get them and got behind the decks while we waited for them. The problem was only one of the headphones worked, and most the records were 808 ones, and most of them were white labels; no titles, and no RPM, and so I had to gamble. I was actually playing some of them at the wrong speed, but the American audience were loving it! I was shitting it; I'd just had a big line, was pissed out of my head, and the last thing I expected was 'Get up on those decks!' This lasted about half an hour, and I managed to avoid a heart attack dropping the needle, before Grooverider turned up.

That was very much a full tour, about three months. We started in Chicago, onto New York, Boston, New Orleans, San Francisco and Dallas. To be honest, dance music, especially house music, had only just broken in America, which is ironic considering it comes from Chicago, but we soldiered through anyway. If that tour was happening now in America we'd have smashed it; they're mad on dance music over there now, only they call it EDM, Electronic Dance Music, talk about stating the obvious. To add to that, we couldn't find ecstasy in America at that time, another thing they hadn't caught onto. Then again getting caught with drugs in America is a different thing to here. That said, my job on the tour was to go out into the town centres of places like New Orleans, and hunt for some weed or a bit of coke, and it was hard work! Every cab we'd get into and ask 'Do you know where we can get any weed? Or Coke', the first thing they'd say would be 'Are you a cop?' which is a smart move because you have to declare if you're a policeman, otherwise it's entrapment. Not one of those drivers got us anything either because they didn't believe us or because they were in NA, which basically meant they'd got nicked before they got a job as a taxi driver, they wouldn't risk it.

We did from New York straight across, but half of that tour died on it's arse because, it being America, the venues were massive, where you'd need thousands of people to make it look busy, and 808 were only used to about six hundred; they were playing ice-hockey rinks, basketball stadiums and equestrian centres and Dallas Bowling Alley, without doubt the biggest bowling alley I've ever seen in my life!

The first half of the tour we were all on steaks and really top food, but half way through the money was running out fast, not because of the bands but because they'd overbooked; there were nine bands. Nine bands on nine tour buses, and these were luxurious buses as well, we had Santana's. On top of that we would stop off for three days at a time in places like Dallas and

San Francisco, so all those hotel rooms had to be paid for out of the tour money. This was all Mandy's job. Every town we stopped at we'd just hop out and go on the piss, so Mandy would be looking all over the place for us.

The best place for me was Orange County, California. All day I was walking round there and they were putting up all these Alice in Wonderland statues and lasers through the fountains, and I thought 'This looks right', it was all green and open. One act playing the Orange County show was Aphex Twin. His set-up was a bit weird; it was just a big screen and a huge bed. I never saw the guy the whole tour, all I saw was this bed, I've still no idea what he looks like. LA was the last stop of the tour, and no doubt the promoters were happy to see us roll into California, having shelled out from New York right across the states. The bands still got paid obviously, we did our job, and after all it wasn't us that booked the bowling alley!

THE SALUTATION

In 1999 I got nicked for a bag of E's and they gave me a lot of time on account of all the other shit I had on my person, things like acid, which I didn't even realise I had. They broke it down to nine and a half at the end, thank fuck! Eventually I ended up doing five and a half years, most of it in Strangeways. So that was several years of my life I wasn't getting back, and when I was released in '05 Eric Barker had just recently taken over the Salutation Pub by the university, it was called The Salutation Hotel then. Eric said to me 'Here you are, we've got a room you can have', and so I started making curries at night for the pub. Eric used to have bands on in the main room and DJs in the room at the side, and because we knew people in the music scene we had a load of people in; Alabama 3 after-parties, Mr Scruff doing a video with Dizzee Rascal, we had The Fall doing a video upstairs, with the drummer playing a kid's drum kit in the bath.

Another musician we had in whenever he was about was Nigel Kennedy, what some would consider a proper musician. Well he might have been performing Vivaldi's Four Seasons but he wasn't going home for a Horlicks and his comfy slippers, he was straight to the Sally and getting off his bean like any self-respecting musician! We knew him because a mate of ours, JB, was his tour driver, and so when they came to perform at The Bridgewater Hall, he put us on the guest list and him and Nigel came to the Sally for a drink after the concert. He ended up staying all weekend! Nigel used to get totally fucked up with us at the Sally, I've actually got a photo of him at a table with us, Nigel Kennedy world renowned violinist, with his head in his egg and chips. So every time he did the Bridgewater, he always came to say hello and have a drink. One time he comes in and says 'Hey, after the last concert at the Bridgewater it's my birthday! I'd like to have my party here!' 'No problem' we thought, and then he turned up with forty Polish violinists, a bloody orchestra! How we got them all on the stage I don't know, but it was absolutely stunning having them all playing together. Later we had a jam with him as well; me on the shakers, Billy on bass, another mate of ours on the drums, and we'd all had a load of sniff and joints, what a riot. He's not exactly a wallflower about it but not everyone knows Nigel's mad into his weed, he's big on its uses for creativity, and I'm 100% behind him on that one.

We were at the Grand Hotel in Amsterdam one night, and we all got thrown out through partying all night, and Nigel doesn't have a room with a couple tutting next door, he has a suite, the whole floor! He was blasting the music and waking up all the guests, and he had a gig the next day in Cologne, Germany. The promoters were there, a party at five in the morning, watching him bouncing off sofas, looking at each other thinking 'I knew we should've booked the Happy Mondays.' No one expected him to be this mad but he's always been a proper party-head. We had him at the Sally three times, but we could've never put posters up, 'Nigel Kennedy Appearing Here', because people would've looked at the pub and thought 'Are you having a laugh?'

Being able to live at the Salutation was a godsend, it was great while it lasted, the place was a circus. One night it might as well have been an actual circus, because someone brought in a lion. When the art college next door used to be the polytechnic, there was a guy who taught photography, but he also worked at Belle

Vue Zoo, in charge of the lions. One day years later I was behind the bar and he came in and said 'I haven't been in here for years, I love this pub, I brought a lion in here and no one batted an eyelid. Two guys walked past, looked, said "There's a fucking lion sat there", then just kept walking.' He told me that story then about a week later brought in this beautiful framed photograph with a picture of the lion and a caption, 'The Salutation Lion'.

Eric eventually got married and moved to Poland, so sold the place, or gave the keys back to the brewery, saying 'I'm losing money hand over fist here', we Mancunians have got a habit of putting ourselves in the poorhouse for the sake of a good time, just ask the Factory guys. We used to have weekend lock-ins just to keep the money coming in, and come nine o'clock on Sunday morning, we couldn't get rid of them, so we just carried on, 'It's nearly opening time, let's open the curtains, there's no point in opening the door 'cos you're all still here'.

CHRIS SIEVEY

Chris Sievey aka Frank Sidebottom, knocked about The Salutation quite a bit and I knew him well. What a character he was, Chris I mean, Frank was a creation, but Chris was the real thing. Frank Sidebottom played at the Sally twice a year, and we'd put the posters up 'Friday night, live on stage, Frank Sidebottom' with a picture of his head. He used to use my room as his dressing room, the famous head sitting on my bed and his suits hung up about the place; Sgt Pepper, Timperley Bigshorts FC, and of course the pinstripe. He played his last gig at the Sally on a Friday night, about a week before he died, and sadly he must have known it was coming because he was fucking partying that weekend. He left on Monday morning, and died about a week later, and I thought 'Oh fuck it's my fault. I knew I should have sent him home'. A year or two earlier he'd had a cancer scare and gone off the map, and sadly it'd come back. I'm sure you're aware there's a bronze statue of him in Timperley, and there've been films made about him; all great tributes to a wonderful guy and a real one-off.

MANCHESTER MAVERICKS

BIG UNIT

In about 2012 Darren from 808 State put a band together with me and two other guys; the sound engineer, Ben, and the guy who ran the backline, Easty, playing guitar. Over the years since 808, Daz had been writing songs and so decided to put a band together; Big Unit. We started rehearsing, eventually releasing our first single, 'Get Fucked', which we suspected wasn't going to get on Top of the Pops. We started to get gigs, like going up and down the country with Bez. Through Bez and Rowetta we were very lucky and got the support slot for the Mondays; we played The Ritz, London, Canterbury, all over the place. It was a great slot for us, for a new band to be supporting someone like the Mondays, it was a real leg-up, and we went down a storm.

We've now got a new drummer, Simon Wolstencroft, who amongst other bands used to drum in The Fall, and who I believe is in this book as well! Having him as a new member is great, and it's probably a holiday for him compared to The Fall. Simon's tried his hand in all sorts of different bands, so playing our blend of guitar and dance music is no problem to a funky fucker like him. I've been playing percussion, shakers and the like, for twenty-five years, having spent years playing Eric's festival, One Tree Island, a world music night. Eric was the only guy willing to take a gamble on playing world music, because he loves the music and wants everyone else to get in on it. Mr. Scruff was our first DJ for One Tree Island, before any bugger knew who he was, Eric got him to play, and he played for us for years. Sadly now there isn't a club scene in Manchester where once a month you can go to a world music night. We used to have guys on djembes, ten or twenty of us, playing along to whatever Scruff was spinning. We've been talking about bringing it back.

Eric used to bring out One Tree Island albums, called One World. Scruff was on one of them I think, with 'Chicken in a Box', which is a fantastic tune, it's pure African but once you add the electronic stuff, it takes on a new form, and most importantly you can properly dance to it. A lot of his stuff uses African influences and instruments; kalimbas, flutes, djembes; an interesting choice in what you want to make the noises on your record. Having people dancing off their faces to instruments they'd never heard before was a beautiful thing, because we've all been off our heads to 'Voodoo Ray', but tripping to the sound of a Tuareg tribe is another thing. We'd have a big drum full of shakers and hand them out to the audience, so everyone would be shaking along to whatever record was on and getting in the groove.

GIO-GOI

The Donnelley brothers, who started Gio-Goi and used to deck out all the Hacienda bands back in the day, were approached by Daz with a song, called, 'Gio-Goi'. They said 'It's fucking great this', and they'd since gone into making music videos for the likes of Plan B and won awards, so they said 'We'll make the video for it'. They brought their own film crew to this warehouse, kitted us all out from the racks and racks of clothes, and shot the video, which looks top. It took twelve hours to film it, and we got a load of students off the street for it, saying 'Here, free beer and sandwiches'. That video is Gio-Goi's main advertising film, and not to mention Big Unit's best advert as well. The Donnelley's now do a lot of summers in Ibiza, they've got a big Gio-Goi party bus, and are busy with new projects, like YO, Your Own. 'Gio-Goi' is actually Vietnamese for 'What's happenin' man?' They've got a book out as well, 'Still Breathing', and in it they talk about Eric giving them their first E, saying 'Eric changed our life, man', and him saying 'Don't sell drugs, make clothes', and they became millionaires! They give page after page of credits to Eric, who truly is a Manchester Maverick; not the first name that gets thrown around, but a true originator. He's not known to the likes of the normal person, but in the Manchester music scene, to people in the know, 'Eric Barker, what a fucking legend!'

ERIC BARKER

Back in '88 when Ecstasy was changing the world and Manchester in particular, the one club that never gets talked about much but was up there alongside the Hacienda for us locals was The Thunderdome. However as it was stuck in the middle of a council estate in Miles Platting its punters were all from Manchester and Salford and few outsiders fancied it. The place itself had been a converted Irish club called The Osbourne but when Acid House hit it became a proper scally dome, where it became the place for the young 'uns to really let loose, it even had all night sessions on bank holidays till six in the morning. What made it so good was the DJ's all being local, better known as The Spinmasters they would later form 808 State. In with these DJs was Eric, the brother of 808 State's Andy Barker and after meeting Eric and getting to know him I was able to enjoy the best parties that Manchester had over a 5 year period without worrying about any trouble. I say that as the big raves always had some kind of trouble at one point whenever they were getting taxed or other shite went down and of course the Hac was shutdown for some time.

Eric was well in with the right people to have his parties, known as One Tree Island, in huge private houses in the best parts of Manchester and never once did the Dibble get involved as they would hardly cost much entrance wise. Also the thing was Eric got on well with all the groups around that time and he had respect and this made his nights out so easy to enjoy and you knew you'd be safe.

I still bump into him over in Hulme and he's always full of life with new ideas so I'm sure he'll have something up his sleeve when it comes to his One Tree Island gigs that pop up every now and then, look out for them!

★

There used to be a gay club off Deansgate called Stuffed Olives, and we knew a couple of guys, Mad Hatter and another kid, who'd started doing a Sunday night there. This was around '88, the scene was pretty young so there were only about sixty people involved in it at that time, and these two had been playing at parties in Hulme, at places like The Kitchen.

ERIC BARKER

*Eric Barker (left) and Roufy at Heaton Park
before the Stone Roses gig in 2012*

They'd started this Sunday night so we were going down there every week, and coming over from Ancoats and Miles Platting saying we were going to Gaff X, because there were so many people trying to get in on this party, and we were still quite protective of it. That's when Anthony and Chris, The Donnellys, started hanging around and when I, according to them, introduced them to the Acid House scene and all that came with it. So we were all knocking about at this night at the Stuffed Olive called 'Sunday Service', a good name to keep things underground but also a great name for the start of what would become a religion for some people.

Those Sunday nights were unbelievable, and this is when Es were Es, paying £25 a pop and probably only needing half. There'd be sixty, seventy-odd people in this space and it was dripping wet. It probably opened about seven o'clock and went on until midnight, but by ten o'clock it was packed to the rafters and the only person in that club that wasn't off their nut was the owner. It wasn't generally open to the public; the door was shut, you knocked on, they looked out, "You look like you're off your nut, get in." That went on for a while, in the end the police put a bit of pressure on the owner, because it was getting slightly out of hand; when it finished about twelve, one o'clock, everyone was on the street then, on a Sunday night on Deansgate in 1988. Normally there would be tumbleweed going down the street at that time, so everyone would have their car radios on. After nights there and at the Hacienda that's what people did after kicking out time, because there was nowhere to go. This is how places like The Kitchen in Hulme started; people needed somewhere to go after these nights and keep the party going. The Crescents in Hulme had been abandoned by the council about four years before, so they took up residence there, knocking the walls of three flats through to make one big room, and that became the place to go after The Stuffed Olive and The Hacienda.

Week by week The Hacienda went from ten people taking up a corner of the room to the whole place packed to the rafters. This was when you started seeing smiley faces on badges emerging, like a secret handshake; you'd be walking down the street, see someone with the badge on and knew you were both part of the same thing. Obviously everyone knows now what the smiley face means but for a while it was your passport into that world, well before *The News of The World* caught on and made it like the mark of the devil. Up north we were all jumping in with both feet, baggy clothes and the lot, but it seemed everyone else in the country was light-years behind, still trying to look cool in their leather pants. Mike Pickering went to play at Spectrum in London and they booed him because he was playing Acid; up here we had our hands in the air and in The Smoke they didn't have a clue. He went back a few months later and obviously they'd caught on by that point, talking bollocks about how they were the first to come up with it. Things like Boy's Own playing wish-washy Balearic; Paul Oakenfold and that lot went to Ibiza and came back with 'The Ibiza Sound', which was Alfredo playing Café Del Mar stuff like Robert Palmer. That worked on the island, but when they brought it back to London and created their own little scene, whereas the Acid House scene really started here, 808 and A Guy

Called Gerald.

One Tree Island came from me getting fed up with the rave scene, because by the end of it the whistling came in. I was one of the first people in Manchester to blow a whistle, in The Hacienda, but when that caught on it caught on very quickly. I was using a referee's whistle, and when you're off your nut and someone blows a whistle, it does something to your head, gets people going, so that became very popular, and it didn't take long before every cunt in the club had a whistle. So before long things like white gloves and silly dancing came in, and we were getting very disillusioned with it all by then, plus The Hacienda was having a lot of problems with gangsters and guns.

So I happened to be at Glastonbury one year, E'd up and that, and stumbled upon the World Music Stage. There was an African band on, and they blew me away; what was going on in my body just resonated with what they were playing in a mad way. I thought it's one thing dance music making you feel good through having an E, but this African band were a different story. So I came back to Manchester and decided that's what I was going to do, a world music festival. There was already a guy doing it in Manchester, called Guy Gondwana, and he was into world music already, but not part of a scene just a straight member really. He had a night going on at The Roadhouse at the time, so we went down to see him and see what he was doing. So I said "I want to do something with you". We started doing it at Jabez Clegg every fortnight on a Thursday, £2 in. We used to dress the whole place up with banners and camouflage nets, and we had two rooms upstairs; an ambient room all in black with UV lights and UV jugglers. The world music scene seemed to share a load of people with the trance and techno scene, people who went to the trance nights also came to a lot of the One Tree Island nights; lots of people with dreadlocks and Day-Glo shirts.

One Tree Island ran for thirteen years, the only reason it stopped was because I left the country, because it was really my night. I did it in a lot of different places around Manchester but I did it because that's what I wanted to hear, I just happened to make it more popular by getting more people into it. We had a core audience of about two-fifty, so wherever we did it, we always had a good night. We did it in venues that would push people together, not too big, so that everyone in there was dancing next to each other and it was busy, and that goes a long way. Then we started doing the party in Chester, it started off as One Tree Island's Magical Mystery Tour, and it was the first one we did there so it was a mystery where it was. That became a regular occurrence and we did it every August Bank Holiday for six or seven years at this particular place. That was a fantastic place. Now that I'm back in the UK I'm thinking about going and speaking to the farmer to see if he'd let me do it again. The farmer's quite eccentric, it's a dairy farm, and in his garden he's built this fucking great maze, so we used to have a sound-system in the middle of it, and so you could hear the music but couldn't see it. There was a small lake there with an island on it and one tree, so this place was made for this party, and we had people camping in a field at the side, so it felt like a mini festival. You could turn up Saturday mid-afternoon, put your tent up, around about ten we'd kick the music in, finishing about five or six in the morning, go back to your tent, stay there all day and leave when you want, it wasn't a 'Get off our land' sort of thing. The added attraction to this place was that a quarter of a mile down the road the farmer had built something called 'Crocky's Trail'. It's like an assault course but it's for children, with slides and climbing frames, so all the party people used to go onto the Crocky's Trail, all falling over and hurting themselves. It's still there today and he does really good business. The problem he had was that the price of milk had hit rock bottom, so he was trying to make money and people still go there for bank holidays and the kids love it. He'd built it all himself from raw iron and metal with a welding kit. Along with that he'd built these big metal statues, forty feet high, of people, all welded by himself, they looked incredible. The guy was great, and he loved us, he loved our party, it was right up his street.

The One Tree Island core audience were just nice, normal people, and they all knew each other. We created a scene that was a bit like the E scene when that started out, in that everybody knew each other, for about six to eight months everyone knew each other on that scene. One Tree Island was built on that sort of ethos. At one point we had about a hundred and fifty people who all knew each other, and that was part of the party. The music was another thing, people love dancing to world music, especially if you've had drugs; you think you're on your fucking holidays. You could be in a club in Manchester with it pissing down, and you will think you're on your holidays, because it gave you that buzz, and you knew everyone you were dancing with, that was One Tree Island at its purest I guess.

The thing with the world music scene is it's timeless. I've been playing a CD that I recorded live at the party back in '97, and you couldn't tell whether it was made yesterday or twenty years ago. Now all these world music acts are putting dance beats behind their music, getting more advanced, so now they're releasing music that sounds like a dance record, but it's got all the instruments from their countries. If I'd had that back in the day, it wouldn't have necessarily made it better, but it would've been great to hear the beats that you had in House music. The beats are there in world music anyway, but having electronic sounds coming in just takes it forward another step. We had a really good set of DJs, there were about ten on the roster in the end, and they were all right up for it. They all played house and other stuff, but all had big sections of their collections that they could play at One Tree Island, all World-orientated. I'd definitely love to get One Tree Island up and running again, I've mentioned it to some people and everyone's gone 'Fuckin' hell yeah, get that going again, bring it back!'

ANDY BARKER

Manchester's best known nightclub was the Hacienda, but the fact is the first few years after it was opened it was rarely full. There were leaks in the roof and it was if anything a bit too trendy and in a part of the city not known for its night-life, hidden away at the wrong end of Whitworth Street. The only time it got a half decent crowd was if there was a live band on - The Smiths and New Order nights were always packed out and we all know Madonna played her very first gig there when the TV hit show "The Tube" came one Friday night but the place was a huge empty shell for at least 5 years.

I went to a band competition there and The Happy Mondays were signed on the strength of it by Tony Wilson. They were certainly different - just a set of scally lads having a great time. Around that time I got chatting to a lad called Andy Barker who was gutted him and his mates from Miles Platting were just short on equipment and time to get on that night as 808 State. Anyway a year or so later the club was moving in the right direction and even made it on to the TV show called "The Hit Man and Her" presented by Micheala Strachan and Pete Waterman. They had cameras all over the club that night even though they didn't have a clue that most of the punters were off their trolleys after taking Ecstasy. Now the fact is this is the only film you can see of the Haçienda in full swing. Just go to YouTube and wait till a top tune called "I like to Listen" comes on you'll see a young funky ginger haired Andy Barker up on a podium doing his acid house moves. Almost 30 years on and Andy and 808 State still play live, so here's a bit from the man himself...

In 1991 808 State played the G-Mex for two sell out nights, which was quite an achievement for a pretty faceless band at the time, getting ten thousand people a night. The fans kicked in the fire doors and got about another two thousand in that way; we had a great time, and made about £2.79. We spent all the money on the sound system, lasers and big inflatables, and had Bjork onstage with us, who no one knew at that time. Only about two months before this we'd supported The Happy Mondays there. We set up a big DJ booth in the centre of the crowd, so it was just a big party basically. Every penny we earned from the

ANDY BARKER

808 State and guest, a then relatively unknown Bjork, at their legendary GMEX gigs in 1991.

G-Mex gigs went straight back into production. This was right at the height of what the press called 'Madchester' and it was one big party.

At the time it seemed that not only Manchester but the whole of the North West was off its nut, so loads of raves started cropping up around places like Blackburn. You'd finish partying in somewhere like The Thunderdome in Manchester and hop in the car straight over to Blackburn as there was bound to be something happening there. You'd arrive and there'd be thousands of people congregating, all looking for the same thing. Online you can find photos of those huge convoys of cars on the motorway into Blackburn, with the police directing traffic; they couldn't stop it, and knew they couldn't, so just wanted to work the overtime and talk to girls who were off their heads all night. There was a bit of cat and mouse about it all; if the police found it before you'd started then it's a no-go, but if they get there and you're already in full swing, then there's nothing they can do. There was a place called Sett End, where everyone would park up, put some tunes on and wait to find out where to go. Eventually one car would set off, followed by another, then another, and lead us to the warehouse, and before the police could get there we're in, it's on. This went on for just over a year, and there was nothing the police could do because there were just too many of us, and we weren't doing anything wrong or causing trouble, we just wanted to dance. The whole thing started to die when the gangs from Manchester started getting involved, and therefore attracting the police; they were taxing the door and selling drugs, which made it a police matter, and that's when the riot vans started rocking up. Me and Eric were there one night when there was a running battle with the police, running at each other and throwing stuff, we saw a guy throw a police dog through a window.

The Thunderdome was an old rock club that was doing nothing, and a local lad who was a future mate of ours thought he should put a night on there. He asked the guy who owned it if that was alright, and he said fine, but to be honest he was happy to have it empty because as far as the taxman knew it was full every night. He opened up a can of worms by saying yes to the night, because all of a sudden he's got fifteen-hundred people in there, the place has turned into a sweatbox and there's queues round the block, it's just a shame he wasn't selling much booze. It was the alternative to the Hacienda, because a lot of the kids at the Thunderdome couldn't get in there, so created their own scene in Miles Platting right in the thick of the estates. It went from one big night at the weekend, to suddenly being chocka from Wednesday to Sunday, and he had such a hit on his hands he didn't know what to do with it. There were a few naughty people knocking around there, but mostly it was just for the music; you couldn't get in the Hac because your face didn't fit or you didn't have the right clobber on, so it'd be 'Right, off to the Thunderdome.'

A lot of the Hacienda crowd would not have gone in the Thunderdome; too scary for them, even though it wasn't scary, but it looked it. Unlike the Hacienda, the Thunderdome took no time at all to get going, just word of mouth. The Hacienda really made Tony and New Order work for their money (not that they saw any of it). It was quiet as a grave for years, then Tony and New Order went to New York and came back with a ton of New Order money and a load of big ideas. Peter Hook wasn't too happy at the time with being the cash cow, if you read his book it'll say 'Thanks to Eric for sorting my head out with the finances'; me and Eric were at Glastonbury one year, and Hooky's saying 'the fucking Hacienda's costing me millions', so Eric says 'Where're you from, Hooky?' 'Salford' 'Exactly, thank yourself lucky you're not in jail. Get over here and sort yourself out.' For some reason he paid attention to that particular comment. There's some horror stories about the Hacienda but nothing compares to looking at those accounts. If the Hacienda had opened in 1987, they'd have made a fortune, but it opened in '82 and sat dormant for years, until the scene appeared and it became the exact type of building you'd want, a warehouse. They never made any money though; everyone was on the guestlist, no one drank booze, they had to turn the water off in the toilets just to get sales up, and even then water was only 50p. It went against them in every sense it could; 'Everyone's on the Mondays' guestlist, drinking water, and who's selling the drugs? Not us.'

That was a special time for music I think, and an amazing thing to be a part of. The tools you had at your disposal, especially the Roland 808, meant that if you had a sound in your head that you wanted to achieve, it was possible. Much like the dawn of psychedelic music, 1967, and the advent of the 8-track tape recorder, when you're given a new set of instruments, you experiment. For example people like DJ Pierre, who was experimenting with this machine that was meant to be a bass accompaniment to a guitarist, and he saw that it made lots of weird and wonderful new sounds, and so just ran with it; tinkering around with new equipment and experimenting can bring out all sorts of new noises, whether it's DJ Pierre or 'Tomorrow Never Knows'. New scenes can even grow out of these little experiments, like the truckload of scenes that have come out of dance music over the years; drum and bass, dubstep, even that EDM shite. It's the willingness to experiment and really head down the rabbit-hole that can bring out some amazing sounds, and all the best from Can to Giogio Moroder have understood that experimenting and manipulating equipment can make something brand new. Some of the old equipment, like the 303, were quite cheap back then because nobody wanted them, saying 'I'm a guitarist I don't need one', and so someone's bought one for fifty quid, thought 'That sounds a bit weird', hooked it up to his drum machine and there you go, they've got house music.

At that time, if you bought the latest equipment in say '87, like an Emulator sampler, it would've cost thousands, but little companies like Casio were starting to make their own keyboards with a microphone on them, so you could sample two seconds or something, where an emulator could record ten. Trevor Horn had made a fortune producing Frankie Goes to Hollywood and that sort of thing, and so bought a few studios, which we used to use, and also bought an emulator,. He had loads of the old technology that we were really interested in, Moogs and that sort of thing, and so we went mad for them rather than the newer stuff that was all pre-set, Roland's and the like where you could push a button for strings but you couldn't manipulate them, so we were going back to the old stuff.

Whether it's tape loops in '67 or samples in '87, it's all history repeating itself but moving in a different direction, it's all the same ethos; picking up equipment and making it do something it's not meant to. It's that experimentation that brings about new forms of music, and up until now there's not been any new ones. We were into Hip-Hop before House music and would've kept on with it, but House suddenly was like a juggernaut that just squashed everything around it and got under the skin of music. Dance music is a strange thing for record labels to try and tame and package, because it's faceless; it's music, not a hairstyle. ZTT, Trevor's label, who we were with, signed Seal and then dropped us, and neatly put House music into his sound and image. They asked us to write the music for him, to which we said no; we've said no to far more things than we've said yes to. Integrity's far more important than a pile of money. I think the nature of these massive cultural movements like Dance music is that eventually it gets dressed up and packaged, and you know it's all gone wrong when 'Cream Anthems 43' and 'Now That's What I Call Cream Sessions' starts appearing, but the real stuff's always going on, you've just got to seek it out.

SIMON WOLSTENCROFT

Simon Wolstencroft has a unique distinction having been the only musician to play in both The Stone Roses (technically Roses forerunners 'The Patrol') and The Smiths. Quite some accolade for a humble lad from Sale. Yet it was with The Fall that he made a mark; surviving for a remarkable 11 years under the autocratic and capricious rule of the legendary Mark E Smith. Having travelled the world Simon has a few tales to tell, as he did in his autobiography 'You Can Drum But You Can't Hide' which covered everything from tour bust ups, groupies and drug addiction to his gypsy lifestyle as a drummer across 4 continents.

If ever there was a Manchester Maverick, then it's Si...

I was like a lot of teenagers. Stubborn. Single-minded. Knew better. 'You won't be told, Simon,' my dad used to sigh. 'You just won't be told.'

Dr Peter Wolstencroft was a general practitioner who held a surgery in Baguley and could not understand why his son showed little interest in school. I was obsessive about hobbies. I went from planes and football to music and fashion, and later, as obsession slid towards addiction, a long relationship with drugs. Through all this, music, as other interests came and went, has been the constant. Starting back from my mum's Motown records and glam rock on Top of the Pops, I took a particular interest in drumming. I would find myself fiddling with the radiogram to get the maximum bass sound and improvising drum kits from biscuit tins and pans. It's hard to know why, as a lad, I took especially to the drums. There was something primeval about it.

I could never have known it would be my job for a large part of my life, aided by the burgeoning music scene in Manchester. There is this idea that punk created the local explosion and I tend to believe it – not necessarily punk music but the DIY ethos. Me and my mates at school thought: if they can do it, why can't we? Ian Brown on vocals and Woolworth's bass, John Squire on catalogue guitar and homemade practice amp, Simon Wolstencroft on drum kit nicked from school. Hey presto. We're a band.

We practiced on Thursday evenings, listening to Sex Pistols,

MANCHESTER MAVERICKS

Generation X and Clash records over and over, learning the parts. Ian was more of a Pistols fan while John and I favoured the dulcet tones of Joe Strummer. I idolised drummer Topper Headon. He could play anything. I spent most of my wages, scraped together by bagging tomatoes in a greengrocer, following the group. In the canteen at South Trafford College I was introduced to our new lead singer, Andy Couzens. He was kicking someone's head in. It seemed about par for the course. It was a violent time.

Andy had a mustard coloured MG Midget, immediately replacing the need for any audition, and we crammed in the back of it, tooling around, winding up CB radio enthusiasts while arranging rehearsals and plotting shows.

We were called The Patrol. We cobbled together a set, drew up flyers, and toured the Badlands of Cheshire, backed by Stretford punks Corrosive Youth. You want some, I'll give it ya.

The music scene was always changing back then. Glam rock, prog, punk, disco, reggae – totally different styles – had all emerged since I started school.

The latest one was Ska revival – we got shiny suits and cheap crombies from Carnaby Street. I had a flat top. We looked the business. After a year or so, though, the group started to be less tight knit as other interests took root. John and Ian started going off on scooter runs, tinkering around with Lambrettas. It wasn't for me. Quadrophenia – so what? My first love was still the drums and I wanted to carry on with it as far as I could.

Drinking in The Vine, I was introduced to a hotshot 17 year-old guitarist, name of John Maher, ex of White Dice with Corrie bin man Curly Watts. He had the gift of the gab. He was going to be a rock star and needed a drummer. Did I fancy it? Yeah, why not. Johnny Marr, as he would become, blew me away. Straight away. He could play anything, unbelievable musical knowledge. His mate, Andy Rourke, was equally impressive on the bass. We started hanging round at Andy's house down the road. Andy's dad was always away on business and we'd sit around, smoking weed, listening to tune after tune through a pair of humongous speakers. Bands like Parliament and Grandmaster Flash. So many different sounds.

SIMON WOLSTENCROFT

*Simon with fellow Red former Stone Roses front-man
Ian Brown at Old Trafford*

We'd all hang out at Pip's or Legends, in our Johnsons threads and soak it all up, getting high on 'poppers', which I hated. I got into other things. Namely, heroin…but that's a whole other story. The three of us became Freak Party, recording industrial funk at the Beehive Mills in Ancoats and looking for a singer to contribute to our demo 'Crack Therapy'.

One night, whilst rehearsing in Decibelle, there was a persistent knock at the door. Finally relenting, we went to see who it was and in burst four blokes in crombies and shiny shoes.

It was the serious crime squad.

'Which one of you is Johnny Marr?' one of the burly coppers asked.

Johnny identified himself. We were bundled into unmarked Ford Granadas and whisked off to Longsight nick. The police were investigating the theft of an original Lowry and Johnny's name came up through his association with Kev 'The Smoke', a fence from Wythenshawe.

We saw less and less of Johnny after this – he kept his head down and probably wanted to steer clear of Andy's house, where, without any parental oversight, dealers had more or less begun holding shop. Months later Johnny rang me out of the blue, excited.

'Si, will you be the drummer in my new band?'

He explained how he'd met a singer called Stephen Morrissey and he needed to record a demo, pronto.

'We're called The Smiths,' he said.

My first thought was: what a crap name.

The Smiths?

Though I wasn't sure about this band, I felt duty bound to at least sit in for the session. So, a few days later, we were back in Decibelle running through a depressing song about the Moors Murders, 'Suffer Little Children.' You can say what you want about The Smiths and Morrissey's singular streak of genius and what a fool I must have been and anything like that, but here's the thing: I didn't like Morrissey's voice. It was light years away from what was turning me on musically at the time. I didn't like the cut of his jib. I was into jazz funk.

Within a year The Smiths were massive. If I'd have known what they would become, of course I would have stayed with the band. I'm not that much of a purist. And I did love some of the songs they did, but I'd made my bed and I was going to have to lie in it.

Since I wasn't in The Smiths, I carried on working at the fishmongers in Wilmslow, slicing fish like a fucking champion and getting stoned in the evenings. I did, however, remain good friends with Johnny and he hooked me up with a few auditions, which led me to the seat in Terry Hall's new band, The Colourfield.

This, I thought, was a lifeline.

Terry Hall was an icon. I loved The Specials and Fun Boy Three – I quit my job and threw in my lot with the band but it just didn't work out.

I had only seriously begun to think that you could make a career being a musician from The Smith's rise, but the rejection from The Colourfield seemed to make this dream as remote as ever.

If I'm honest, things got a bit low for me then. I was working in the council canteen. My habit got worse. I was falling out of love with music. I wrote my car off. I ended 1984 spending a couple of nights in the nick for theft.

I needed to turn things round.

Via Johnny, I met Andrew Berry, a hairdresser who ran a salon under the stage at the Hacienda, a club we both frequented. We started a band called The Weeds, after a little hobby one or two of us got up to. It was a great laugh and got me back into playing again. We played a gig in Corbieres supporting The Happy Mondays, who Factory Records supremo Tony Wilson had come to sign. That same night, he offered to sign The Weeds, but Andrew had it in his head that we were going to get picked up by a major label. I thought he was daft to turn it down.

By the start of 1986, the Weeds were touring with the Fall, a band I had been aware of since my school days, but only recently begun to take notice of after hearing their latest album, 'This Nation's Saving Grace'.

As luck would have it, The Fall's leader, Mark E Smith, had just had another bust up with his regular drummer, Karl Burns, after the gig in Bristol. He must have been watching me earlier on and as I was loading my kit into the Transit he approached me and asked if I wanted to join the group.

It was a paid gig, so like a flash I accepted the offer, jacked in the chip frying, and by the summer was in Abbey Road Studios tanning whizz and recording 'Mr Pharmacist'.

What a turnaround this was.

So began 'The Glory Years'.

We played all around the world: small clubs, festivals, plays, ballets. You never knew what you were going to get with the mercurial Mark E Smith. I liked Mark – he was dead funny and could be very generous. We became good mates for a time. But he also had this paranoid, dictatorial streak and, if things seemed to be going too well, an urge to throw a spanner in the works.

He stuck to his guns. I'll give him that. He didn't like fads or marketing because he thought it was ridiculous and dated very quickly. He had a point.

MANCHESTER MAVERICKS

So it was, at the height of the Madchester scene, with major labels falling all over themselves for a piece, he insisted I help him move to Edinburgh.

'We're from Salford. Not Manchester. Do your homework.'

Much as he cultivated this outsider thing, though, he wasn't above hob-nobbing – showing he belonged in musical circles.

We went to Barry White's 50th at a club in New York where the 'Walrus of Love' himself serenaded the ladies, sat behind a white concert grand. Rochdale crooner Lisa Stansfield wandered over, pissed up, and shoved her tongue down Mark's throat. Mark looked proper chuffed. I thought I was going to be sick.

I survived eleven years in the band and if you know anything about The Fall, that's pretty good going. There were plenty of reasons for leaving, but basically, I stopped getting paid regularly and along came my daughter, Emily.

I wound up, again through a combination of effort and luck, in my old mate Ian Brown's band for a couple of years, finally reaching the heights I'd long hoped for in The Fall. Credible pop but with a wider audience - Top of the Pops and the like. You need a certain amount of skill and commitment to get ahead in this game, but you also need a big dirty slice of lady luck.

Extract taken from Simon Wolstencroft's memoir, 'You Can Drum But You Can't Hide,' published by Strata Books.

ALAN LORD

Like most Mancs, we're all aware of Alan's life behind bars after his fame following the Strangeways Riot which started on April Fool's Day, 1990. I was sent down myself for three months for drink driving on Monday 2nd April, and all the talk was about Alan and co up on the roof.

It sounds crazy but we were all buzzing our bollocks off, with chit-chat and reports coming in over the radios while we were all locked in the Central Detention Holding Block on top of the courts. The rumours and speculation about how many prisoners and screws were dead was untrue, but it shows you how people's minds work when a crisis arises.

When I was eventually sent to Durham, the talk just got more intense and we all openly enjoyed seeing the news as Alan and the lads seemed to be tearing down what we deemed an evil, Victorian prison, and making fools of the prison officers that seemed hell-bent on using their power over all cons, whether they were serving short sentences or doing life. Once it was over we all knew there would be one hell of a price to pay for the likes of Alan and co. It was great to see the recent TV show which reconstructed exactly what went down with both sides telling the truth, at last. What stuck out for me was that Alan wasn't trying to add any bullshit, it was all from the heart. If anyone embodies the spirit of the Manc Maverick it's Alan as he made a genuine difference to the prison system and got the prisoners' point of view into the public eye for the first time.

Some weeks before this book was being finalised, I was waiting to go for a scan at North Manchester Hospital, and I heard a familiar accent. I knew one hundred percent who it was, and across the waiting room I saw Alan. He looked like a bodybuilder. It turned out his frame was too big to get into the CT scan machine, there so the doctors were talking about transferring him over to Bury where the machine was a touch bigger. After 32 years behind bars, following an original sentence of 15 years, he now runs a gym up near Bury and my brother, Mark, has been up to see him a few times. So I took the chance to ask him, before the ambulance took him away, if he'd be up for penning a few pages for Mavericks. I'm glad to say he was well up for it, so here's a chapter from someone who has the DNA of Manchester in his genes; what us street people term a real Manc Maverick.

MANCHESTER MAVERICKS

★

I was put into care at 18 months old. My mum and dad just couldn't cope so me and my sister were farmed out over the next ten years and we went through 7 different Foster homes and 4 children's homes during that time all over the north west. Thing is at that age you get attached to the people who look after you. I was with one Foster family for ages with my sister and the Welfare people just came along one day and moved us on. It was soul destroying really. It definitely has an effect on you as a kid. I can't blame it for my criminality but it definitely made it easier for me to slip into it. It also made me unemotional about certain things because I'd had to hide my true emotions as a kid. It also gave me a huge mistrust with authority something which obviously continued through my life.

When I returned to my parents' home after 10 years, I immediately away back to the Children's Home I'd been at in Liverpool which was Strawberry Fields, made famous by the Beatles song. As a result of moving about all the time I didn't really have a proper education as I'd just play truant all the time, so I'm basically self-taught.

When I was kid, it wasn't about educational achievement, it was about survival. When I got a bit older the gang I ran with was for survival really. For example we'd go down to the Student Union in town and sell them cooking Thyme instead of weed. You'd get £4 worth of herbs from the shop and sell them for £40. It worked cos the students just saw a black lad selling them weed and thought 'cool'. We always had to have each other's backs – it was a violent time and we had to stick together to survive. There was the gang thing breaking out in Manchester at the time and then there was the police who were by and large NF or borderline NF.

We were petty criminals and housebreakers but we had morals. We tended to target rich people's houses for example because we knew they had stuff we could sell quickly like the family silver but we didn't destroy property needlessly. We saw it as a business, a matter of survival. We wouldn't break into a working class house, mainly cos we knew they had as much or not much more than us.

I've never drunk alcohol in my life. My dad was from Belize but he hung around in the Irish pubs in Manchester because he liked the craic. So one day when I was a kid he let me have a sip of his pint and I hated it and decided then and there that it wasn't for me. Same goes for weed and cigarettes, I just didn't fancy them. It didn't stop me going to pubs and clubs around town but I was more into the shebeens around Moss Side. Sometimes we'd go out to clubs like Genevieve's or up to Oldham to the disco there but generally we stuck to the shebeens.

At that time, which would be late 1970s, I had dreadlocks - I was never into fashion labels. It was a time when black people were becoming aware of their roots and questioning how we fitted into UK society. I was definitely into that. It all culminated in the 1981 riots but by then I was inside…

Walking around town today I love a lot of the older buildings such as the Fire Station on London Road – it shows a level of craftsmanship that you don't see in modern buildings that just seem to be thrown up. But I'm not one for being an Uber Manc. I don't think in terms of where people come from. It takes me back to my days in Borstal. They would always separate the Mancs and Scousers and we'd only meet very occasionally, in the canteen or on Sports Day and there would be this huge tension. On Sports Day they'd set us up against each other as a form of entertainment for the screws so I've always rejected it. Divide and rule I think they call it. People are people in my opinion and we should judge each other regardless of where we born. In prison if you weren't a nonce or a grass then we were all in it together basically. We were all equal.

I ended up inside following a botched robbery in 1981 which started off as a mistake and ended in disaster. We were going to do one shop and found it was shut. So we were all arguing among ourselves about the cock up as we're walking home in the snow when we saw a jeweller shutting up his shop in Cheetham Hill so we decided to follow him. Now, I had a knife on me but it was for self-defence really as I was walking around Manchester and there was an ongoing thing between Cheetham Hill and

Salford. I tapped the shopkeeper on the shoulder saying 'give us the brief case' and he started hitting me. This guy turned round and started battering me with his briefcase and instinctively I started to fight back and there was a scuffle. I didn't think much of it but later that night it was announced on the news that this guy had been stabbed to death. So I panicked and went on the run. I was hiding out in people's houses and then in a park. The police soon narrowed it down to me and by the Monday they'd cornered me. I was charged with murder and taken to Moss Side police station, then they started working me over, my feet didn't touch the floor between the entrance of the police station and the interview room, they just kicked me up and down. My interview was conducted without a solicitor and then they chained me to the interview table and bounced my head off the table for half an hour while others were booting me. On top of all that my confession was false. When it went to court they all denied it and stuck to the same story, the cops stuck together like glue and I was fucked.

When I went into Strangeways at 19 on remand it was not my intention to be violent but the screws were on to me from the moment I got in there, presumably tipped off about me by their mates in GMP, so I just said to myself 'what will be will be'.

The screws in Strangeways were racist to the extent that a lot of them were in the NF. For example I wasn't allowed a comb for my hair because I had an Afro, whereas a white guy would be allowed a comb for their hair. And then it became a thing between me and a certain screw to get an Afro comb and I had to fight my ground.

Strangeways was different to other prisons. When lads would get sent there they would be walking in all cocky but they didn't realise the hard cases and lifers that were in there already. It was ruthless and that swagger soon disappeared. Even for relatively hardened criminals this was on another level. You had guys in there who would never be let out.

Conditions in the prison system were grim. After I was sentenced I was sent to Wakefield which had a high proportion of nonces so it was very tense. By the time I returned to Strangeways in 1990 I soon sussed out that this was a nightmare and I wanted to get out so I got some tungsten files smuggled in and was working my way through the bars. I'd also got a 40ft rope disguised as laundry in a bag and I'd replace the bars in their slots by using porridge as cement. One day they turned my cell over and these screws walked out with the bars in their hands so that was that. Mind you, the riot happened a few weeks later so my planned escape was quickly forgotten!

The riot had been coming for months. Certain people were being victimised for no reason and conditions were bad and getting worse. It's well documented what happened…When I first got up on the roof, it was exhilarating. It was great to see the whole of Manchester laid out before me. Then I could see all the press and media setting up and running around like headless chickens to catch a glimpse of us. I suddenly realised the power we had. The Strangeways riot was a huge media circus but it brought the moral issue of how prisoners were housed at Her Majesty's pleasure, into the public domain. It ended up as a good thing because it led to the Woolf Enquiry which improved the lot of prisoners immensely.

I don't classify myself as a ringleader but I took control eventually because I realised this was a chance to educate the outside world about what was really happening. I became famous for the blackboards. The only reason I brought one on to the roof was because the police would drown me out whenever I started to talking to the press so I needed another way to communicate with them.

I also became famous for appearing on the roof naked because the police were using fire hoses on Glyn Williams, so I came up with a bar of soap and shouted over 'I need a shower anyway'. They knew it was illegal and it soon stopped. It was all about getting across that we weren't animals and we had a sense of humour. Of course it had started because some lads needed to let off steam but it got out of hand. For example right at the start a load of them went in the kitchen and ransacked the place and poured all the food onto the floor, which was obviously a self-defeating exercise. That's when a few of us started storing provisions because we were in it for the long haul.

Back then we only got six visits a year and were allowed one letter a week. The meals were the same thing every day. When I got to the kitchens I found steak, chops and all the other delicacies we had never seen in there. Then there were the daily abuses and abuses of power that were regular occurrences in Strangeways as well as the indignity of slopping out. The prison, designed to accommodate less than 1000 prisoners had a population of over 1600 at the time of the riot. The situation was out of control.

The police got up to some daft schemes to get us out. They were frying onions to try and tempt us down for example. While I was up there I knew it was my job to expose the system and get the message out. I knew this opportunity would be short lived but while we were up there I knew we had the upper hand in terms of the media. I have been involved in 5 prison riots but the others were confined and this made a difference because this one made the press and went worldwide.

During the riot I was acting as a negotiator with the Home Office. I just told them "you let this happen" because the day before there had been the Poll Tax Riots and I am certain that they let this go on to deflect attention. Bear in mind 7 people held off all those police officers - how can that happen unless they are being allowed to do it? Without us holding out nothing would have changed. Of course they snatched me on the way back from a meeting with the Home Office. I'd lasted 14 days.

In the aftermath of the riots I had a woman visit me from the Woolf Enquiry and she was shocked at the number of screws who were accompanying me. And when I told her about the various conditions inside she was surprised. But I pointed out that whenever they had an inspection they would always tell the prison in advance - of course they reverted back to their old ways once the inspection team had gone.

It was noticeable that they spent £50m on refurbishing Strangeways when they could have knocked it down and built something better for half the price but it was a case of 'We're still here' - it's their bastion, to knock it down would have been to admit defeat.

ALAN LORD

Alan Lord at his gym in Radcliffe

After the Woolf Report, the prison system improved but they still have old school people looking after things and the cutbacks will soon lead to conflict. For instance they have banned cigarettes now and this will inevitably cause problems sooner or later as 80% of prisoners smoke.

The common misconception among the public is that prison is there for rehabilitation. I am now on Life License. If I choose to move I have to inform the authorities. If I go for a normal job there's no chance I would get it having spent 32 years inside. So where is the rehabilitation? I am permanently marked by my time in prison as it's on all my records. The state hasn't just said, 'oh he's rehabilitated now'. In fact it's the opposite.

Now you have two types of prisons: private and public. The conditions in private prisons are miles better because of the terms of the contract these companies sign. My first experience was an eye-opener, they called my by my first name and offered me a cup of tea! The landings are clean, the warders are approachable and so you only need 2 warders to watch 90 men – this all makes sense because the fewer men, the bigger the profit, so it's in their interest to keep prisoners happy and resolve any niggling conflicts quickly rather than using the prison population to cause tension.

Then biggest difference after I came out was the technology. Then I struggled with the sheer amount of people and thinking their eyes were on me but I got on with it. Then there is the abruptness of prison speak which people on the outside would take the wrong way but I'm slowly adjusting to life on the outside.

ANTHONY DONNELLY

Anthony Donnelly comes from pure bred Manc/Irish Maverick stock. His father is Arthur Donnelly and his Uncle Jimmy was 'Jimmy the Weed' who were allegedly both part of the fabled Quality Street Gang of Mancunian myth. Anthony, along with his brother Christopher, went a different route to their elders, capitalising on the cultural explosion in Manchester with their fashion label Gio-Goi. The label soon became a money spinner and made the pair rich and famous but Anthony and Chris have always stayed close to their roots. So just how did a couple of lads from Wythenshawe become multi-millionaire businessmen?

My first earner was selling toast on the school bus to my classmates. Every Friday morning our class would set off for Sharston Baths from Benchill Primary on a bus and I'd sell slices of cold toast to those who couldn't afford a packed lunch or whose mum and dads just weren't looking after them. To be honest, I probably didn't make that much money as I gave away as much as I made, that's still the story of my life. I also used to steal biscuits from the biscuit box at school, which the teacher would keep at the top of his wardrobe and hand out at lunch time. I'd take them then sell them in the playground, these were probably the first rackets I had on the go. One of my next enterprises was when I was about 10 or 11 years old, selling badges outside the Buzzcocks and Slaughter and the Dogs punk gigs from a badge board I'd made up, that and working in my Dad's scrap yard stripping copper-wire, I was raised in that scrap yard it was a hard upbringing and my mum did her best with three kids on her own for most of our early years.

My early memories are of visiting my dad in Walton jail with my mum. My Dad was always in jail so that was when I think I became a petty thief. We couldn't afford the luxuries like most kids on our estate so helping yourself became a way of life.

So by my early teens I was smashing it on the estate as I had become street smart and was as game as any of the older boys and

MANCHESTER MAVERICKS

I soon come to the attention of the main lads on the estate being a cheeky lad sticking my nose into everyone's business where money was concerned. Some people starting calling me 'The Count' in reference to the Sesame Street vampire character, as I was selling anything and everything including coats that cost £100 for around £50 or whatever the price was - I usually halved it as I only paid others a third of the price for stock.

The landlord of the church pub in Northenden bought me a silver tankard which had 'Champagne Charlie' written on it for my 16th birthday because I would often drink on nights out when we made money. I had my first car when I was 14, everything I had was a banger but the fact was that I had a car was bizarre at that age, me and my pals started to get around different areas meeting new people in the motor which was an absolute shed, I loved it though. We would drive to other youth clubs even though I could barely see over the wheel.

It was around this time I met my first love Kathleen Delahoyde. She was from a strict Irish Catholic family and her mum chased me away from her for one reason and another, I was just out and out trouble apparently. Being a colourful character you can often be blamed for just about everything, I suppose that comes with the territory - you just have to live with the plusses and the minuses. You had to learn the hard way, nobody could or wanted to explain the life lessons to you.

Pretty soon I was attracting as much attention from the police as I was girls, weirdly I loved all of it; I just loved drama, I was addicted to it. It was different back then if you got pulled over by the police there was no ANPR so you could just blag the police saying 'I'm insured, my tax is in the post, my name is such and such' and they could only give you a note to produce your documents. There was no CCTV back then either so you can just imagine the shit that the police had to put up with from us!

We learned a lot of moves from the people who came before us, original pioneers like John Sullivan aka Sully and Beaner, the author of this book - they were the first at it internationally that we knew. They were coming back from all over Europe with the best clobber you would ever see, they were bringing in the

ANTHONY DONNELLY

Anthony (left) and Chris enjoying a cuppa and a smoke

new labels and watches and gems for sale and living like playboys. Everything seemed to be falling into place for us back home and as the young ones we were learning from them. We'd see them all either on the street, stopping at my mums or on the terraces or at the gigs so it wasn't long before I set my own team because I thought anything they could do, we could do better.

One person in particular round the Manchester area I got inspiration from was Barry Valentine, he was the coolest thing since slice bread. He and his brothers were on the same page as us with the football and fashion and he represented North Manchester, he came from Ardwick which is where I was born and although we were South Manchester, it was good to meet new people. One of my first overseas escapades, grafting abroad and learning new skills, was when my Mum and Dad took us on holiday to Corfu of all places. I took Christopher and Tracey out to the town centre in Corfu and leaving my parents at the pool. I got Tracey and Christopher to attract attention from the staff in a supermarket whilst I snuck in the back and rifled the safe - who would of thought these three angelic kids would be up to so much mischief! I have to say Chris and Tracey were innocent as it was all my idea and I ended up giving my dad the money for some of the holiday. He never asked where the money came from, nor was I quizzed on all the new Lacoste clothes I'd bought with the proceeds.

On my return to the UK I remember asking my Dad if I could go away with the older lads who were grafting abroad, though I was younger than them I was rather nimble and extremely game, a prolific villain in the making, very well dressed with more front than Blackpool, it was a special time. You hear about people who profess to be connoisseurs on brands or claim to be instrumental in the development of the casual/ terrace scene. When I hear some other people going on about their history in fashion and football I have to laugh. I am convinced they think they were part of what went on because of the garments that they were wearing. In fact they were influenced by our lot, the fact that they had been involved in a tear up at a few games they attended made them part of the firm when in fact it doesn't actually work like that – it's actually a clique that these kids probably did not even know existed.

I knew most of the people who kick-started these wonderful times in fashion; a few small crews from Man United and Man City who were the pioneers with other groups of lads be it from Liverpool or Everton - our mob was in the thick of all of it. We would often meet these crews on our trips to Europe on the ferries heading away or returning from our travels. You were affiliated through the football and other things we won't mention that were going on. We were definitely one of the first Manchester terrace fashion crews - we were up there. Mancunians and Scousers have a lot to answer for, I think we have the smartest firms on the planet and always have done.

Eventually the brands became more widespread and the garments became more accessible and travel became much easier with overseas holidays and our thing was not as special as it was back in the day. Things change and people got into taking hard drugs – some died and others went to jail, children arrived and some wanted to put the past behind them and start businesses. It was time to grow up and move on and I suppose it was time to move over as it was someone else's turn.

ANTHONY DONNELLY

These days life is different; we have had a rollercoaster journey with fame and fortune, fashion has always been a prominent part of our life and always will be. Crime obviously pays for some people and doesn't for others but I find it hard to believe that so many people from my type of background get anchored by what they're born into - for us the less we had the more we wanted and it was out there if you worked hard and travelled.

Gio-goi has served us well; we have had the front cover of Vogue and we have had nights out with the best of them - we have lived life to the best we could and though we have had our ups and downs we keep going. I truly believe that my misspent youth on the streets and terraces was instrumental in our success as businessmen. I would most definitely not recommend crime to anyone - prison and violence is costly in more ways than one and there are a tonne of legitimate opportunities out there, you just have to go find them

Manchester is the greatest city in the world - the best football, the best music, the best swagger, the best bitter, the best nights out – George Best (and not forgetting Colin Bell to keep it even) and the best days of my life apart from Acid House!

KAREN WOODS

Karen is Manchester's most prolific novelist. As of November 2018 she had penned 20 novels on life in and around the city since her first book, Broken Youth, was published in 2011. Her books have touched on all aspects of modern life from wife beating and paedophiles to online stalking and swinging sites. She has a sizeable world following but has stayed loyal to Mancunian publishers, Empire…

My earliest memories are of St Patrick's School. The nuns were seen as a gang not to be messed with. Sister Anne was feared by all who met her and I can remember being swung around the classroom a few times when I crossed her. Mr Cassidy was the head teacher whilst I was there, he was nice enough. Which leaves Mrs Brett, Mr Barlow and Mr Dunn. Mr Dunn taught me how to play chess and I'm sure he thought I was really interested in it, in fact I hated it! My favourite memories were predominantly with the school athletics team, I was a part of the team who helped win "The Mother Catherine" memorial trophy!

St Patrick's taught me that being second didn't really count; they wanted winners and would always push me to seek the gold medal. My friends were Teresa Dalton, Marie Andrews and Catherine Regan, we were all part of the crew back in the day and I still see Marie and Catherine. The lads were Martin Hamilton, Gary Quinn, and a few others. I went to High school with all of them and we had some great times. In all honesty I was a naughty kid, but I have loved to make people laugh from an early age. Unfortunately this often led to me getting the strap from Mr Gribbon. His strap was like a block of wood, but coming from Collyhurst I was immune to it after the first few times. They could never break a Collyhurst kid, we were far too head strong.

After leaving school I had a few jobs but the one I loved the most was working in the local newsagents in Harpurhey. As you can imagine the local kids all knew me and would often run inside the shop helping themselves to all the sweets. It was funny to watch them, but hard to keep my job when the stocks were down. But you kept your trap shut if you knew what was good for you. Everyone hates a grass.

Like many people in North Manchester one of the highlights of the year were the Whit Week walks as it was one of the only times we got new clothes, including new shoes and underwear. I don't really know what they were celebrating, but we all got new clothes and that was all that mattered. Kids ran freely in the town centre and would often be found swigging a pint of bitter that one of us had had away from a drunken parent. Those were the days.

In the 80s I had some major fashion disasters. Drain-pipe jeans were one of the best things I have ever worn, but they belonged to my brother and I had to steal them to look cool. I was more of a tom-boy back then and my Monkey-boots were something I treasured. They were a must for fighting too, every time we attacked another estate my monkey boots always came in handy.

A bit later when we started going out properly we would often be found in 'The Bottom Derby' or 'The Forresters' pub. I started drinking in there when I was only 14, dressed to the nines in my mother's dresses and her high heeled shoes, I must have looked a right state. My friend Tina Burton was my partner in crime and we often fell out of there at the weekends unable to walk. My mother thought I was at a youth disco or something, sorry Mam! I was living it up with all the mad heads, loving every minute of it. The hangovers were horrendous, especially on a school night. Those two pubs have a lot to answer for, that's why my education went downhill! But ay, I learned the rules of life, which was much more useful than science or history.

Then later still we started going out in town. My favourite nightclubs in Manchester were 'Rumours' and 'Brewsters'.

MANCHESTER MAVERICKS

Everyone I knew was in these clubs and I always felt safe even when I was steaming drunk, somebody would always make sure I got home safely.

My entire family are big United fans and I have been to Old Trafford to watch them, so it's in my blood to follow the team. As for concerts I've been to see 'Take That' at the MEN. It was a fantastic night and brought me right back to my youth. I also went there to see Neil Diamond but you mustn't tell anyone, he's my guilty secret!

As for heroes I suppose Nobby Stiles and Brian Kidd because they went to St Patrick's, they set the bar for us wannabes at the school and even looking at the photos of them inside the school let all us kids know that if you believed, your dreams were just around the corner.

I'm not one of those that think the kids of today are animals. Kids have always been kids. The difference lies in how schools are allowed to deal with them nowadays. We got a quick slap round the head and a kick up the arse and it stopped us in our tracks. It let us know that if we messed about we would have to pay the price if we got caught. The lesson is simple kids: learn how to not get caught!

Coming from Harpurhey and Collyhurst has always meant you knew the local coppers. I have had involvement with the police but I'll keep that to myself. At the end of the day they are just doing a job; it's just one of them jobs that will never get the praise it deserves. I fully respect them and understand how hard it is for them to cope with the youth of today.

Finally, my biggest regret is not taking my education properly. I should have studied more and not been the class clown. And my ex-boyfriend, I should have kept my legs crossed!

TOMMY DUNN

Tommy Dunn shot to fame as the brains behind 'Britain's Biggest Hoaxer', a Channel 4 documentary featuring his close friend Karl Power and his son performing various friendly pitch invasions impersonating famous sportsmen and, in one particularly famous (but unfilmed) incident, a legendary passage of play where Liverpool goalkeeper Jerzy Dudek dropped the ball and Uruguayan Diego Forlan 'made the scousers cry', in front of the away end at Old Trafford.

Tommy and Karl's antics earned them notoriety and the friendship of the likes of Damien Hirst and Joe Strummer. Today Tommy is a Maverick at leisure with perhaps at least one last trick up his sleeve.

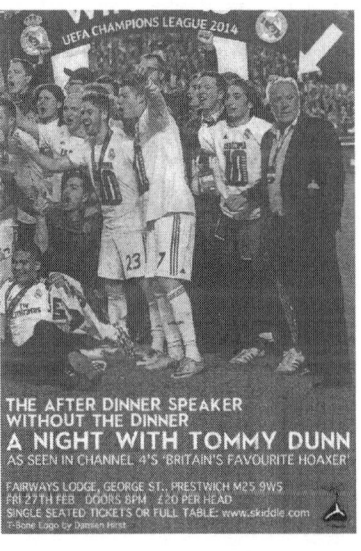

I grew up in the same area as Beaner, Miles Platting. It was a great area, with brilliant people in it. We learned early doors not to pay for anything. I am of the belief that if you haven't got the money to pay for something, take it. I knew Beaner from the area, and he was my idol in those days. Looking back now, that was the wrong move! I looked up to him. His mates were all hoolies but Beaner wasn't, he was different. The rest of his mates were workers but he was a thief. As a kid who are you going to idolise? Gerry, who does a hard day's work for someone else, or Jesse James riding the 88 bus to Old Trafford in Italian fabrics? He was always dressed smart in the best clobber and I thought 'Yeah, that's me.'

Miles Platting was my training ground; I honed the skills there that I would use later as a blagger. You'd start out pretty small; going to the post office for your dole and, when they gave you your cash you turn away for a sec and slip a tenner away and say 'I'm a tenner light here'. There were always money moves going on. I still tend to have a move going on even today, but it all started in that post office. Even today, I could be at the bar and say 'I've been left one in' and they'll just pull you a pint. Just daft things like that. It all makes the same point; don't pay for anything unless you have to. I will never voluntarily pay for anything, I've got to be asked. If I was passing the buck I'd say that seeing Beaner in his clobber made me the man I am today, but it's all been my own choice, and in my own way.

In the early days, Beaner was the first person I knew that went abroad before me. He'd come back in all this new clobber, and he was a cool guy. So the next step for us was abroad. Not with Beaner, though. On our own; Germany, Belgium, Holland, Switzerland, Austria. From the age of 15, to being about 40, I was abroad. Those were great days. We went to jail a couple of times but for me that's part of it. When you're on to a good thing and you're earning plenty of money for your age, it's never-ending. Your mantra becomes 'I'm not going to stop until I get nicked'. When that happens, you go to jail, do your time, and then get another move going, a different one.

I had my first spell in a detention centre in 1978 for robbing shop safes. That was three months, then when I came out I got nicked again and went to Borstal for a year. When I came out in '79 I just wanted to get abroad as quick as. Then again, I've seen some jails abroad as well; Sweden, Norway, Denmark, Germany. The Scandi prisons were civilised but Colditz would've seemed cosy after going to Strangeways at 15. Yeah, 15. You've got to be 16 to go to Strangeways, but for some reason I got sent there while I turned 16 on remand from Borstal. I got there and thought 'Fuckin' hell man', but I knew that I deserved to be there. I've never complained about getting nicked because that was the path I chose. As far as I was concerned, it was going to be my career. Just as those tossers working in The City have good days and bad on the stocks, we had good and bad days on the rob.

One thing I take from what I've done is that it's always been banks and businesses on the receiving end; sneak thieving, no violence. At the time I probably said it was a 'victimless crime' but now that I'm an old bloke I know it wasn't; the woman behind the counter probably either got in trouble or got in therapy. I understand that now, but in those days I thought 'There's nothing better to do than scam a bank'. We made better and better scams and made a very good living off it; scamming banks with foreign money, exchange rates and a good poker face. I don't meant to come off all Robin Hood, but knowing what we do now from the 2008 crash, the banks were full of criminals before we ever stepped into one. We got smart, to the point where in the prime of this thing I was earning £10,000 a week and that was twenty years ago. That's footballer's money. It was crazy; I got onto something where I thought 'This can't be real', and so I'd try it again, and it'd work, and I'd try it again, and it'd work. I was on that for 6 months on my own, and didn't tell anyone. Then I got nicked in the Isle of Man, ironically the place where everyone stashes their money. When I got out after that I told a couple of my mates, 'here's a move'. I said I was out of it but I couldn't stay that way; I patched the move on to a couple of mates, and they started earning big money, so I thought I had to get back into it. I was scamming banks for about 15 years, with nothing to show for it now other than great memories. I had plenty of money, eating out every night with my family, a top car, six holidays a year, properly living it up.

Then, now, and always, I've hated the system. It doesn't apply to people like me or Beaner, who are loyal to one another, and the system has no loyalty itself. When people say there's no honour amongst thieves they're talking bollocks; we remain loyal to one another, and avoid certain things like the plague. I would never rob a person, it's just the establishment I love robbing. There's nothing better than robbing a bank, because they're legalised thieves, they rob us all. When you go over your overdraft they charge you every day. What's the difference between that and a loan shark? A fancy letterhead. It was a thrill taking their money, and I couldn't have taken it from better establishments.

I was earning mad money, and looking back now I think 'Jesus, I had that much', but I gave it away to friends and family. That's why none of us grafters have any money now, because we gave it away. I should have my own house and all the rest of it, but I've no regrets. Looking back, yeah I should have bought property, but I had a different mindset then. I was a young bloke with a darling girlfriend, travelling the world and buzzing my tits off. I thought 'I'm living the rock star life, and I'm from a council estate in Miles Platting', that's social mobility for you.

So nowadays I'm unemployed by choice, so I have to fill my day. You have no rota, you wake up when you wake up. I spend my days either with my kids or in the boozer. My local, in Prestwich, is full of top people. We're all close, and not being from the Northside it would've been easy for me to just dodge the place and go elsewhere, but I love it and I love the people there. I met most of them at United. A lot of the lads I know, from all over the city, I met at football. We all met at games and shared in a fantastic lifestyle. Whether it's for business or a day on the piss watching the game, the hub always seems to be Old Trafford.

With time on your hands and a city to explore, you start noticing a couple of things. Mostly that Manchester is a totally different place to the grey 70's shithole I grew up in. It was a shithole, but we loved it. It was our town. There were about three clubs in the city, and now there's three on every street. Loads of bars, restaurants and cafés; it's a different world. I think two things changed the city forever; The Hacienda and the IRA bomb. The Hacienda changed the cultural fabric of the city, gave it a new set of DNA that wasn't to do with the industrial revolution or Coronation Street, and suddenly you had Berliners making the trek to Manchester for a night out. If the Hac changed how the city felt, the bomb changed how it looked. Before '96 no one really lived right in the centre of town, then after the bomb they restructured that whole part of the city; Deansgate, St Anne's and St Mary's Gate. Then Shudehill and Oldham Street started to become the bohemian part of the city, now known as the Northern Quarter (rather than just the knocking shop). After Oldham Street the change just spread, and has kept going to this day.

Everywhere you turn there's a new hotel being built, and at the weekends they're all full. The foreign journos you meet at Old

TOMMY DUNN

Trafford say "the Hilton's fully booked, I've had to book at the other Hilton". Other Hilton? In Manchester? Crazy. It's changed beyond recognition. The Northern Quarter used to be a slum, and now it's the trendiest gaff going. A few of the old haunts still remain, The Millstone, The Wheatsheaf and The Unicorn, but the area's totally different. Great Ancoats Street used to give the Gaza Strip a run for its money and now it's home to sheen glass apartment blocks. Walking down Pollard Street into Miles Platting you can see the place transforming every ten metres. It's worth a fortune now, and if I'd known at the time what I know now I'd have bought the whole area. Where Beaner lives, in Collyhurst, a construction firm bought the block of flats off the council for £1 per flat. Give it three years then pick a sum and triple it.

Like it or not, this is part of the new identity the city's forming for itself. The two massive pillars of Manchester's cultural identity, The Hacienda and Fergie's United, have both gone, and something has to take its place. We can't spend the next twenty years still talking about Blue Monday and Ryan Giggs, although the temptation's always there. I, like everyone else, has to move with the times. That doesn't mean I'm 100% behind it, I can sometimes feel a stranger in my own town, but you have to adapt. Admittedly it knocks me sick to pay £4.50 a pint, but that's just how the world's going.

Mancunians have a certain disrespect towards authority. We don't bow and scrape, we don't sell out, but we still get the result. That is Manchester for me: we'll talk to anybody, we'll help anybody, but no one can fuck with us. That's Mancunians; "You're very welcome, mate. But if you take the piss, you're not welcome any more". I was in my mate's bar the other night, and this young cockney lad of about 21 was pissed and saying "I'm really glad to have met you" and all this. I said "I'm nothing special here, you know. We're all like this, anyone will talk to you." He couldn't believe I'd gone over and talked to him, "Y'alright fella, how're you doing?" That's Mancs I think; we're hospitable. One thing I've noticed is wherever I go in the world and people ask me where I'm from, I say "Manchester" and there's immediate respect. I like that; we've got a good name. It seems everyone from the cockneys to the scousers respects Manchester to some degree. We'll talk to anyone. I said to the cockney lad, "There's a lot of ignorance in London. If someone's lying on the floor nine out of ten people will step over them." You wouldn't get that here. When you're on the tube in London no one chats to each other, and I'm sat there like "Are we not allowed to talk?" It's total silence. Fair enough, sometimes when I'm on the met in Manny I don't necessarily want to hear the whole sexual history of the guy in front of me, but I'd rather that than a carriage full of mutes.

Another thing about Mancs is we're funny bastards. We love a joke. Whenever I'm out, whatever mob I'm with, it's always the same thing; we have a laugh. We don't do boring, we don't do conversations that goes something like, "my capital gains this, my tax band that". What a load of tripe, crack a joke and enjoy yourself. We take the piss out of each other. I'd think any mate of mine had had a stroke if he came into the pub and went "Alright Tommy you're looking great, have you lost weight?" I much prefer "Alright Tommy you knobhead, how's it going?" We keep each other honest, and if someone gets flashy they'll get the piss taken. I remember being on trains where my mates have grabbed my passport and thrown it out the window, I go "You bastard" and as soon as I got the chance his passport's gone. When we'd go grafting out of town and be on the return journey, whoever was last out of the service station was being left, the only person who was safe was the driver.

Another strong quality in us Mancs is the ability to blag. There's no secret, it's just confidence; looking like you're meant to be there. When you've got a whistle and flute on you're invisible. Whenever I've been somewhere for a stunt and I've got a suit on, I'm the gaffer. That's what's in my head, "I own this place". I'll walk into the back room of anywhere and as long as I'm suited up no one says a thing, people are scared of pulling you in case you are the gaffer. And when we get fronted, we front them back, we don't fold. Never crumble; we've learnt that since we were in short trousers. "Who are you?" "Who am I? Who are you?" This is coming from someone who's been going to Old Trafford since 1970, and I've never paid to get in. I've not paid for a car park in five years. I won't voluntarily pay for anything, it's got to be dragged out of my hand.

I guess the blag I'm most proud of, as a blagger and a Manc, is interviewing Fergie. When United won the treble in '99 I went to every away game, from Lodz to Barcelona, and I filmed pitch-side for every one. I spoke to Ferguson at each press conference, asking silly stuff like "If you were manager of England would Andy Cole be starting?" "When are you gonna take the City job?" Another year we were in Valencia and I came out of the ground to see Ferguson heading towards his car. I walked towards the driver and indicated to the driver like "I'm with him." He opened the door for me and I hopped in. So there's the driver, the minder, who are both Spanish, Ferguson and me. Alex turns to me, "What you doing?" "Alex, do me a favour man. Give us a lift into town." "Where to?" "Just United's hotel, I'm gonna meet the lads down there" He just paused and went, "Yeah alright." By this point he'd seen me in loads of press conferences and knew me, so he asked "Who do you want in the quarters?" "Inter Milan" "Yeah, same here". We got to United's hotel and he said "You alright here?" "Yeah," I said "I'm good here, nice one Alex." I went in the hotel and sat down with my mates, "Ferguson's just given me a lift here" and they're like "Fuck off!" A while later we were playing away at Dynamo Kyiv, and as the team left the airport for the team bus and I followed with my camera and called "Alex!". He turned round in full view of my camera and recognised me, "Alright, how you doing!" "Cheers for that lift in Valencia!" I said. "Oh no problem, it's sweet." That was it, straight back to the lads with the footage, "Here it is!"

So over the seasons we got to know each other. Then a few years later after he'd retired I went to Yeovil with my kids, and he was there. We bumped into each other and had a chat and my son grabbed his phone to film it. Ferguson said to me "Have you had Van Gaal yet?" "No" I said. "Go and do Van Gaal". I think Fergie wanted a baptism of fire for the new manager.

Throughout the '99 European run I'd asked Fergie a question at every press conference, and when we'd won the final in Barcelona I couldn't miss the opportunity to say something.

MANCHESTER MAVERICKS

There were about a hundred journalists there itching to ask a question to the man who brought the European Cup back to England. I put my hand up and his press officer looked at me. The PO looked at Fergie, who nodded like "Give it him", and he gave me the go-ahead. "Alex, what were the fans like in that ground?" a near 100,000 capacity stadium. "They were brilliant, kept us going until the end, which we needed." He paused, looked around the room to the journalists and said "This guy's been to every game we've played in this competition, he's not a journalist, but he's been to every press conference. Good luck to you". I had all this on video, and it was a very special, proud moment for me. I went outside to meet the lads at the hospitality round the corner, and Fergie had finished the conference so came outside, and I bumped into him again. He came up to me, "How do you do it? How'd you get into all those press conferences?" "Alex, I just said I work for MUTV", he started laughing, "Seriously though, Alex, you've made a lot of people happy." He just said "Thanks, son" and walked off. Even though I've never had a drink with him, I reckon if you asked Ferguson about me he'd remember. It'd be hard not to the amount of times we've bumped into each other. The other year I went to the Ryder Cup with my son in Scotland. We were in the hotel at Gleneagles and me and junior were walking down this corridor. Who comes walking towards us but Ferguson and his missus. My son goes "Alright Alex!" and Fergie gives him a jokey slap on the head, "Hey you cheeky bugger". Junior loved it, looking to me, "Dad, I felt like Giggs and that!"

The thing I'm probably most famous for are the stunts I did with 'Fat Neck' Karl Power. The one that really made our name was getting in the United line up in Munich. I had been videoing on the pitch at every away game in Europe, and knew I was in a position to do anything. So I thought, "we've got to do something here", and it occurred to me; the team picture. When I got back to Blighty I went to Fat Neck and said "the team picture. Do you fancy it?", "Yeah" he said. "Right". We planned to do it at the final in the San Siro but we lost the first leg of the quarters against Bayern 0-1 at home. I know we'd pipped them in '99 and had every chance of going through, but no one ruins a party like the Germans, so we thought it best to pull the stunt on the return leg in Munich instead. Just like that I got the plane tickets and we were off. I'd been there the year before and filmed on the pitch, so knew the layout of the ground, which routes to take, which to avoid. We had *Loaded* magazine in tow to cover the stunt, and they brought three United kits with them; Home, Away (white) and that blue and red third kit. Obviously Karl couldn't turn up in the wrong kit and mess up the whole stunt, so I headed to United's hotel to find out what they were playing in. I saw Peter Kenyon in the lobby, so I walked over, "Alright, Pete. My son wants to wear the same kit as the team tonight, what are they playing in?" He turned to me with a knowing look, "The white one." I relayed the message, Karl got his kit and tracksuit on and we left for the Olympiastadion.

We arrived and Karl looked at me, "Are we doing it?" "Yeah we're doing it," I said "follow me." I had my bib on and we were in, before you know it me and Fat Neck are behind the goal. Karl was shitting himself, "He's looking at us!" he said looking at a guy in hi-vis. I calmed him down and gave him the plan, "when Andy Cole shakes the last player's hand, that's your cue to go." The players were coming out, so we headed to the half-way line and were in the middle of all the journalists.

So there we were; all Karl's waiting for is me to give him the go-ahead. Andy approaches the last player and I say "Right, Go!" and Fat Neck was right out of the traps, whipping his tracksuit off, and the timing couldn't have been better. I was about fifteen yards behind, filming it, and could see it clear as day. Andy Cole came round and shit himself when he saw Karl, they all did really. Once he realised Karl wasn't a threat Cole must've thought, "Yeah alright then" and just stood with him. They all looked baffled, and Gary Neville looked down the line, "Who the fuck-". Karl stuck his head out, "Shut it, I'm doing it for Cantona!", and they all gave a face like "Fair enough".

After the photo Karl walked back to me, and I said "Karl. No one has seen that" believing we'd just dipped in and out too quickly to be noticed. Anyway we walked around the pitch and went behind the goal at the United end to watch the rest of the game. At the end of the game we went back to the hotel and Barmy was there with Jed Lyons, so we got pissed and then went to bed. The next morning, at about 7am, Barmy was banging on the door. We opened it and he went "Fucking hell, man. It's mental down there." "What do you mean?" we said. "Just get in that lift and go downstairs."

The lift opened at the ground floor and the lobby was rammed with journos. They turned round and shouted "Here he is!" stampeding towards the lift. So we sat down with them; The *Daily Mirror* and *The Sun* are scrapping it out for a deal and we're playing them off against each other. We came to a deal with *The Sun* and they gave us £20,000 for Fat Neck's exclusive story. They said "Right, don't go back to England yet. Come with us" and took us round the corner to the Marriott Hotel. They gave me a suite, Karl a suite, and even Jed Lyons got a suite! "Right" they said "Stay here for a couple of days, lads. Let it calm down". Not forgetting we were getting loads of calls from home saying "It's mental here man, what's gone on?" Even the ITN News at Ten starting with BONG "Who is Karl Power?"

So we were at the airport for the flight back home (a private jet I might add!) and a woman came over to Karl, saying "Excuse me, the pilot wants a word with you." So Karl went in the cockpit to give the pilot his autograph.

We landed in Manchester, went through immigration, and the passport guy went "Lads, it's mental out there". So I said to Karl, "Right, you walk out on your own, me and Jed will be behind you". Jed was pushing the trolley with all the bags as penance for that free suite. We walked out and I've never seen anything like it in my life, it was chaos. They were all trying to grab hold of Fat Neck as he walked through. The Renaissance Hotel was across the road, and our mates were in there, about 30 of them all up the wall, so we went into the hotel and got battered with the lads, a true victory lap.

Looking back at it now, and the fact it went all over the world before the days of the internet, it's crazy. I reckon it was one of the best stunts of all time. Can you think of a better one in terms of execution, the amount of people who saw it, and the amount of carnage it made in the media? The attention from that was massive. Obviously later there was the F1 and batting for England in the Ashes but lining up with an unwitting United team in a Cantona shirt? It doesn't get better than that.

All these stunts ended up on a Channel 4 programme, Britain's Favourite Hoaxer, and to be honest I didn't like it for a few years, but I'm proud of it now. At first I thought "We look a pair of knobs here" but now I love it. I haven't watched it in about five years but some of my mates in London watch it often and call me up, "I've just watched Hoaxer!" so I'm proud of it. The thing is though, we've done better stunts than those that didn't get media attention. Like Crufts. We filmed it but the police took the tapes off me. How I'd love to have those tapes now. That was a beautiful stunt.

My sister's dog had never been out of the garden in its life. It's a mongrel, it's got mangy sleep in its eye, it's an ugly bastard. So we took it to Crufts, the World Cup of Dogs. So we're inside the NEC and Jack the dog was with us; rope attached to his collar and him walking around with a big hard-on looking at the Bichon Frises. I was filming it all and my mate had Jack on a lead, and the plan was that as soon as the announcer says "The Best in Show" he goes. So the guy goes, "And 'Best in Show' is... Rover" (or something), and I pushed my mate out into the arena. He walked out onto the mat, dragging Jack behind, and the geezers clocked him so grabbed the cup. All you could hear on live TV was a lone voice in the silent crowd, "Get off, ya prick!"

Princess Anne's in the crowd and the police dive on my mate, nicking him and Jack. I was filming, and this copper sees me, points and shouts "Grab hold of him!" About ten police dived on me, grabbed the camera and ripped the tape out of it. So my mate and Jack the dog had been nicked, and I had to call my sister and explain that her dog, her baby, had been arrested. I said "Pauline, you're not gonna believe what's happened." All she could say was "Where's Jack!" We went down to the RSPCA in Birmingham and got to the reclaim desk or whatever, "Hi, we're here for Jack". The guy on the desk says, "How do we know he's yours?" I said

MANCHESTER MAVERICKS

"Listen mate, bring him out here and you'll see his tail going, alright?" We got him back home safe and sound, and he took up his usual spot in the garden, but I'm sure Jack will never forget his day out in Birmingham.

Anyway, that's enough about the Midlands. It's not the most interesting part of the country, but you know what it's got? Some truly great films, mainly from Shane Meadows, the best British film-maker around today. The key is that they're about life in the Midlands; a snapshot of life there (exaggerated or not) not some poncey London exec's idea of it, "What's for dinner, Mam? Oh, drippin' again!" The same goes for Trainspotting and Edinburgh, Snatch and East London, and the Scousers are a regular little Pinewood the amount of films they produce about Liverpool. Say what you want about them (and many Mancs will), but Liverpool has such a strong sense of its identity through its films; Letter to Brezhnev, No Surrender, Educating Rita. Manchester's got everything except for a raft of great films about the city. Fair enough there's the old kitchen-sink classics and a few belters like Control and 24 Hour Party People along the way, but is that it? We've had enough films about the Hacienda and the rave years, we need some about Mancunians. Now this isn't a long-winded way of saying I've written a script, but I've written a script. I'm not suggesting it's the Manc Opus at all, but I wanted to see if I could do it, and after many years and many re-writes I finally wrote 'Dreamer'. It's about a guy who gets wrongly sent to Strangeways and on release (by judge and chambers) he and his friend go over to Germany to pick up the World Cup. It's a comedy and I'm really proud of it. Even if nothing comes of it, I'm glad I paid tribute to my city and the people in it. We need a truly great Manc Film. I'm not for a second suggesting my film is it, but we still need one. Mancs spout script-writing gold every day and yet nothing has emerged that really pays tribute to this city.

Even if nothing comes of that, a tribute has still been paid to Mancunians in this book. I'm honoured to have contributed to something that gets to the beating heart of this city; the proud, progressive, piss-taking people of Manchester.

SUE CUNDALL

In the summer of 1987 My ten year relationship with a mix-raced lady from Moss Side, Beverley Ayo, sadly came crashing down whilst living in Rotterdam. With me working all over Europe on the Michael Jackson 'Bad' tour it had its effect on us both. We had a trail split which saw me going back to Manchester to see family and find a place to chill. I ended up living in what Sue named the 'Home for Battered Husbands!'

Really it was Roufy's terraced house in Whalley Range, but fact was three other mates had just split with their women as had Roufy so you can kind of understand Sue's naming the place. Saying that as believe you me all of a sudden we had gangs of women calling in almost 24/7. Sue was round every day but never to look for a fella just for the craic as it was so lively for almost two years, it just got better until Roufy done a deal down on Liverpool docks and got ripped off and had to pay back and got a loan on The Home for Battered Husbands, but as you would expect ended up losing the gaff. Never mind we moved on and Sue was able to help us all out finding bedsits near by which would fill the gap for a year at least till we moved on again to better places.

Fact was I knew Sue's brother Sid from a few years before I met Sue, he was a in Moss Side. Sid always spoke highly of the way Sue was when out with people, I suppose he meant she was Old School but I know all the lads who knew her say the same thing she's a proper Manc - oh and by the way can she cook!

Thinking back my earliest memories were of being a 5 or 6 years old in Wythenshawe. There were not many schools when we moved up there so we were placed in Shadow Moss on Ringway Road. The school is no longer there and I believe that part of my schooldays was probably the happiest. All the kids, or most of them, were from the farming community and we had no problems at all, just happy memories. Unfortunately the school was housed in a very old building right at the end of Ringway Airport's only runway (as Manchester Airport was known then). The school used to shake when the planes took off and inevitably had to close for safety reasons.

My next stage was a move to Woodhouse Park Junior School.

MANCHESTER MAVERICKS

I met with quite a bit of name-calling and kiddie racism there, some of it from the teachers. For a couple of years my younger sister and I fought our way through that school. When our younger brother joined he was a tough little blighter; six years old and cock of the school in no time. We were in our element then. All the kids were so scared of him that they were really nice to us. Thinking back, even though we were one of only 5 mixed race families in a huge area, we didn't do too badly.

Dinners were odd. Nobody really wanted to sit near us, maybe because we didn't have much. We were clean but our clothes were either what my mum had made for us or were jumble sale bought. One of the Deputy Heads actually called my sister dumb at a parents' evening and said she would "never amount to much". I remember my mum being really upset but I couldn't grasp why.;that sister grew up to be a British Diplomat fluent in three languages. Shows what some teachers know.

I remember mostly being our own little gang. We had mates but it was always our little crew. We ran away from home once after Mum said we couldn't have any sweets for a week because we'd popped a hot water bottle. We made it to Moss Side to my Auntie Audrey's house. Picture the scene; three little brown kids trudging down Princess Parkway. My little brother was saying "All we've got to do is find the docks then we can get on a banana boat to our Nana in Jamaica". All the kids used to say "Your dad came here on a banana boat, he's a monkey" - I wonder where they heard that?

The holidays were good. I can only remember ever going to one place, Penmaenmawr in Wales, and it was full of such nice people. There were a couple of convents with orphaned kids in. I think that's why we felt so at home there; nobody felt like they fitted in. Some places we tried before we discovered Pen wouldn't even consider putting us up. It used to be awful seeing signs for vacancies at B&Bs but as soon as my dad knocked on they decided they were "full". My Mum's Irish temper really used to come out then. Finding Pen was a blessing. Until the day they both died my parents visited Pen every year. Their grandchildren still go now.

Leaving school and starting work was the next episode in

my life. I learnt a lot then. My Mum and Dad used to say to us, "You're as good as anyone else and don't ever let anyone tell you you're not". I was good at Art, and to be honest the headmaster made an exception and let me leave school early as I had a job to go to. I think he was suicidal when I decided to stay on in the lower sixth. The poor sod. When my mum rang and asked if I could leave school before the end of the year he said "Of course she can Mrs Reynolds!" I had applied for a job as an apprentice Tracer at Ferranti in Wythenshawe. My dad was buzzing, telling all his mates at work about his second daughter who was going to get a good job. He came home one night and was really quiet. When my mum asked him what was up he told her that a bloke at work had said I wouldn't get the job because they don't employ blacks at Ferranti. My dad was really upset. When I got the job he was walking on the moon, couldn't brag enough, and I felt really good for him for about six months, then I ran right off the rails. I went on the machine as a dressmaker with my mum after that. She used to take us in work with her on school holidays so I think I got a feel for the factories. I loved my work.

I started going out, and of course underage drinking was the in thing in those days, and much easier to get away with. The Benchill Pub was a favourite with a chosen few mates back in the day. Another was The Sharston, when it became a nightclub. Genevieve's in Longsight was my home from home, I loved that place, and The Cock of the North (later known as The Talisman) was the biggest Red pub in Woodhouse Park. We had amazing times at all those places, and it's a time and a social life we probably couldn't return to now. I tried to go to The Reno once but apparently my brother had told them not to let me in, so I ended up in the Capitol Club and the Nile. My Uncle George was the founder of The West Indian Centre in Moss Side and I used to end up in there most Sundays. I remember going to the very first one he started on Nelson Street when I was a little kid of six or seven. When I became more of a fly girl I was a regular in The Blue Note. Most of the young kids of colour would go there, and I was going from the age of sixteen so I told my mum I was staying at my mate's and vice versa. They had an all-nighter on a Saturday and then Sunday morning we'd get the bus down to the Top Twenty in Hollinwood. I guess my one big regret in life is not accepting that if I carried on with my career at Ferranti I would have a good life in the future. My head was on a different plane then and I just wanted to have fun. At a certain age short-term fun always trumps long-term gain. Now I see where I could have been and what I could have achieved, but you can't torture yourself over things like that. I still enjoyed myself though, and wouldn't have it any other way; I made some great lifetime friends and had some wild, wild times.

Moss Side carnival, what a scene. I remember when it first started; all the old-timers, people selling booze out of the boots of their cars; new up and coming bands playing; some delicious brown stew and jerk chicken getting cooked on wonky stoves. What a spectacle it was; wonderful costumes, all colours and races sat about on the grass enjoying the day. In its modern version the only thing that's the same is the parade. You can't beat West Indians when it comes to parades. The council even had the cheek to move the venue to Platt Fields. No comparison, the carnival has always been in Alex Park. We petitioned the council and last year they moved it back. It was nothing like the old times, everything was really expensive and just impersonal. I saw a couple of people I knew but the vibe wasn't like it used to be. I'm hoping it changes back, I didn't go this year because of it and I had friends in the parade dressed to kill. Though making a point sometimes means missing out on fun.

I was living in Wythenshawe in '81 when the Moss Side riots started. Boy did it go off. I don't know what sparked it in Wythenshawe but lads I'd known all my life were petrol bombing pensioners' bungalows, shops, houses, cars, people were looting. It was bad. I'd say testosterone and alcohol had a lot to do with it, not a great combination. There were big fights outside certain pubs; the landlord would get word that the mob were heading his way and the lads in the pub would go outside with pool cues. It wasn't a nice time; no one wanted to walk home. The strangest thing was the mob would split up and then go drinking in their locals like nothing had happened. There was a strange mentality in those times.

Despite the occasional bit of carnage Manchester wasn't as much like the Wild West as people think, the city was booming culturally and there was plenty going on. The three live music nights I remember and will always remember are Free at Radio One Club, The Temptations and Junior Walker & The Allstars at the Odeon, and finally the ultimate band, The Small Faces, who were absolutely unbelievable. These four bands were huge at times in my life when big changes were happening; I had tried to leave home and get a flat in the middle of all this amazing music, but arriving at the place I was told that I "didn't sound black on the phone" and that the flat was not available. I still saw a few signs on flats, B&B's and pubs in those days, 'No blacks, dogs or Irish', sad people hanging on to the past while the city grew into the multicultural place we know it as today. Nowadays I think my top Manchester bands are New Order, Oasis and Happy Mondays. They tell the story of Manchester in their music, not the words. It's a sound that we all relate to and an era that will always be remembered.

For a city known for taking in people from all over the world, it's no surprise we have plenty of Adopted Mancunians. My favourite would have to be George Best, who brought glamour (as well as a European Cup) to a city that needed an injection of pizzazz, and what a good-looking bastard. I am impressed with Miss Ariana Grande too; the guts that kid had to come back here and stage a concert. Big up girl! Sir Bobby Charlton will always be a beloved adopted Manc too. I don't really admire too many people, I think due to my father being my biggest hero. I saw that man go through hell and high water for his kids and his wife. You have to be a certain kind of person to gain my respect but I feel Tony Wilson may have just peaked with my dad. He fought racism, homelessness, drug addiction and countless other wars for Manchester and not for some place on the board later down the line, but because he cared. R.I.P.

Aside from Tony Wilson's cathedral to the city he loved, The Hacienda, Manchester is spoilt for great buildings. My favourite would have to be the Museum, I remember it opening and thinking how wonderful it was. A building full of knowledge is better than one full of shops or insurance companies. The University would have to be a close second. I went to see the first computer there and wow, it was huge. When I sit at my desktop now I smile and wonder how they crammed all that into this little piece of hardware, considering it used to need an entire building. I am quite in awe of the G-MEX building too; I went to see New Order there and the architecture of the place is amazing, adding to the atmosphere of whoever you're seeing. I saw some WWE there too with the son, showing it's a good space for anything.

I really feel for the youth of today. What do they have? Nothing. Nowhere to go, nothing to do. They drink or smoke weed to have fun then a bunch of bullying boys in blue turn up and lock them up, then push them around so they end up with no respect for anyone. I was in a pub in Hattersley and some bizzies came in with a couple of specials and started making two young lads empty their pockets. The lads were saying, "We've not done anything, why do we have to empty our pockets and let you search us?" It was downright embarrassing for them. I was never one for keeping my mouth shut, so I had to say something and asked why they were giving these lads a hard time. This 'really nice' special just said "because we can." I then got my dander up and asked them what they were looking for. Drugs was the reply. You could tell these kids were not on drugs, the true perpetrators were big mean-looking young men in the other room, but the cops were too sad to approach them. This sort of treatment of our youth is not on. We then breed a society of young people who grow up to hate authority, which creates unrest. Here's a start: legalise weed. It can't be any worse than it is now. They've done it in Spain and Portugal and crime has decreased. The UK is so behind Europe where drugs are concerned. Because we've dragged our heels on something the whole city smokes anyway, we've ended up with something worse, Spice. Now that's another kettle of fish, and extremely dangerous. It's ripping people apart in a way a few puffs of weed never could. Greater Manchester Council, take your tail out from between your legs and do something. You never know, it might just work.

SUE CUNDALL

Manchester, my home town, is a great city, a city of love and diversity. 'Live and let Live' is the motto and I have seen great changes growing up here. I find it hard to accept the morons who are now turning the clock back by advocating racism after the Manchester bombing. I have had car loads of people shout "dirty Paki" to me as I fill my car up at the petrol station, and people I have worked with for years make derogatory remarks about people of colour. One man performed that atrocity and he has paid with his life. We know what he did was unacceptable but you cannot make a nation pay for one man's deeds. The people affected and the city's response to the attacks is all that should be remembered. How we came together and unite through love was a truly inspiring thing to see, and only made me love my city more.

RAY BANKS

Born in Kirkcaldy, Fife in 1977, Ray Banks tried university and a number of different careers, including stints as a wedding singer, a double-glazing salesman, an office temp and a croupier before establishing himself as a crime writer. His last job came to an abrupt end when the casino was ram-raided one night and Ray decided it just wasn't worth the personal risk for the sake of other people's money.

Ray currently lives in Newcastle-upon-Tyne with his wife and a fat, black cat named after a dead country singer.

Ray Banks is a liar. I think it's only fair that I tell you that. The bloke writing this, the one calling himself Ray Banks, he wasn't Ray Banks when he lived, worked and played in Manchester about six years ago. Banks was a pseudonym that became a legal name with a dropped thirty notes to the Deed Poll. Not only did Ray Banks look better on the cover of a book than my birth name, but there was also the sense of a new name meaning a new life. Why? Well, bear in mind that I'm possibly lying here, but it could be something to do with my time in Manchester. I spent three years there, give or take. To be honest, my memory is a little fuzzy. When you work nights, the days and months tend to shift into one long blur. Throw alcohol in there, and you're lucky I can even remember I was in Manchester.

I went to Manchester because I needed a job – it was that simple. I was unemployed in Newcastle for quite a while, didn't want to go back to the factory skivvying and door-to-door sales stuff that I'd done before. And besides, there just didn't seem to be any jobs that far north. So when the opportunity came to become a trainee croupier for a national casino company, I was on it. I was interviewed by a casino manager who had long fingernails (the man played bass) and got the job the same day.

Then began the training – American Roulette, Blackjack and Caribbean Stud Poker – surrounded by a guy who'd been made redundant from his factory job (and then lost his wife and daughter in a particularly messy divorce), a white guy who believed Eminem was the Second Coming, and a numerically-dyslexic cross-dresser (which made those blackjack games so much fun). The training school was a good cross-section of Newcastle society, and we were all in the game for the glamour. After all, there weren't many jobs where your trainer would turned around and tell a story about that time she was land-based in Ukraine and the Russian Mafia shot out all the windows of the casino. This was excitement. Once we managed to get our chip-handling skills up to snuff.

My first place in Manchester was a part-furnished house in Longsight. Quiet, pretty safe, and it had the benefit of being within walking distance to the library where – in leaner times – I found Jack London, Eddie Little, Hubert Selby Jnr, Edward Bunker and Iceberg Slim, writers who I'd come back to once I'd discovered that writing was what I wanted to do. Then there was Longsight market where I stocked up on ex-rental videos, culture-clash sounds all around and the smell of Halal cooking up the way. It was a good place to be – though I hear it's not as welcoming now. On to Salford, opposite an off-licence that did a good line in bargain crates of green-tinged Kronenburg 1664. The place was walking distance to where I worked – the Salford Riverside (though where they got off calling the Manchester Ship Canal a "river" was anyone's guess).

Finally, I lived in Cheetham Hill, where the air smells like yeast from the Boddingtons brewery and your most stable neighbours are those doing time at Her Majesty's Pleasure across the road in Strangeways. Skip shops, phone shops and a lot of warehouses. When I walked to work in the evenings, the main drag – Cheetham Hill Road – was already thick with prostitutes, some of them braver than others, the "Got a light, love?" refrain in the darkness.

While all this was going on, there was the work. Us trainees were moved around from Whitworth Street, up to Cheetham

MANCHESTER MAVERICKS

Hill, back to George Street before we ever got to Salford. The Whitworth Street casino was precisely as it's described in The Big Blind, the smell of aging leather, sweat and dust in the air. George Street, in the heart of Chinatown, was the birthplace of the Mah-Jong Derby. At two o'clock every afternoon, a gaggle of little old Chinese ladies would gather outside the casino. At the final slam of the lock, the ladies sprang into action, elbowing each other out of the way to bagsie their favourite seats at the Mah-Jong tables. The casino would then rattle with the sound of the tiles until four in the morning.

There were stories: some Triad bloke going apeshit with a machete, hacking up punters and dealers alike at a Stanley club in town; the alleged Triad boss at Whitworth Street who could clear a table of Chinese with his very presence; the problem punters who'd swear they'd take a claw hammer to your skull as soon as you stepped out of the place. With the new flagship casino in Salford, the kick-off merchants arrived in droves – a new casino meant a clean sheet for them.

And so I got to know a bulk of the characters in The Big Blind and its follow-up Double Down. While I managed to stay out of the pit some of the time, on poker nights I couldn't help but be surrounded by ten or more sweating, griping players. Now I look around, I see the resurgence of Texas Hold 'Em as a hobby-sport, I remember the games I used to deal, the games I used to be a part of after work that went on all night and sometimes gave me enough money to drink.

When my wife and I visit Manchester, I keep passing pubs and slowing down – "I think I got drunk in there once". Some of them make it into the books – The Commercial Inn, The Mutz Nutz (imaginatively renamed "The Dawgz Nadz" in The Big Blind) and the Press Club all feature pretty prominently – but there are a wealth of pubs that I haven't used, simply because I don't remember where they are or if I've been in them enough to remember what the interior looks like. I remember getting my nose broken in the Press Club, blood all down my blue uniform shirt. I remember fights in the city centre. I also remember those "quick drinks" after work that ended up miles from home and left me with pockets heaving with change, or the suited old drunk crooning his way through The Stranglers' Greatest Hits on the karaoke.

That's why now, when I'm asked how I view Manchester in the books, I always answer that I try for an emotional accuracy rather than a geographical one. I get called on the fact that both Manchester and Newcastle seem to be populated with a series of ugly, violent freaks, but it's true that when you feel home in neither place, and when your brain automatically clings onto negative energy, a certain Expressionist cityscape emerges. Couple that with a noir sensibility and the "vile psychic weather" that Derek Raymond wrote about, and you're looking at characters who'd choke on the word sympathetic. That includes the police.

Let's be frank about this: I have nothing against the police. Individually, they're human beings like the rest of us, and individually (without uniform), they can be as genial or as brutal as anyone else. I've met good officers (worked with an ex-CID on the doors when I sold windows) and I've known judgemental arseholes whose singular purpose in life seemed to be a trophy cabinet of collars, regardless of their suspect's culpability. My early memories of the police were formed at age seven as the constabulary beat down striking miners at Orgreave. Whenever I saw police in my childhood that seemed to be their pose: batons at the ready, riot gear helmets masking their faces. And it's always tempting to drop to that characterisation whenever I can. With Detective Sergeant "Donkey" Donkin (who appears in both The Big Blind and Saturday's Child), I hope to get a little more into him before the series is over, deal with his damage the way I've dealt with everyone else's because I'm a firm believer in there being many sides to every story. A criminal isn't just a criminal, a cop never just a cop. A murder can be for a myriad of reasons, some of them premeditated, others pure accident. To steal a phrase from Lawrence Block, all us writers are "telling lies for fun and profit", but I'd go so far as to say that if a writer invests a lie with depth, it has the potential to be more truthful than any stone-cold fact. But the only way to score that depth is through empathy, something which seems to be in constant short supply these days.

MANCHESTER MAVERICKS

My only regret stems from my lack of empathy in my previous life. Those that I'd discarded or judged too heavily, which is the main reason why the bloke who lived in Manchester had to disappear, and why Ray Banks feels the need to lie through his teeth in the name of fiction.

STELLA GRUNDY

Actress, musician, songwriter and scriptwriter Stella Grundy came to fame as the lead singer with local band Intastella as part of the second wave of the indie music scene of the early 90s alongside the likes of New Fast Automatic Daffodils and World of Twist. Yet like many of Manchester's music stars Stella grew up on a council estate in Moston and worked mundane jobs until she realised she wasn't cut out for the nine-to-five.

A maverick to her bones, she's also starred in the play she wrote based on her own life story called 'The Rise and Fall of a Northern Star' and continues to play and perform across the country.

My first job was at the age of 17. Education finished for me at 16; I left school in a hurry, fire flying from my heels with 3 GCSE's in my hand: Art, English Literature and English Language. I started out as quite an academic kid, mainly because my Mum wanted me to be a civil engineer, which I didn't want to be, but I tried for her sake. I was an only child growing up on quite a tough estate. I read a lot, mainly 50's and 60's Americana, Sci-Fi and biographies about infamous characters like Charles Manson and Aleister Crowley. They might be interesting characters but they offered little help in engineering, so that hope dwindled as I ploughed my way through five years at North Manchester High School for Girls. I clashed often with the teachers and there were lots of fights between pupils, some of them including me. It was a harsh place. I started off studying Latin and ended up on special report in a class of just one. I never took the rest of my exams, deciding school education was pointless. I just wanted to be shown how to sign on and play in my band.

I couldn't remain at home, so on my 17th birthday I moved with a friend into a one bedroom, freezing cold, damp flat on Spath Road, West Didsbury. It had a shared bathroom and there was never any hot water. So I got my first job as a trainee machinist at Dance Step on Red Bank, Cheetham Hill/Strangeways. I remember the mornings were dark and cold. Usually I'd had little, if any, sleep. I was in the habit of taking my mate's mum's slimming tablets, easily prescribed back then. There was never any food at the flat so it was a good way to stop hunger. I'm really not sure how we survived the year in that house.

I'd get dressed in bed as the flat was freezing. My hair would still be spiked up after a mid-week night out; a Wednesday at the Hacienda when it was like a youth club in an aircraft hanger. On the way to the bus stop I'd pinch a bottle of milk off a doorstep from a proper family's house. The bus would be full and I'd fight to keep my eyes open, and keep the milk down. I'd get off in town and do the long walk across to work.

The factory was divided into two halves; the cutting room and the sewing room, with an office in the back. It was all women machinists, of course, and I was the youngest. The fellas worked in the cutting room, cutting cloth and patterns and dragging big heavy things about. I remember they did their best to make it seem like the most dangerous place in the world in there. Telling me tales of how so and so lost an arm because the guards don't work on the Guillotine and how I'd be squashed flat under the rolls of fabric. I thought it was a wind up but to be fair hardly any of them had all their fingers.

I met some ace female characters though and heard some eye opening stories of affairs, sexual deviance, perverted bosses. There was always some drama unfolding on the fag breaks, and I'd proper flush up. I thought I was street wise but sex, no way, I was very naive for a 17 year old.

I've had a lot of nicknames over my lifetime. At work it was Sid Vicious, because "I had spikey hair and never smiled". It was 1982, I was never a punk but let's say I had unique dress sense; most of my clothes were handmade or from Oldham Flea Market and I had stuck up white hair, sometimes with blue tips, which I suppose made me stand out a bit. I felt quite suited to the role of weirdo. It was the same in school and on the Miners Estate.

Life at Dance Step revolved around dinnertime. We spent our mornings waiting for it and then spent the afternoon recovering from it, burping up onions from the dodgy pies. As the youngest it was my job to go and get everyone's dinners along with the youngest lad from the cutting room. We didn't have a lot in common and looking back now I think he was trying to be friendly, even chat me up, but nah I completely blanked him. I had no interest in lads younger than 23 for some odd reason, I thought they should be at least 5 years older. Fuck knows why, I probably read it somewhere.

Basically he irritated me; always talking, asking questions, 'how I was liking the job?' giving me tips on how to stop my machine jamming, blah blah. I truly didn't give a shit about the job, "it's just a matter of surviving mate!" He eventually gave up and we did our duties in virtual silence.

Yeah I suppose I was an unfriendly cow. I preferred to daydream, that's all. The reality of this job was beyond boring and as soon as I left the building at dinnertime my mind wandered. I was dead nosey when we went to get the dinners from the cafe. I liked all the gaudy hand painted signs. It was like the Blackpool of buttie shops. I was always a bit of a voyeur and there were plenty of broken looking people in those cafés. I imagined their back stories; prostitutes stoking up for the afternoon trade; tramps who had secret millions buried in shoe boxes. I ignored the pleas from the lad to "hurry up". It was made clear by the manager that I was in charge of the buttie run, she obviously thought a female would be better at getting everyone's food. She was wrong. Chips, pies, onions, no onions, drinks, chocolate, the list was endless and stupidly complicated. They took the piss really and I always got it cocked up and brought back the wrong change. That caused uproar on the shop floor and heated phone calls from the manager to the cafés. I was not at all arsed.

I did meet someone who I had something in common with. A young woman, 20ish who was already married with a young kid. We both loved music and spent our breaks discussing bands, swapping vinyl, making cassettes. She was a bit more heavy rock than me but we both loved Devo. She lent me three albums which I actually still have! I know, bad one, but I didn't last long at Dance Step. I lasted 6 months or so and left before I had the chance to give them back, I can't remember if I jumped or was pushed.

I then entered the world of the black economy. Signing on and earning bits of money here and there. It wasn't that black

actually. I was still poverty stricken but you just survived. I was a hair model at Vidal Sassoon's, so got free haircuts. I'd blagged an honorary membership to the Hacienda as I was mates with the Stockholm Monsters, who were an early Factory band, so got in gigs and nights free. My friend made me my clothes, we took our own booze out (Pernod) and we would regularly hitch home, or of course there was always the night bus. Taxis were a rare treat and often ended in a horribly funny but exhausting runner.

From then on it's blurry in terms of going out for me. I went to loads of gigs and got a job at The Belle Vue Dog Track on the Tote Ticket Booths. I loved the atmosphere of that place; the floodlights and noise. I used to get given tips on dogs, had the odd bet and occasionally won. The customers were usually half-pissed old fellas who left it until the very last minute to place their bets then got all shirty because you couldn't get them all on in time. The Tote machine was this semi circular contraption with a handle and numbers on a plate which you had to punch in. Some of the women were really fast. Banging them out. I wasn't, and having a red faced, grumpy old get glaring at you through the glass window didn't help. It wasn't all bad; I'd finish my shift, get my wages and head to town.

I then came to my senses and realised a dead end job was

STELLA GRUNDY

exactly that. It took up too much time and was mind-numbing. With my Mum's encouragement and some minor miracle, I went to do an Art foundation course at Abraham Moss and worked part time at Pizza Hut. That was a really happy time in my early life.

My memory is fragmented about clubs and gigs, with dates, names and faces all out of order. However, I do know that by the age of 19 I'd been going out in town for 5 years already. Being from North Manchester we started early and tended to go to the first club we hit after getting off the number 80 or 77 bus in Stevenson Square. There was no Northern Quarter then, just the hell hole that is Piccadilly.

The first club we hit was Brewsters. I think it was on the station approach or somewhere close. It was full of Moston and Miles Platting and extremely territorial. I kind of knew it wasn't the escape I was looking for. It was just like Moston Youth Club only the music wasn't as good. It felt like it would kick off at any minute. The lady's toilets were full of empty handbags, robbed from the girls by other girls as they danced around them on the sticky floor. This was hardly Studio 54. I did my homework and found the other side of town was where I wanted to be. So me and a couple of friends ventured over firstly to St Anne's Square and Horts, where the hairdressers hung out. Then on to Berlin and The Exit and of course the ultimate weirdo hang out The Hacienda, which it is was back then. I went to its opening week and saw Cabaret Voltaire. I know many people claim to have been there but I was. I met Hooky and Bernard from New Order and many others who I am still friends with today.

I also remember Manchester being quite Jazz-orientated in my late teens. Clubs went small again. We would always start off in Corbieres; it was our gaff and had a good Jukebox. I loved the style too. It was slicked back hair and Audrey Hepburn fringes. The obligatory black ski pants, polo neck, waspy belt and red lipstick. The fellas wore baggy pants and braces. It was 50's beatnik crossed with working class 40's. I remember a club called Manhattan Sound. I saw Sade sing there and, to be honest, it sounded dreadful but she was still uber-cool. I also saw James there and hung around with various bands. I was mates with ACR and The Jazz Defectors. All the fittest lads went there too. My libido had eventually kicked in and I had a brilliant time in the pubs and clubs of Manchester. This kind of melting pot of styles and music did, I think, influence the so-called indie dance crossover that came later on in the decade and proved so massively popular.

I'd say it influenced it musically but not culturally. The early and mid 80's Manchester club scene was sexy and intelligent; more Berlin and New York than London. Many of my friends were male. They were hairdressers, musicians and wrote books. Some wore make up. I was in a band too and I wrote songs; odd little poetic outbursts. I didn't feel that was unusual in anyway. It was escapism but there was no ambition attached to it. None of the bands I liked were on Top of the Pops. I didn't sense any misogynistic overtones or macho posturing then really. That came in later with the Joe Bloggs *NME* portrayal of this whole so called Madchester Era which in my opinion was a double-edged sword. Although it brought a lot of attention and got bands like mine (Intastella) major record company interest, they were actually looking for repetition, copyists of the Roses and The Mondays. Some did okay but bands striving to be different lost out.

In the late 80's when the shoplifters, Perry boys and football hooligans (basically the people I grew up with) turned up at The Hacienda it was alright. The balance between the original people and the new influx worked; it was great to have a dance with a plumber from Wakefield off his tits on ecstasy. The 'lads don't dance' thing was gone. The music and drugs of the time did contribute to this shared experience that has been documented so thoroughly. The freaks outnumbered the hooligans still. Everyone from different areas, classes, tribes were united under the influence of acid house, ecstasy and LSD. Brilliant bands that were your friends were making it big. It was a high old time, but after a while the territorial mentality crept in. There was a lot of money to be made out of all these kids coming in from here, there and everywhere. Such euphoria could not last long, and it didn't.

I did make lifelong friends around this time. I enjoyed the colour, the 60's references. I loved my hipster flares and crop tops,

Adidas shell toes and sneakers. I had the long curly hippy hair, all connected with the '88 explosion here in Manchester. But I never wore a hoody or big daft 24 inch flares or anything with the word 'Manchester', or even worse 'Madchester' written on it. I've never been fond of uniforms and that's kind of what that was.

By the mid 90's the hooligans outnumbered the freaks in the Hacienda. The ecstasy wore off. It was more about the Cocaine and I saw a lot of casualties and personality changes. I only went there to play or to see friends DJ or for an occasional Flesh night. The Macho shit had taken over. It was edgy but not in a good way and the music was just unremarkable. I gave the place a swerve after that. Too much hassle.

Two of my favourite people are John Cooper Clarke and Nico. I first saw them both at The Library Theatre. She was performing, he was in the audience and at the end they walked out past me, he actually said 'Iya'. I felt like I did when I first saw Bowie in Cracked Actor on TV. They were like Aliens, they had an aura you could see. I remember it so vividly, and they became two of my favourite Manchester 'Icons'.

We were smoking black hash joints in the Library Theatre. Imagine smoking joints in there now! It's not even there anymore, it's become HOME. Somewhere I've yet to get to know or grow attached to.

Another guy I like and respect is Damon Gough aka Badly Drawn Boy; I saw how hard he worked to record that first album, which I still love. He's not your usual front-man type, but his ambition was immense. He would drive around in this big maroon car and turn up everywhere. He really did the networking bit as well as write some beautiful tunes, and he's a great guitarist too. I knew him and saw his drive and ambition and I admired him for that. He had the right approach, "I will do this, I will achieve this". I was so pleased when he won the Mercury Prize. Having seen him recently and hearing how good those old songs still sound I hope he gets around to writing more. He sort of shows that success perhaps isn't always what you wish for. I'm sure there is a lot of love around for Damon Gough but I think he is an unsung hero.

MANCHESTER MAVERICKS

One of my favourite buildings is Affleck's Palace, and thank goodness it's still there. This city seems to like flattening things and it's criminal in every sense of the word. Me and my then-boyfriend Spencer had a stall selling handmade suits and dresses. It was called 'North' but our mate Bendy renamed it 'The Titanic', and he was right. Everything worked out too dear and so we'd sell about one suit a week. The owners Richard and Elaine would often let us off with the rent on bad weeks. I sold most of my 7" vinyl to Rob's records. He was shrewd, well actually he ripped me off, but there was a good vibe in Affleck's. I ended up working on other stalls and I was there for the big boom time of '88-91 where we were literally selling the shirts off our backs. Hordes of Japanese tourists trooped to Salford Lads Club to take photos, they still do. It was a boom time in fashion and we all made a few bob and then spent most of it in Dry Bar after work.

The International 1 remains the city's best ever gig venue for me. I remember watching Echo and The Bunnymen there, I don't remember the year exactly but I think it was around 1982. The sound was always brilliant and I really liked the all-dayers. I think that's where I got my real determination to sing in a really good band. Intastella played their first ever gig there, supporting World of Twist. I was bricking it, and we didn't really know what we were doing but I loved every minute.

Another cultural highlight for me is the famous Crusty Cob in Ancoats. They serve the best meat and potato pies in Manchester and Salford. It was round the corner from Intastella's rehearsal room on Pollard Street. We lived off them for about 4 years. ACR, Happy Mondays and Doves also rehearsed round there and I'm sure they enjoyed those pies too.

Recently, I've been touring a play called The Rise and Fall of a Northern Star. The blurb is "Unique and incendiary show blends comedy and tragedy in rhythmic, pacey dialogue, interspersed with Stella's original music". The story is a cautionary tale of rock 'n' roll wannabe Tracy Star trying to make her mark in the male-dominated Manchester music scene of the eighties and early nineties.

It's essentially my experiences of being in a band, combined with my over-active imagination. I've also recorded a concept album at Gadget Lab Studios, Manchester. It was produced by myself along with Jonathan Hurst and features legendary bassist Jah Wobble. It's to be released on the Louder Than War record label and there will be an official album launch taking place next year.

What I'm doing now and in the future is what I've been doing all my working life; following the compulsion to be creative in the arts and provide a stable family life for my daughter, Nico, who is my favourite ever Mancunian.

Who knows what I'll be doing when this book comes out but it will involve performing, writing and, I hope, getting wiser.

IAN HOUGH

Born and raised in Salford, Ian Hough went on to write 'Perry Boys' about the rise of the Casual football hooligan in the late 70s and early 80s from his perspective as a United fan. He has since moved to the US and turned to writing fiction.

By the time I was finally settled into a primary school, aged five, I had already been to at least two or three others, due to my family jumping about the northwest side of Manchester like a rip-rap on Bonfire Night. As a little kid, I remember going to a summer school at Langworthy Road School in Salford, prior to the term starting, and my cousin Debbie and I hated it. Thankfully, during one of the breaks, some older lads from our street, Laburnum Street, came to the railings and lifted us over, and we escaped into the rainy cobbled maze that was home. It was our second such escape. A couple of years earlier, our parents had put us in a little play-pen in Laburnum Street, and left us to our own devices. There was another kid in there with us, too. We soon felt the urge for freedom, and we quickly realised that we were actually strong enough to lift the thing up and move with it. We lifted it over the bewildered third kid and simply ran off round the corner carrying the cage with us as we went. This need to break free has never left me.

As a kid, I had a memory that amazed the adults around me, and this capacity continued into adulthood. I was always able to recall events from when I was an infant, and the degree of detail in which I'd describe these events left no doubt in the adults' minds that I really did remember things from a time most people are not capable. I believe there's a really good reason for this, an incident that triggered my ability to recollect things from an early age; one afternoon in Salford in the mid-60s, my mam and my Auntie Viv were wheeling my cousin Debbie and I in our pushchairs down a busy shopping street. This was back when you went to the greengrocer for all your vegetables and the bakers for your bread, and there were no superstores for DIY or wholesale food and clothing. The street we were shopping on was packed with people, all unaware of what was about to happen. For reasons that remain unknown, the sky suddenly darkened, far beyond what you'd expect from an impending thunderstorm, so dark, in fact, that all the people went scurrying into the shops, cowering towards the back, as far from the windows as possible. My mam has always been a nervous sort, and she just legged it into the greengrocer's without bothering to grab me, but my Auntie Viv grabbed Debbie and the three of them were in there with the rest of the throng, all panicking while I was left out on the street.

Amazingly, it became as dark as midnight, and it happened in seconds. I remember a sea of terrified faces peering out towards me, and a large oval-shaped white light came over the middle of the road, which even as an infant I reasoned had been turned on by the council to combat this alarming plunge into darkness. I felt utterly safe and special and was perfectly happy to be out there. Auntie Viv eventually ran out and hoisted me into the shop, and I can still see the large illuminated shelves containing late-afternoon's last few bunches of lettuce, cabbage and cauliflower, strange and inappropriate in the electric lighting, as we never visited such shops after dark. This incident was so unusual and profound that it became the yardstick for weirdness for my entire life. In time I came to believe it had been an eclipse, until I witnessed an eclipse in the mid-80s. The eclipse was a piddling shadow of that shocking day, and I was forced to rethink what it could have been that sent the world into instant darkness.

Funnily enough, despite being quite obsessed with UFOs and aliens throughout my life I never once considered the possibility that the event might have had a paranormal cause. A few years ago when I was in college here in America, I was sat at the dinner table, studying calculus. Occasionally, when I came to a difficult equation, I would doodle in the margin, and it was always the same thing I doodled, a thing I'd been doodling my entire life; it was an oval-shaped thing, with facets which shone like a diamond or the plastic cover of a car headlight. It suddenly hit me that I had been drawing that oval light my entire life, and for a brief instant I was engulfed by the notion I had indeed been abducted by a UFO, and the entire street full of Salfordians had been rendered inanimate, their memories wiped clean by alien technology. The "instant" darkness wasn't instant at all – they had all been knocked out by some unknown bluish beam during daylight, and had simply been reanimated once the mission was accomplished.

The aliens had left me in my pushchair outside the shop, and upon regaining consciousness the people became terrified, as several hours had passed and it was indeed now dark. The white oval light was my final glimpse of the craft upon which I'd been transported, and it was farther away than I realised, hence its relatively small size. I gulped when I realised I'd been subconsciously scouring the streets of Manchester for just such a light since that fateful day, and had never seen one quite like it. My pen dropped from my hands, and I fancied I even remembered my Auntie Viv sometimes remarking that I had actually been in cousin Debbie's trolley and not my own when she'd ran out to grab me, a mystery she's never been able to fathom. It all started to make sense, and during the next weekly phone-call from America to my mother, I pestered her for details. I was called a 'daft get' for my troubles. *A daft get.* And that was the end of that.

One of the schools I went to as a kid was Saint Augustine's in Pendlebury. The yard was hemmed in on all sides by a covered walkway and a wall, and only a small gate in the wall allowed people access between the street and the yard. The school had its own church which loomed Gothically beyond the wall, and every morning we had to attend a service, with proper blokes in dog-collars, and choirboys, the full Montezuma.

At the time, Brooke Bond Tea had introduced a set of dinosaur cards, which you could collect and stick in a book they issued for that purpose, and I was already well into my second or even third full book, as I loved reptiles and my family drank a lot of tea. Every morning in church we'd sing "When a Knight Won his Spurs" and when we sang the line, "and the dragons have fled", I always thought it was a reference to the Brontosaurus and Tyrannosaurs that sadly weren't around anymore. I thought those knights were a load of shitbags dressed up in armour with a shield and lance, while the poor "dragons" had nothing to defend themselves with. I imagined the poetic justice of one such monster who, having somehow survived undetected since the age of chivalry, might suddenly come smashing through the large stained glass window of the church, sending the modern humans scattering in terror. I've sided with non-humans against humans my whole life, and I'm not sure why. It probably has something to do with the fact I believed people did cruel and destructive things for their own sake, while non-humans only did what they needed to, and killed what they had to. Whether or not this is actually true I have no fucking idea.

As kids my cousins and I would all descend *en masse* on my nana and granddad's house in Salford every weekend. They lived on Littleton Road in Kersal, which was one of the routes for the Whit Week Walks. My nana, who had a head of eye-catching red hair, would send us all out into the rhubarb field at the back of their house, and we'd return bearing handfuls of the ruby coloured prize. Nana would proceed to bake several large and fabulous rhubarb pies, which we'd set to avidly after we'd eaten our Sunday dinners off plates on newspapers across the kitchen floor. When we were all little kids, Nana knitted all her grandkids a red and white bobble hat each. My cousin Trevor received a sky blue and white bobbler, and he stood out like a sore thumb, a lonesome blue among twelve or thirteen reds. In later life he converted but memories are long when it comes to such things.

When we moved from Salford to Pendlebury, and then Prestwich, we would sometimes go to visit other friends from the old neighbourhood who had been decanted to weird and horrifying areas in unknown quadrants of Greater Manchester. I would always note the ugliness of the architecture, or the too-well kept foliage lining the sides of the roads, or the utter lack of soul, or the ineffable diluted stench in the air of peasant diasporas mingled from numerous inner-city hives, colliding on bizarre and cold housing estates and merging to form vile hybrids never before seen. I was glad we lived in Prestwich, as it was quite uncultivated and green back then. There were lots of old mansions along the quiet roads, in the shade of big sycamores and horse chestnuts to climb and knock conkers out of. Most people in Prestwich had come from Ireland or Salford or some part of proper inner city Manchester, and it made for a very tranquil casserole. I was relieved not to have been carted away from Salford to one of those other places, where the locals were hard-faced and confident enough to make life uncomfortable for our misplaced brethren. They were shitholes, and everything about them stank of backwardness, unhappiness, and fear.

My first holiday abroad was a school trip to the South of France. It was May 1981, and I was 16 years old. The casual culture was about two years old in Manchester, and the thought of travelling to France filled us with expectations of mind-blowing Adidas training shoes, incredible Lacoste sweaters, and hitherto unknown species of Fila tracksuits. I came home with a cracking pair of Adidas Easy, strap-over tennis shoes made of amazingly soft leather with a thick white sole with blue bottoms.

It was also my first proper exposure to alcohol, in the form of the bottles of red wine the French drank with all their meals, and I have to admit I spent the entire time I was there drinking, drunk, or recovering from being drunk. The teachers were having a ball, and not really keeping much of an eye on us (as testified by a couple of mad rampages which went totally unacknowledged by our chaperones) and after a few days we'd settled into a grand old tour of the great cities and towns of the French Riviera; St. Tropez, Nice, St. Maxim, Ramatuelle, Monaco, and Cannes. We spent days swimming and pedal-boating in the Mediterranean, drifting through the amazing boutiques, ragging the odd bits and pieces, and the warm nights were electrifying and novel. The place where we stayed was a fantastic network of stone alleyways and guest rooms, and was a two minute walk from its own private beach. There was a swimming pool, and a collective dining hall, where the locally produced wine was kept, which we ragged vast quantities of.

My mate Sean and I enjoyed the company of a couple of

young girls in our party, and even at that young age I was totally swept along by the romance of it all. The moon always seemed enormous and golden, and the hilly country pulsated with aromas and ancient buildings. The vineyards were everywhere, their tell-tale neat rows furrowing across the local topography like a picture-label on a wine bottle. I'd never seen so many trees in my life. It was nothing like Manchester, and it planted a deep seed of curiosity in me that served to inflame the ones already there. Liverpool played in Paris in the European Cup Final while we were there, and right as we went to the TV room for kick-off, Emma Burney pushed me fully-clothed into the pool. I had to dry all my money out and leg it to our room for a quick change. Emma was my mate Dave's sister, and she helped me pick presents for my family in Saint Maxim, as I was too pissed to function. I remember sitting outside a café, slurping down a large Knickerbocker Glory and trying to get my act together while Emma thankfully furnished me with some decent gifts to take back to England.

It was my first taste of continental café culture and I was hooked. I loved the way the cafés had large roll-shutter doors across their fronts and the long bars with glass cases displaying all kinds of delicious breads, meats and cheeses ran down one side. I was mesmerised by the little beer-taps with logos, crests and names on that looked and sounded so foreign and ancient, and the breathtaking style of the furniture and architecture. Sitting out in the sun under an umbrella with *Cinzano*, *Martini-Rossi*, or *Dubonnet* emblazoned on it, sipping gorgeous aromatic coffee, nursing hangovers and lusting after all the women and the designer gear in the ritzy boutiques became par for the course every morning. We knew we couldn't run complete riot because we'd be caught and sent home, so we made do with a prolonged skulking marathon, slipping in and out of the boutiques like little serpents, waiting patiently for opportunities that almost never came.

A funfair had arrived in Heaton Park the week before I left England, and there were thousands of kids making the pilgrimage from all over north Manchester every night, posing in unidentifiable European training shoes, tracksuits, and knitwear. There were a few skirmishes, but even with those numbers present representing myriad neighbourhoods, it was more of a fashion extravaganza than a battleground. It was scheduled to stay for a week, but upon returning I was delighted to find they had added another week or so onto the time they were staying, as it had proved enormously popular. As a result, I was able to move among the crowds at the fair wearing my Adidas Easy, and privately enjoy the thrill of having heads turn everywhere I went. Fortunately there were mates on hand to back me up if anyone tried to have them off me, which was definitely a possibility.

When I was in my mid-20s, I realised that there had only been three occasions in my entire life when I had felt absolutely relaxed. The second of those occasions was a Friday afternoon before we broke up for the six weeks of summer, lying hidden in the tall grass on the "out-of-bounds" banking at my primary school, Park View, in Prestwich. Even as we risked falling foul of the teacher, should she spy us there in our little illegal spot, I was intensely aware of the endless summer holidays and it made my head swim with possibility.

The third time I was in that state I was 20 years old, sat on the edge of a vast crater in the Israeli desert, getting drunk with Jane, a Canadian girl I'd met on a kibbutz, watching buses disappear round a corner on the spiralling road directly below us, only to reappear an hour later, a distant speck moving slowly across the floor of that gigantic dent in the sandstone earth.

But the first time I ever felt utterly blissed out, the one that sticks most in my mind, was when I went to Belle Vue Zoo as a child. We lived in Salford at the time, and back then I didn't get around much, being a little kid. Salford buses were a deep green colour, a huge contrast to the Manchester buses, which I never saw unless we went to Belle Vue, as I wasn't old enough to regularly trek through town yet. Manchester buses were red, and there were always hundreds of them packed all around the breathtaking expanse of Piccadilly, as well as a small number of Salford green buses, which were usually clustered in one corner. I came to associate the red buses with the fabulous zoo-park as a result of this, and called them "Belle Vue buses". Salford was an extremely tight-knit place back then, and one thing I knew was that our accent was the best in the world, but on those red buses I was transfixed by people who virtually spoke the same as we did. This was a revelation to me, and it was always the bus conductor upon which my attention was most firmly fastened. There'd be dozens of buses flowing past in the traffic, and I loved the ever-open door at the back, with the bone-white pole you grabbed to hoist yourself aboard, and the furrowed wooden floors with numerous cigarette dimps, silver foil off cigarette packets, and spent tickets between them. My dad used to make me little FA Cups from the foil back then, in that entire ancient world constructed from unnecessarily durable and toxic materials.

In the summer glow of Woolworth's and other elaborate frontages, opposite the statue of Queen Victoria, the crowds throbbed, and the old architecture appeared magnificently surreal. I'd stand admiring the procession of shiny red buses, and when we paid and jumped aboard, slowly drifting down London Road, the conductor would appear, smoking a cigarette with one hand and administering tickets from that mysterious little machine he hefted from hip to hip, all the while swapping the cig from hand to mouth to other hand and back to mouth in a lightning exhibition of hand-eye coordination. And of course, that accent would boom out, that virtual-Salford sound, as he rapidly pushed buttons and churned out his endless ticket-tape, ripping it at select locations, and giving change from a bulging pocket that jingled heavily. The Manchester bus conductors had an air of arrogance about them that seemed lacking in Salford, and I took this to be a symptom of their plying their trade around the giant glittering attractions of their Piccadilly wonderland. I particularly admired their ability to remain vertical as the bus accelerated and lurched wildly round corners through an alien world called Gorton. It was my first exposure to the fact our little cobbled street was attached to a larger realm, and in that realm was paradise – Belle Vue.

On my first ever visit I walked cockily through the turnstiles, and hurried down to where a crowd of people were paying attention to something through a fence. It was the first exhibit

MANCHESTER MAVERICKS

you came to in the zoo, right near the water-chute that towered high behind the barrier and could be seen from Hyde Road outside. I arrived just as a terrifying dinosaur suddenly appeared from nowhere, drooping its huge horned head over a fence that looked a hundred feet high, down right in my face. I can still see its eyes; big dark saucers that looked directly at me, transmitting disappointment at the fact I had no banana to feed to it, as the other people were doing. I remember it was covered in large orangey blotches, and its neck was insanely long. I burst out crying in terror, thinking that even my dad wouldn't be able to save me from this dirty big fucking monster, and indeed spent a few minutes shaking and sobbing in his arms, while he carried me around the edge of the giraffe enclosure and patiently explained that it was harmless and we were there to enjoy ourselves.

Once I'd got a grip, I found myself entering that blissful state, and could hardly contain myself, as we looked at polar bears, snakes, and monkeys. But the animals I wanted to see the most were the crocodiles. That day, as we took a break for a picnic and rolled a sheet out on the ground, with my mum and dad and sister Jane, and Auntie Viv, Uncle Dave, and cousins Debbie, Paul and Andrew, I remember thinking that I could have stayed under that tree forever, on that lush lawn, surrounded by exotic beasts. It was heaven.

A few years later we went on a school trip to Belle Vue and as we walked round in the drizzling rain, I found a silver sixpence and quickly slipped it in my pocket. It was worth quite a bit in those days. My mate Steve was dead chuffed, and we discussed the lollies and crisps we'd buy with it as soon as we found a kiosk. Unfortunately, before we found a kiosk we went in the reptile house. One look down at a large crocodile with innumerable pennies on its back, and many more on the bottom of the pool around it, sealed the fate of my silver sixpence. Steve frantically tried to talk me out of it, he was a canny little fucker even back then, but I was immovable; if people had made wishes with pennies on this ancient creature (which was still my favourite animal at the time) then imagine what a fantastic wish I could make come true with my sixpence! And it was free!

The school party was drifting away as I licked my lips and hesitated, a nervous wreck that I might miss from my vantage on the little bridge that spanned the croc's pool. The animal was right there, though, not too far below, and my confidence grew. I was shaking as I dropped the silver coin, trying to land it right in the middle of that broad, scaly back, while Steve cursed and called me an idiot. It missed. In fact, I had no idea where it had gone, to be honest, and the two of us walked dejected through the rest of the zoo. I think Steve had been secretly hoping I at least hit the thing, but he stubbornly refused to console me, choosing instead to freeze me out and sulk as we walked faster to catch the rest of our party, past the colourful ice-cream vendors and hot-dog vans.

Belle Vue had so many famous attractions, such as the Scenic Railway, and the Bobs – a roller-coaster eventually sold to an American that was said to be the fastest in the world at the time, if my mother's account of it are to be believed – but to me it was always about the animals, even though I no longer believe zoos to be a humane form of entertainment. Steve was always a bit of a character, and many years later he did proper time for smuggling amphetamines through the Channel Tunnel. I sometimes picture him sitting out those years in his cell, mesmerised by that glittering coin, and the things he'd do to put his hands on it. That silver sixpence was a bit of a come-down from idyllic previous visits to Belle Vue but to this day I wonder if that old croc is still alive. And I think I can speak for both Steve and myself when I ask, *where the fuck did that sixpence go?*

I always love walking around town, and have been proud to be from Manchester my entire life. The city centre has so many great boozers that it's almost impossible to pick favourites out of them all and say they're the best. So I'll probably just mention a couple, and deep down I'll know that I've missed some real beauties.

In the 70s there was a pub built into the façade of the Arndale Centre right next to Top Man called the Samuel Pepys. Walking past and looking in, it always seemed to be packed, with plenty of interesting heads on show amid the pall of smoke through the many tiny Georgian windows along its frontage. The Samuel

MANCHESTER MAVERICKS

Pepys was renamed Seftons at some point in the late 70s or early 80s, and I started going in there quite a lot then. I remember they had one of the first video jukeboxes I ever saw and whenever I went in there it was always pretty lively, being close to the very centre of town. Seftons became one of our meeting points before we went on to clubs in town, along with Mr. Chesters around the corner. Every time I went in there I saw someone I knew, and often spontaneous little squads of lads would form and go on a mad one. I remember painting a sign one week for a new nightclub called Chelsea's off Albert Square. It was a steak-house, and the bloke who owned it was a right character, from Ireland but based in Ancoats. Every day, as the Town Hall clock gonged out its noontime twelve bells, he would bring me an ice-cold pint of Becks. His brother and his mates would turn up, and we'd end up standing in the little street throwing ale down our necks like it was going out of fashion. They were a proper crew of grafters. I would go on to Seftons from there, and regale people with secrets I'd discovered, such as the fact that Old Trafford was built by alien technology from Area 51, or that the earth wasn't actually round at all, but was instead a vast planar plateau shooting through space, enclosed by inscrutable laws of physics we could never hope to understand. I was probably a proper pain in the arse.

Off Saint Ann's Square, down a staircase on a little back street, is a bar called Corbiere's, which is definitely one of my favourites. Many a time I would go and walk around the bookshops, art galleries, and museums, transfixed by the primitive or technical antiquities, and Corbiere's would be a good place to grab pie and chips and a few pints. Being down the stairs and out of the way didn't mean people didn't know the place, and this was another pub always full of heads from far and wide. You could easily find your way into a decent conversation, and the place would be packed with chattering people, drumming up a right old atmosphere (and temperature) down in that secretive vault. Corbiere's was right round the corner from Brannigan's in the Royal Exchange. We went in there a lot as well, sometimes ordering food and doing a runner without paying. It was too easy, as Brannigan's opened right out onto the market in the Exchange, and you could be out on Market Street, into Marks and Sparks, and up across the skywalk into the depths of the Arndale before the security guards had a sniff there was anything amiss.

Another cracker was surely The Beerhouse, right outside town to the north. They sold myriad real ales and it was always packed to the rafters with locals from Ancoats and Collyhurst, as well as dozens of students. The jukebox was legendary, and favourite hits from previous decades would boom out and amaze you, as you hadn't heard them in years, or even forgotten about them completely.

Even though it was a Man City haunt, my mates and I often went to the Cyprus Tavern, or "The Cypriotic Tower" as my mate Kezz called it. The Cyprus was like a youth club for adults, with its little serving hatch at the back dishing up chips and sausage late into the early hours, all the stoned punters grabbing a scran to quell the munchies after dancing berserk to techno and indie sounds for hours. We knew the City lads, like Chris F., Meesey and Lofty, and some nights there'd be up to twenty of us in there, all having a laugh and singing Roy Orbison or Englebert, big time. The DJs were alright in the Cyprus, and the light shows completely fucked your mind to the point of heart attack material if you were suitably bollocksed on powerful substances, which we always were. There was a point in the late 80s when a little group of us were literally in there seven nights a week, up to no good and grooving to the tunes. Some nights we were the only ones in the entire place, and perhaps some girls from places like Longsight or Moss Side would come in and invite us to a party in the flats down their end. They say Manchester is the city that never sleeps, but some nights I think it was just me, Andy, Howard and Dave B. who were keeping the entire camp-fire burning!

We sometimes went in the Continental round the corner as well, as it was an interesting shady place where we could run free and live life to the full. They played a bit more mainstream music in the Conti and the crowd was different from the Cyprus, more straight heads that we'd take the piss out of in one way or the other. One night my mate Andy sold a guy two hits of "acid" – actually two tiny squares of red Rizla paper he'd ripped off a packet of skins, almost in front of the kid – and off he went, chuffed as fuck. An hour later the same guy was back for more, giving it the big thumbs up, his personal seal of approval. Andy obliged and sold him a few more. You couldn't make it up.

The pubs of Manchester are the best pubs I've ever been in, and I've been in some pubs. I could go on forever but should probably stop now. Nah, fuck it, let's have a couple more for the road, eh? There was the Auld Reekie, down some narrow steps between shops right on Market Street, which was a major meeting point for a certain United crew before going to the game in the early 80s. Lads like Batesey, Goody, and Salty introduced me to the Auld Reekie, and to the after-match haunt, the Old Vic in Crown Square, where hundreds of lads would converge after the match, again in the early 80s. Then there was the Brunswick, at the top of the run down to Piccadilly, where the same mob would be ready for anyone coming off the train, on the rare occasions when we expected an unescorted crew, which I have to say was almost never. But the memories are a fading kaleidoscope of crazed disjointed and malformed fragments, each one bearing the holographic likeness of a perfectly atmospheric boozer as it arcs through my mind's eye and dissolves to become yet another at the edge of my tortured and homesick vision, kicking back across my brain like an Olympic swimmer in a pool full of frothing ale.

What about the magnificently tiled Peveril of the Peak, or the Lass O' Gowrie with its ornate bar and hanging plants? What of the Swinging Sporran, so beloved by the bikers and students, right next to UMIST, and then there's The Phoenix, built into the first floor of the modern brick structure opposite Manchester Business School on Oxford Road, where you go up a moving staircase and get smashed on cheap cider. And then there was the Crown and Anchor near the old Victoria Bus Station, a Holts pub which has been changed in recent years, but once held a gorgeous array of earth tones and had an ancient two-faced clock protruding from the wall, viewed from both directions, held in place by a nice wrought iron bracket. There was always an old geezer or old dear on their pissed up way home to Salford, willing to get up and belt out a classic tune or three late on a Saturday afternoon. Then there's the Crown and Cushion, that lovely Holt's place down in Red Bank full of smoking wrecks and colourful bawdy birds who are dead confident and always game for a piss up. And Band on the Wall up near Ancoats, where some of the best music I've ever heard is played, week in, week out, by bands and artists from all over the world. We've had a full crew in there many a night, all dancing and whizzing and steaming the ales like a mad troop of amphetamine-maddened baboons from the jungle of Prestwich Clough. The Mark Addy on the banks of the Irwell was a cracker for a big plate of cheese and paté, and the Pen and Wig across the street was another, now sadly long gone. The Pen and Wig was a daily haunt of the motley crew I used to work in town with, right opposite Salford Station. We used to play pool with the office workers and blokes running the Metrolink construction. There's also the Egerton, and the Brown Bull across from the Pen and Wig, not to mention the Chapel Street selection of the Albert Vaults, the Black Lion, the Ship, and the now extinct Tallow Tub, a truly ancient and putrid little hole full of trolls and weirdoes supping the most alarming real ale you've seen in all your life. And there's the King's, off Chapel Street, past the Salford Arms, a semi-circular shaped place with wild butties, fucking ace beer and a knock-out jukebox...

To be honest, I was always fond of a couple in the greenish-glass domed bar in Victoria Station, a plush leather place full of mirrors and large rubber-plants that resembled a train station in India rather than England. It was always full of drinkers who "looked like they were waiting for something", to quote Dave B. The little bar in Piccadilly Station was also a great place to get gabbing with a total pisshead or two. I remember one old alcoholic homeless feller in there one Friday when I was on my way to Nottingham, trying to convince me he'd seen a dinosaur crossing the road outside earlier, but he kept collapsing in fits of mental giggles and uproarious laughter each time I asked him to describe it. He was so funny I actually let myself miss a train just to hear him talk his fantastic brand of Mancunian shite, and buy him a few pints.

My first ever job was working at a steel stockholders in

MANCHESTER MAVERICKS

Ordsall. I drove a stacker truck and cut and weighed immense steel bars with a giant circular saw. The company I worked for used to be very big on getting out for a liquid lunch as often as possible. It was there that I was first introduced to Holt's Bitter and I never looked back. We would go in the Broadway pub off Trafford Road, and I used to leave my chicken paste butties wrapped in greaseproof paper on a window ledge above the door until I came out later with the munchies, craving salt. We used to booze hard in all the pubs in Ordsall such as the Clowes, with its cavernous rooms, pool tables and revolving door. The Oxford further down Trafford Road was even more massive, again with a revolving door (which they said were installed so the bouncers could eject trouble causers more easily back in the grand days of the Barbary Coast), and big snooker tables and multi-level lounges, all kitted out with big tables and loads of chairs for the huge numbers of people that called it home. The Bricklayers on East Ordsall Lane was another pub we would get smashed in, sometimes not returning to work until after two or even three o' clock. It was no bother though, because the bosses were out with us, and egging us on to drink more as they continued to get the beer in. They were happy days, but things have changed now, and such lunchtime practices have been outlawed.

My favourite fashion was very likely the suede Adidas training shoe range that began in late '79 with Adidas Jogger (blue suede, white stripes, white sole), and Adidas Bali (blue suede, blue stripes, blue sole), and the all-brown Adidas Hawaii. I loved the texture of the suede, and the moulded rubber soles which were durable yet soft, flexible yet strong, and I owned several pairs of those comfortable shoes from 1980 to 1982. The only thing that really challenged them was the slightly later white Adidas tennis selection, which began creeping in from Europe in late 1980. By 1981 everyone wanted a pair of Nastase, ATP, or Wimbledon, with the blue-bottomed soles and red and blue stripes.

The worst fashion, in my opinion, was the green MA-1 flying jackets, which were often worn by cockney skinheads and Scousers. They looked like the cheap windjammers we wore when we were nine years old, and I couldn't stand the silly elasticated waistband and the shortness of the things, as they barely covered your belly-button. Rubbish.

The city always seemed to be hosting some form of big parade when I was a kid, and Whit Week was one of the biggest, if not *the* biggest. I remember watching the most dynamic marching band ever, storming down Regent Road in Ordsall, while a massive, bulging crowd cheered them on from behind the railings that ran along the road. Back then, Regent Road was an arm of Manchester city centre, and was home to some pretty elaborate architecture and large department stores. These buildings loomed over the street while the uniformed buglers, drummers, and baton-twirlers marched noisily between the sea of faces at either side, the music reverberating madly off the walls of this enchanted Salford canyon. I was always fascinated by the stick the band leader carried and twirled, especially by the ornamental knobbly bit at the end. It seemed to transmit an almost religious significance, like it was the magic stick of a shaman or witch-doctor, its brilliance wrought by the spit and polish of angels or other supernatural beings.

Everybody would have their new smart clothes on and it was in Whit Week that I first learned the concept of wearing a blazer with matching or non-matching pants, as well as a tie. As kids we wore elastic ties, and our dads wore real ones. We got new socks, new shoes, new everything. My blazer had red and blue vertical stripes, and I had a new pair of pale green shorts, some knee-socks, new sandals, and a very fetching elastic tie with a pastel floral pattern on. To top it all I wore a new cap, which matched the blazer. It all seems so ritualised now, as it was part of an earlier culture, one rendered extinct these past few decades. This was an unbroken tradition, as old as the hills, and probably traceable to long-forgotten pagan festivals, as many supposedly "Christian" pageants are. It might be my imagination, but the weather seemed more consistent back then, and the air of conviviality saturated the entire occasion. People would mob the pubs, and the aroma of beer was never far away. Relatives would give you coins for no apparent reason, and the whole world took a holiday, with no exceptions. It seems that many of the festivals and special occasions in the yearly calendar have been removed, as people are just too busy these days to prepare and make something of times like Whitsun, but it will always remain as a glow in my heart, and I'm proud to have at least caught the tail end of it all.

I was part of the generation that invented binge drinking and the so-called Casual culture. As a result, my mates and I had a massively snobbish attitude towards whatever wholesome and outdated music was considered "cool" by the mainstream. In fact, we felt we held the power of absolute judgement over the various acts performing in Manchester, and we thought it was all complete shite, so never bothered to attend any of the "big" gigs in town. Thankfully I outgrew this attitude later in life, and started listening to music people had actually heard of, because to a large extent my attitude was, well, wrong.

By the end of 1985, a fair-sized little mob of us had been using psychedelics and getting off on some underground sounds for about three years, and my personal musical tastes rarely ventured outside the realm of the original and strange. We turned to sixties music because the charts in 1980 and 1981 were garbage, and the Beatles, Kinks, and Stones sounded better. But those innocent early years of beat-bands in suits and ties quickly gave way to drugs and the consequent search for meaning of the late-60s, and we relived it ourselves avidly. Within a year or so, we were listening to music that was loaded with symbols, feedback, and spontaneity, while the New Romantic music played on the radio we considered utter rubbish. We never expected a demand for information regarding the nature of the mind-set we were involved in (though we believed there should be), especially as most of the music we listened to was now being played by emerging modern bands nobody had ever heard of, or apparently wanted to.

One of my favourite concerts was when Robyn Hitchcock played UMIST on October 26, 1985 – my 20th birthday. I went with Kenny Lewis, a long-time mate. My other mate Dave Burney couldn't go, his dad sadly having just died during heart surgery, so Dave gave Kenny his ticket. Hitchcock was wearing a mental patterned suit like a camouflaged octopus, and did a set from his latest album, and when he came out for the encore, I jumped on the stage and wrestled the microphone off him and took over the singing. Needless to say I was swiftly launched down a corridor and out on my ear by the security, but it was a nice way to end a couple of years of admiring the guy from a distance, just before I took off for the kibbutz and Israel. Kenny and I had been drinking pals for years and we got in a right state that night, the UMIST bar being an old haunt by then due to its hipsters selling top notch speed and acid.

A couple of weeks later, Dave Burney and I had tickets to see more of our heroes, Los Angeles bands Green on Red and The Rain Parade, perform at the International. We had been making a habit of doing an acid or three on Saturday mornings and going on mad all-day benders with a Walkman around this time, and this day was no exception. We even went and obtained a copy of Arthur Conan Doyle's *The Lost World*, to throw at the stage, as an answer to the outlandish lyrics in some of Green on Red's songs (and a testament to our undying fascination with giant lizards). We embarked on a pub-crawl all round Prestwich Village, and at some point we were split up, and I couldn't find Dave (or *The Lost World*) anywhere. That night I was meeting a girl called Carol for our first ever date and she was going to come to the club with us. As I walked out of the pit in the Wilton pub on my way to meet her, I slipped on a step and landed right on the bridge of my nose, which began bleeding profusely. I was wearing a white shirt, and by the time I'd made it round the corner to meet Carol, I was a right sight, covered in blood. She cleaned me up, and we set off in her car, minus Dave, who was considered MIA by then. Funnily enough, a few seconds after I'd walked out of the pub, a thirty strong mob from Salford had steamed in and wrecked the place, doing a lot of damage to people and property, and I literally missed it by seconds, thank fuck.

The bouncers were reluctant to admit me in my blood-spattered state, but Carol talked them round. When we entered the rocking club and squeezed our way through to the front for a better view, we were amazed to be greeted by the sight of Dave dancing on the stage, right next to the band, arms outstretched, still tripping his brains out. He dived into the crowd and we danced all night. It was a special time for me because I was due to leave for Israel in a fortnight, and the pressure was building. And once again it was a rush to actually see some of our heroes in the flesh. We never did find the book, but the Walkman remained in Dave's pocket throughout the day and night. The acid, the Walkman, and the music had become embroidered into our entire lives by then.

My third favourite concert is remembered because it never happened, and in fact the night was almost a disaster. It was now 1987, and the California band Thin White Rope had announced plans to play The International. The whole Madchester scene had begun to stir, but we barely noticed, as we were jaded travellers on different chemical pathways and our music was timeless. The band had rocked our world with their alarming blend of buzz-saw guitar, weird vocals, and cold moonlit drumming, and we knew we couldn't afford to miss this one. I went with a mate, John McGrath, who'd recently been diagnosed with a tumour in his spine. John was originally from Sunderland, but he'd lived in Canada for years, and now lived round the corner from me in Salford. His cupboard was always stocked with plentiful supplies of painkillers, and until that night I'd never touched them, as it wasn't really my thing. When we arrived at The International, pumped up and unable to believe we were actually going to see Thin White Rope in the flesh, we were confronted by a small notice on the door. It said, "Tonight's Show Cancelled". Just eleven tickets had been sold; the world wasn't ready for Thin White Rope.

Utterly livid, we jumped back in the same taxi that had brought us and trundled grimly back to Broughton with an electrical cloud over us. We stopped at an off-licence and picked up a large bottle of cheap Scotch called High Commissioner, which had a picture of a bloke in a kilt on the label. Back at John's flat, I embarked on a self-destructive assault on the Scotch, beer, and unlimited supply of opiates, saying, fuck it, Thin White Rope hadn't bothered turning up so I was gonna get wasted very quickly. Unfortunately, I took it a bit too far, and when I awoke the following morning on John's floor, I was quaking and shivering like a man possessed. A serious dent had been put in a bottle of morphine and the Scotch was all gone. I dragged myself across the street to the taxi place at the Rialto, and the queue of punters actually let me go to the front, I looked that bad with my shaking, doubled up in pain and horror. I spent the day in bed at my parents' house in Prestwich, and will always remember the Lonny Donegan song, "Cumberland Gap" playing on the radio, as I fought with my sanity and my physical well-being. It was no ordinary hangover. That non-concert took me days to get over, and I really believe I could have jossed it that night, but for sheer good fortune. By the time I was in the pub with Dave the following Saturday drinking Holts' bitter, I truly felt like I'd had a brush with death.

I love the atmosphere and architecture of Manchester, but to try and name my three favourite buildings just succeeds in making me realise that the task is impossible. John Rylands Library is one of my definite top picks though. The Central Library in Saint Peter's Square is probably another. Old Trafford's United Road and Scoreboard End original cantilever, now dead and long gone, has to be my third.

Ryland's Library is a rust-coloured mass of intricate brickwork, showing myriad functional and ornamental devices, and it houses one of the best collections of rare books and documents in the UK. I love where it is, bang in the middle of Deansgate, among the strange doorways that lead up to old offices and other official chambers, which are often illuminated at night by a mysterious orange glow, as some night-owl is working late. The area reminds me of old New York, from some 1970s *Spiderman* story, and the ruddy library, which looks almost like a church, lends a dark attractiveness to the place.

The main library in town is a gorgeous round building, and it has rows of columns running along it. I have spent many happy hours in there, reading books at the large study tables in the cavernous heart of the amphitheatre-like structure, cradled in the warm arms of my city. The central library oozes memories and ghosts like a fabulous curved alleyway where it's always safe to go and every room is crammed to the rafters with books. I used to love nowt more than to grab some chips, sausage, egg and beans in a lively Piccadilly café, and pace rapidly down Mosley Street, past the bizarre shops set into the base of Sunley Tower, past the art gallery and the glimpses of Chinatown, homing in on that circular wonderland of information.

Old Trafford was a space-age monument to footballing madness long before I was born, and the sight of the cantilever supports running along the roof of the alarming stadium always used to set my heart racing like it was the first time all over again. I always wished Old Trafford would one day be finished off with that same style all around. The mass of red seats with the wall beneath them, and the long paddocks with their mighty crush barriers set in concrete supports, was a world-class template for a working class sporting venue. On rare quiet moments during the match, people would clap, and the echo would bounce back and forth off that awesome steel roof, causing the noise to distort and quickly fade in a twisted whistling sound. The away fans would be fascinated by this, and they would try a few claps of their own. It was suffused with a sense of magic that I think died with the structure itself and it was a powerful advert for Manchester's ability to build pioneering forms on a large scale.

A fourth building I really like is the wavy glass office block that towers over Piccadilly Station Approach. The silvery combination of solidity and fluidity embodied in its contours makes me proud to be a Manc. We shouldn't forget though, that many beautiful buildings have been demolished around the city, due to misguided fools working on the city council among other things. I could easily mention the now gone Rialto in Salford, or Tower Buildings in Prestwich, both similarly grand, with their long and massive façades, with a dome set in the corner at the end, made from shining white stone.

My favourite Mancunians are the ones from Salford and north Manchester, the ones with the accents outsiders always mistake for Scouse. The cheeky monkeys with the cute grins and lightning wit, always up to no good, eye out for an opportunity of some kind. They are the ones that sound nothing like their Lancashire neighbours, the ones who gave us a sense of being different, in the same way that Scousers feel different, when we were growing up and slowly coming to grips with the accents of people from the rest of England. They are the essence of what people are talking about when they mention Mancs in the modern sense.

Two of my favourite famous Mancs are the actors John Thaw and Ian McShane. I most admire John for his stellar performances as Jack Reagan of the Flying Squad in the 70s detective series *The Sweeney*, which everyone of a certain age gladly acknowledges as one of *the* highlights of the 1970s. Ian I admire for his intelligent, hilarious, and moving depiction of crazy saloon owner Albert Swearingen in the series *Deadwood*. John Thaw and Ian McShane have starred in many other things, such as *Inspector Morse* or *Lovejoy* (and assorted bank robbers in McShane's case) and they always manage to emit an aura of authority and confidence in what they do, with a dash of jaded humour. I think it's the humour that makes them special, and what makes them Mancs. And let's not forget that Ian McShane's dad, Harry, played for Manchester United.

The practice of mugging or simply beating up people for a thrill seems to have gained momentum in Britain over a long time period, but has recently turned extremely serious. This is partly because some youngsters today carry knives and are prepared to use them on innocent defenceless people, even to the point of committing premeditated murder. I remember watching a Youtube video of a young man in Essex, a student who was causing no bother whatsoever, attacked by other youths, and repeatedly knifed in the side and back. As I watched the video, I actually thought the attacker was patting the student on the back as he lay bunched up and shocked on the ground, presumably a thank you for the money and wristwatch he'd just stolen from him, but those "pats" were actually the rapidly repeated stabbings that ended the guy's life. The people who carried out that attack were caught, I believe, and I truly hope they get what's coming to them, if not in prison then when they are released, as they sadly will be one day, for some stupid reason.

These modern kids know they are murdering people when they do it, and some are even reported to laugh about it as they walk away. This makes my blood boil, especially as they always pick on those who are either outnumbered and/or don't appear particularly aggressive or tough enough to fight back. We've all heard of the youths who've attacked elderly women and men, and subjected to them to vicious beatings, and we think with horror of our own grandparents (and other old people we know personally) as this is a natural reaction to the unfairness and evil inherent in it.

It's a radical thing to say, but I think the only way to sort it out is for organised groups of men to speak to them in the only language they understand. Cowardly bullies such as these will quickly be brought to bear, but not without this secret police force doing what they know needs to be done. Apparently it worked to some extent in Dublin with heroin dealers, and there are neighbourhoods in England where it's been done, but obviously it has to be on the q.t. due to the stupidity and impotence of the law. I'm sure many a policeman would agree with that, and be prepared to look the other way if known menaces to society were being targeted. If you know the names and addresses of your local trouble causers, and you have the correct set of conditions at your disposal, you can arrange to play them at their own game. Sooner or later people are going to fight back, and that's when we'll see what these bullies are made of. Hopefully it will only require some muscle and bats and a few cracked skulls, but if that isn't enough then further measures must be taken. These little twats need their ringleaders made examples of, and a good way to do that is to take a couple of heads apart and let the rest watch and know in no uncertain terms that they're next if they either grass or don't turn it in rapid. Most of them are only petty criminals and wannabes so there wouldn't be any danger of comebacks, as real gangsters don't have anything to gain from murdering innocent vegetarians and OAPs in deserted shopping arcades. Only pure shithouses do things like that, because inside they're small and insignificant and secretly terrified of how weak they are in the face of having to be a man in a cruel world.

I think the police have a job to do and we all need them once in a while, for all kinds of reasons, as life can be very complex and spontaneous. That said, the idea of a bent copper doesn't just disgust people, it *frightens* them. It means that anybody could end up in a prison cell, regardless of whether they're guilty or not, all to satisfy someone else's dark agenda. The police have a very difficult road ahead of them every day, as their basic task is essentially to go around telling people what they can and cannot do, and this is a guaranteed trouble causer. Unfortunately, the police force contains as diverse an array of personalities as the rest of the world, and different policemen inevitably respond in different ways to the facts of their occupation. When it comes to the police, we only remember the bad ones (for the same reason we remember burning our hand on a stove-top as a child) and bad coppers have the power to lock us in cages for a very long time, which is fucking scary indeed. A lot of people will tell you they aren't frightened at all of the police, but they miss the point; it's not the individual coppers themselves, it's what those coppers, and their mates, and *their* mates, can do to you if they really want to. Only someone with psychological issues wants to be locked in a cage. I value my freedom mightily, and as a result I have a tendency to avoid brushes with the law.

Having had the experience of being told by a 'good' copper, "I don't think you did it" while that same copper fingerprinted me, I find the whole realm of the police to be too contradictory and dangerous to respect. Instead I feel fear and mistrust and some of it is paranoia and some of it is well-deserved. But I still appreciate that we need them and that they do an often dangerous job. Some of them could even be considered heroes. But that doesn't help me if I am taken in by the wrong copper on the wrong night, for a crime I didn't commit. Anybody who values their freedom sees dark things in the police, not because they are guilty, but because they are alive. Fear and respect aren't the same thing, and I think sometimes the insanity and technicality of the law, combined with the brute force of those trying to uphold it, causes the latter to dissolve in the face of the former.

In life I have tended to respect intelligent people who live honestly in filth and poverty yet smile and are always patient, even as their babies cry and the rent-man rattles the door of their hovel. I respect those that rob banks and don't hurt anybody and escape with untold millions, or just loose change. I respect the dogs and cats of the city, which trot happily along the pavements oblivious to the traffic and the noise, with broken glass in their pads and a jewelled Manc look in their eye. I respect the blokes who do the hard, dirty jobs in all weathers; the brick-layers, the electricians, the plumbers, the roofers, the joiners, who make civilization *possible* for those of us too far up our own arses to want to get involved.

I respect the gifted creative people; those destined to be incapable of normality before they were even born, instead choosing to entertain, alleviate, and transport the dismal to somewhere better for a while, even as they endure their own demons and madness.

My biggest regret in life is all the pain and anguish and suffering I inflicted upon my family when I was running wild. They didn't deserve it, but I was driven by devils and was hell-bent on self-destruction. My second biggest regret is that I didn't think deeply enough about what leaving England was really going to mean in the long run, when it came to my family and not being able to attend Manchester United matches.

In fact, I didn't think at all.

LINDSEY O'NEIL

Now I met Lindsey via a meeting at Film Wales - they had been over in Manchester to offer me a deal on Grafters. My publisher had signed the deal as they had but I was in need of more info and they were just at the end of a film with my old Collyhurst mate Bruce Jones who used to play Les Battersby on Corrie. Even he said most film companies are full of shite, you see they have to put up the money to get a script sorted then start asking banks and other sources for loans and soon I knew they wanted to do Grafters but put me on like £80 a day when I have to be on the set making sure whoever is acting as a grafter is getting it right. So besides the £80 they explain the contract states I get a percentage but that's all over the place the amount and when it will happen etc.

The meeting was in a top hotel on the seafront in Llandudno and I was glad when it was over as I knew it was all a load of bollocks and came back down to earth. But as luck would have it me and Bruce went through to the main room as we could hear some old school 70's soul music on and at the bar we got chatting to the lady who was in charge called Lindsey. I'm sure you can picture her face when I said I've just interviewed him for a book about Manchester, now? She is a Scouser but had lots to say about Manchester as she's worked in the city for years, so there and then I asked for a pen and paper and she was so easy to chat away with having only just meet her. I'm sure you'll agree it was worthwhile.

I went to Seafield Convent in Crosby when I was younger: schooling was a very important part of my life with my father being a head master, as you can imagine I had a very strict schooling. I was taught by Catholic nuns, my favourite teacher was Miss Stevens who taught me English. I used to entertain everyone by mimicking her though I would always get caught, she was never impressed. She was really goofy looking: buck teeth and glasses.

I didn't enjoy school really, I left when I was fifteen and was quite glad of it too.

My first job was in a hairdressing shop as an apprentice, I

didn't enjoy it much as I was on very low wages. Predominantly it consisted of watching and learning, I'd have to go to college once a week in addition to my shifts. We had a very strict regime really in those days, an apprenticeship was an apprenticeship. I'd be cleaning and sweeping, doing the laundry – I carried out all of my duties. The hairdressers was called 'Herberts'. The man who was there is now on Channel Four, he started off as just a hairdresser himself. When he was a hairdresser in our day you didn't get many male hairdressers doing women's hair, he was the first openly gay guy in Liverpool doing hair. He moved on to open several hairdressing salons and now he owns an academy. He is the best person to have been taught by; if you wanted to learn something this guy was good.

I got fed up of Liverpool and started to work away in hotels. I was sixteen when I started working in the Grand Hotel in Weston-Super-Mare as a waitress, I loved doing that job. I travelled around doing the different seasons in all sorts of different places. I liked the travelling aspect of it, getting away. I remember a lot of parties. With having a strict upbringing you tend to rebel against it so it was great, I had my own money and I could do what I wanted. The best parties would be where all the staff got together and let their hair down; when in work we didn't do much else apart from work so the Christmas parties were very important.

I come from a very big family though sadly I have lost two brothers and a baby sister along the way. We're down to five now unfortunately from eight. I'd have to say my favourite sister is Pat and I'm very fond of my brother Anthony.

When I drove I would take Leon on days out to places like Tatton Park, Southport and Blackpool during the school holidays. We did a lot together as a family. One of the best holidays I've been on is to California which was so beautiful.

We always lived in the South side of Manchester, so I would take the children to Moss Side carnival. We used to love going there, I loved everything about it: the music, the culture and the food. We weren't familiar with the other parts of town at this stage so the Moss Side carnival was always a good day out. I was very much into the reggae music and the culture that came with

LEON AND HIS MUM

it. The jerk chicken and rice was unbelievable. The curried goat was available there too, it was fabulous.

The 70's were good for fashion with the miniskirts; bell bottom pants and the platform heels. I think the worst fashion trend is the maxi dresses the first time round. They weren't like the nice long dresses now; they were always just a plain black. Not for me at all. I love the retro look on girls, I think they look brilliant. With fashion nowadays (especially for the girls) there's so much choice available. There's a diverse range of styles that anyone can choose from.

I was mad on shoes when I was younger and I remember my first pair of shoes were from a shop called 'Saxo' where they were the crème de la crème of the shoe shops. The shoes were like a brogue, they were beautiful. I just remember being so made up about the fact that I'd actually bought them from there as I'd had to save and save for them. They were completely worth it.

I worked in the most charismatic pub in Manchester: Tommy Ducks. I was head barmaid there and it was the most fascinating pub because the walls and ceiling was covered in all different kinds of knickers. They had beer cans which had paper knickers inside so if anyone gave us their underwear to put up they could replace them with the paper ones so that they weren't walking around without any underwear on. That wasn't the only interesting quality the pub had though. You'd get all sorts of people in there like barristers and people from Granada studios, Richard and Judy used to go in there! Any guest that stayed in the Midland hotel would go over and visit Tommy Ducks. The building was probably eighteenth century, it still had the original beams inside, it was unbelievable. You were never bored in there, the hours used to fly by as it was busy all day. On a Friday the office people would come in at three and stay until ten at night, going home smashed. We had very big heavy steps into the pub so you can imagine the amount of people that used to fall down them; it was like an assault course. That place had the most characters in it, at that time, in the whole of Manchester and Salford. We'd get entire rugby teams in there showing their bums, you honestly never stopped laughing. The Sunday nights were on par with what you would describe as a chill out these days, class Jazz bands from all over the UK played 2 hour sessions, I was mortified when they closed and pulled it down almost over night; it was a big part of my life.

Drinking wise I would go to the 'Top Yates' they had three Yates back then on Oldham Street, the 'Blob shop' was always a good place to go, there was never any trouble and 'The Castle' also on Oldham Street. What is now the Northern Quarter was the 'in' place within Manchester then, there was a club called 'Dickens' which was full of your Foo Foo Lammars, it was the big place for gays to go before the village was even planned out. You only had the Union and the Rembrandt in the village. What I like about that area is that there is no segregation or judgement, everyone is accepted.

I used to go to a nightclub called Patty's where you'd find your Jack the lads. It wasn't a bad place to go, it was a daring place to go, if your parents knew you were going they'd go mad but luckily I wasn't at home then. The 'Moonwalker' on Shude Hill was another place I visited frequently. The 'Auto Club' was also brilliant; it was owned by Jimmy the Weed from the Quality Street Gang. You'd have a fair old drink and dance, it was a copping off place really.

I love the library building in Manchester, I think it's beautiful. I did the silver service in the town hall once and found all these little nooks and crannies and little balconies, it was absolutely superb. I was doing some agency work one Christmas and we did a do there. You know when you do Christmas dos how much money goes to the council, everything was free: wine and food. They were a very greedy bunch, I experienced sheer greed. Though it was an absolute honour to be there, it was so beautiful. Also Tommy Ducks (as I've already said) was a beautiful building as was the Grand Hotel which are now old people's flats. I waitressed there for a time and it was so old fashioned. It was for the rich, I could never have afforded to dine there.

My favourite sporting event is the Grand National; I think everyone should do it once in their lives. It's just so intriguing; there are people from all over the world. I could literally see a

LEON AND HIS MUM

sea of Irish. It's incredible. If you ever get a chance go to that. And of course I love my football. My sons are City fans but I'm an Evertonian. I did ladies day whilst at the Grand National: the hat, dress and shoes. The works! That particular year, a friend's husband took us in a Rolls Royce, you felt like a queen for the day. Six of us went: we started the day looking like ladies but returned in the complete opposite state, heels in our hands and our dresses torn.

I'm not a gig person although I did go and see Michael Jackson at Aintree race course and waited four hours for him to come on stage. All's I can say was it was well worth the wait, my son is more of a gig person.

I always loved Les Battersby (Bruce Jones), I had the pleasure of meeting him in the Grapes pup near the old Granada studios, we had a scream all night long. All I can say is what you see is what you get and that's what I like about northern actors like him. I also loved Foo Foo Lammar – he was such a character and tough as old boots underneath all the bravo. And I had the pleasure of meeting Jacky Charlton (the drag act not the footballer) one night in Foo Foo's Palace, what a gentlemen he was.

I think yob culture is rife in Manchester today. I think there's a lot of racism within Manchester, I think a lot of it is caused by drugs as well, they're hyped up. I'm very glad I didn't grow up in this era. If it was down to me I'd line up all the drug dealers and have them all deported to one of the islands up in Scotland and made to work hard building their own Basic detox units where the next lot of Dealers would be shipped out to and work them to the bone. Things would soon change if they were off the streets. And the reason I'm so passionate about this issue is because I lost my baby sister to heroin. You can see how it destroys families and people, it changes them completely. It's all down to drugs. You've got too much racism in Manchester which is a shame, it really hurts me to see the youth of today on the council estates hardly ever mixing with other races; I find the gangs of young white kids the worst, I find them very aggressive. You can see the tension with them in town. People moan about immigration and people taking their jobs yet they are the ones willing to do it and

MANCHESTER MAVERICKS

work hard enough. I'm 100% behind them.

I think there's a few thugs within the Police. I've experienced it with my son. There's good and bad but in my experience there have been more bad than good. But I don't think that applies to the Police in general, I believe it's just the Police in Manchester. I understand they're doing their job and what they're paid to do but some of them go a bit too far.

I'm a pensioner next year so I've been doing a bit of charity work which I love. I've been working in Age Concern charity shop and I also love going to Llandudno. I like to have a night out every month in Liverpool, I love it. Sometimes when I'm in Manchester I feel like I'm in London, you walk along the road in Liverpool and people will smile at you whereas here you don't get anything like that. Maybe I'm biased even though I have had some good nights out in Manchester, as you get older you get that little bit more nervous as you see the danger from your experience and it's a crying shame.

LEON O'NEIL

Back when Mark Hughes (Sparky) was manager at City I was lucky enough to meet Leon Vincent O'Neil on Oldham Street in maybe the last old school pub left there called 'The City'. Thing is this pub was rough and ready but there's never any fighting in here, also the locals

LEON AND HIS MUM

would jump in and stop it first sign more so if it was City and United lads.

As soon as I got chatting with Leon I knew he was on the ball and a great fella to chat football with be it about City, United or any other topic. Now he's an avid City fan who's lived on and off for 13 years in Liverpool, he got to know all about any football scandal that was going on in Liverpool. For example, when Rooney was taking the lads to the local Cat House to get their knobs polished, I found it so funny when he told me and was even more tickled when he told me about Giggs was the person who was being talked about on all the major news TV stations about having an affair in the family and was having to pay to block his name out of the media, yet I clearly remember saying "Leon I could just put it on Facebook that it's him and that would soon do the damage", and that's exactly what went down the very next day. We maybe missed out on a wee wedge that day as there was 1,000 per cent someone out there with few bob to get that story.

We still meet up weekends in the city and have a proper good chinwag. Fact is the better both clubs do, the better it is for Manchester as the money brought in by what's now termed 'tourists' is something else, you try getting a hotel when there's a big game on and you'll soon see how we've moved into the 21st century.

One of my earliest school memories involves a lad called John from when I used to live up on the Racecourse Estate in Sale. Back in the late 70's this estate was the very first in Manchester to sell bags of nasty, or smack. Maybe it was simply because the residents were a mixed bag coming from the slum clearance areas of Collyhurst, Hulme and Moss Side. At the time I'd just moved back in with my mother after being in home care. John played a big part in my early childhood as he was the person who first started to take me to football matches, which soon became a regular thing. As John was a bit older sometimes he would even give me money to go and spend once inside the stadium, he always took me to the pub beforehand and I'd play the space invader games whilst he gambled on the card games, pool or darts. I loved all of these social aspects to the matches and over a full season I visited every pub around Maine Road which always added good times to my memory bank!

MANCHESTER MAVERICKS

I knew him for around seven years and yet once I moved away I never saw or heard from him again, which saddened me for years to think how something like that could happen. One of the matches that sticks out in my mind from the eighties was when City got promoted after beating Charlton Athletic 5-1 on the last game of the season. The whole of the stadium went berserk after the win, many fans invaded the pitch celebrating us going back up to the old First Division. I kind of felt sorry for the away supporters as the full corner of the Kippax Street next to the Platt Lane was like a morgue with barely 400 Charlton fans in it, and the section had room for 4,000 supporters, they had to cope with over 48,000 screaming City fans all the way through that vital game.

With my family moving around a lot I went to quite a few different schools. I'd make good friends but then I'd be off again, so it was hard to stay in touch with anyone. I would mostly then just hang around with Jason McPhee and another lad called Mark Bradley. Mark was one of my best mates and we'd get up to all sorts. I got the strap every day for always messing around, six times across the hand. I think we should still use it on the kids today; it would sort a lot of them out. Kids nowadays talk down to their teachers, it's unbelievable. We'd pull pranks on teachers, sometimes we'd put drawing pins on their seat or hide their hand bag, or we'd even go to the staff room and hide all of their belongings. We particularly used to prank Mr Crawley, he was a floater: he didn't specialise in a specific subject, he'd just teach everything. We used to let his tyres down on his car and hide his gear. We got caught almost every time, and I got suspended a good few times which I would pay for big time really by lacking in an education I needed.

Soon after we were off to live in the land of Hot Dogs, it was a fantastic feeling flying into LAX in Los Angeles. We lived in Anaheim which is in the same district as Disney Land. The first few months of schooling I had some tough Samoa kids on my case mainly after school, which meant I was forever having to jib offside and sneak my way home until I finally became friendly with the Mexicans. That soon put an end to getting harassed

LEON AND HIS MUM

mainly because of my accent rather than my colour. After 18 months we came back to Rusholme and I got my first job, which was at the Contact Theatre on Oxford Road, working the lights during the in house production shows. I always found setting up the lights and the stage very interesting, the shows were mainly what students had put together themselves. However my next job was for an engineering firm in Ancoats; I fucking hated it. Morning, noon and night: I just couldn't stand it. It consisted of welding, painting and cleaning gates, which sounds like a good mixed bag of jobs to crack away with but I found it all mundane. So I moved on to being a maintenance man at the 'Willow Bank' Hotel in Fallowfield for a bit. I was also a hospital porter for a while too though I was sacked after a good year when I was found with one of the nurses in the store room bang at it!

I then went back over the pond living in Palm Springs; the crème de la crème place to chill out, and believe you me I now had the confidence to throw my Manc accent about in the best places. The posh pussy was on the menu every other night for two mega years. I suppose looking back now I was silly to come back to Blighty, but at the time I still missed my city.

With coming from South Manchester we never attended the Whit Walks, our big event of the summer was the Moss Side carnival. It was really good back then, there was hardly any violence bar the odd drunk having a one to one offside in the back alley way. Me and my Old Queen always got ourselves dressed up very sharp. The whole of the carnival was very family-orientated, consisting of all sorts of funky floats. I remember it being so colourful; some people would be playing the steel drums whilst others would be singing away to Gospel. One thing I remember really clearly was the mouth-watering spicy Caribbean food, it was so delicious. A gang of us would sometimes go and follow all of the floats and then get into Alexandra Park where we'd just stay and watch everything for hours on end. We'd sometimes pinch food from the stalls. I didn't have any favourite stalls as they were all a novelty to you, with all the different options that you had you'd be here, there and everywhere. It was always busy and multicultural; I can remember the bright lights when it turned dark and all the different happy people you'd see dancing away to the smooth rhythms.

In my opinion the worst fashion trend ever in my life time was the Madchester baggy Joe Bloggs era. I wouldn't be seen dead in all that cheap garbage. The best fashion items would be what I wore to go to the match in: I'd have my 501 Levi jeans on with a pair of Dunlop green flash topped off with a navy blue jacket three-quarter length, waterproof and it came from Direct works, I thought it looked cool and being well satisfied it gave me a proper buzz. One mate of mine in particular inspired me fashion-wise, Gary Hindle. He was a bit older than me and he was a Manc ahead of his time wearing his yellow kickers. I've got a few mates that go against the grain in terms of fashion; they just wear what they want. Unlike me they're not sheep, I've been a sheep in my life. I've been a bit of a fashion victim really. In all honesty I envy them at times, even though sometimes they look like they've dressed in the dark, they just don't care. They'll just wake up, get their gear on and get on with it. They love it! In the late eighties and early nineties a Manchester fashion trend seemed to be wearing your jeans with a pair of high tech squash trainers, they were white and green trainers but they were very smart.

One of my favourite pubs was Seftons, but unfortunately it was destroyed in the IRA bombing in Manchester that sent shock waves through Strangeways all the way up to Saddleworth in the hills, the impact was huge yet no one was killed, amazing really. I used to like Seftons because it had a good mix of yuppie office workers and wide boy townies. It also contained the best jukebox in the entire city centre. It was the first video jukebox in Manchester. I'd go in there with different kinds of mates really, everybody just loved it.

Another was "The Kings" on Oldham Street; it was completely full of lively odd ball characters. I suppose it's fair to say they were ticking time bombs and nutcases really. The names of them escape me at this moment in time but you would always see the same faces there day in, day out; women in their eighties dressing as if they're in their thirties, a gay lad who was in a wheel chair because he had no legs! When he went to order a drink at the

LEON AND HIS MUM

bar he used to lift himself so that his ribs were resting on the bar so that if you were looking at him you'd think he was standing on two legs. I remember there being a fight in there once and to get him out of the way I lifted him and put him on a shelf. Fortunately he seemed to appreciate it though I do remember him telling me after that he was scared of heights!

One of my favourite night clubs in town was Isadora's because I loved the music. I also went to Konspiracy which was just near Victoria train station. At the time the music was really good as they had 6 separate rooms with everything that was needed to keep everyone happy. I was into acid house and dance music, really good stuff. Tony H Wilson, "Mr Manchester", was always in there rubbing shoulders with the Salford mob who ran the doors there and at the legendary Thunderdome in Miles Platting, which was the hottest club ever, I swear. The sweat would be running off you and it felt like you had just had a bucket of hot water thrown over you as soon as you entered the club. We used to take the happy pills and dance all night without a care in the world; it was something everyone was doing back then. That was a part of the culture and lifestyle in Manchester and Salford.

Believe it or not but my favourite building in Manchester is the Arndale building. I like it because it's so horrible that it makes me like it, if that makes sense? As soon as you see it you know exactly where you are. I think it's one of those buildings that if we got rid of it we'd all miss it even though it is generally frowned upon. To me it represents everything about Manchester. You see the girls coming out with the buggies and Greggs' sausage rolls. Another favourite building would be the Refuge building on Oxford Road, the brick work is unbelievable. The Victorian architect Alfred Waterhouse designed it and it was opened in July 1893. Alfred passed away in 1905 so his son Paul continued the work on the number two building adding the magnificent Cararra marble and bronze staircase and the soaring clock tower making it one of the city's best known landmarks. It used to be an insurance building but in 1994 Principal hotels bought it adding a ballroom and 275 rooms. It's very classy and wouldn't look out of place down town in Manhattan.

MANCHESTER MAVERICKS

The most memorable sporting event for me was when the Commonwealth games came to Manchester. I went a few times to Eastlands to watch the different events. I saw some of the running events; I particularly remember the 1500 metres. I think I also went to some of the track and field events, definitely the high jump. I never did any sports like that, I just played football whilst I was at school, I was the centre forward. Another good sporting event would be when Ricky Hatton won the world title in Manchester. I think that was quite significant for Manchester especially with him being local. He did a lot of good things for Manchester around that time.

In 1988 I went to watch the Stone Roses at the International Two in Longsight, it was my first time going to see them and they were unbelievable. My favourite song that they played was "Sugar Spun Sister". It was the best gig I ever went to. Before I went I'd heard a lot about the band but because there weren't a lot of people there it felt like you were the first to discover them. We went as a group of friends, one of them being a really good mate of mine: Jason McPhee. I went to see them again straight afterwards and followed them to Blackpool where they played the classic concert in the ballroom. They just got bigger and bigger. I used to wear a Roses t-shirt everywhere.

I've been to loads of their gigs since, last one being up in Heaton Park. One show that sticks out in my mind is Oasis at Maine Road in '96, I like Liam's swagger and style, I think he's cool. I'm currently decked out in all of his Pretty Green clobber; he's a proper fashion icon, although it's cost me an arm and a leg. I don't like Beady Eye that much, maybe because I still love Oasis, without Noel it hasn't got that same spark. Oasis were the coolest band in the world for the best part of five years and even the saying from Liam about how Manchester at that time was the centre of the universe felt right. An even better statement he came out with was after he met Maradona at the Etihad and shook his hand, he blurted out, "Now you've shook the hand of God!" I'm pretty sure they'll be getting back together at some point. I reckon their Mother had to bang their heads together, let the lads know it's time to just move forward in life!

LEON AND HIS MUM

I also went to see Pink Floyd in 1987 at Maine Road which was mind blowing, more so as me and Jason were sober and straight. I like going to see someone different from the norm; it makes a nice change from all the different variations of the same act nowadays.

Manchester is considered the second city, but in my eyes it's also in a class of its own. I think it's been the heartbeat of the country for a lot of years. In the words of Noel Gallagher, "it all comes from here" and it's true; from John Thaw to Johnny Marr, it's happening and will continue to happen. From the computer to the bouncing bomb, the birth of Joy Division to the fall of The Stone Roses, washed down with a pint of Boddington's, or if you don't drink, a glass of Vimto, it all came from Manchester. We're always changing as a city, Manchester has become a very multicultural city now, it's a completely changed place from the 70's, but we're a bohemian people so it ain't bad. Even the ship canal has been slowly transformed. In terms of that part of Salford becoming 'Media City', a lot of people think it may be a white elephant, as all the big wigs from down south were rumoured to say they were not prepared to come to Manchester, but we have always been into our arts so it's all good really.

My most loved adopted Mancunian is actually from Liverpool and she's my Mother. She really had to start from scratch back as she came down that East Lancs Road and created a family here in Manchester. Another would be Alex Higgins because he was a loveable nutcase. Higgins was without a doubt the world's first real snooker star. He was known on the drinking scene as a pain in the arse, always being abusive to people and yet he was known as the people's champion. I actually had a game of pool with him once in the Clarence in Rusholme. Thirty quid and he white-washed me, but I wasn't bothered about that at all, it was just to be in his company.

Of course the yob culture exists in Manchester today. I can't say that they need to do a few years national service because I've never done it myself, but they need some form of punishment so that they can sort themselves out. Maybe it's time to lock up the troubled youth and try to install some decency into them?

Something similar to national service for a year or two perhaps? Make men of them rather than allowing them to roam the streets with a free hand causing mayhem for everyone, not helped by the fact that the police are afraid to pull them. I personally haven't been a victim of the yob culture, obviously I've had the abuse on the bus but we all have, haven't we? Though saying that I went to a party in Hulme where a big fight broke out, which is how I got the scar across my face. I got it nine years ago, I had to get stitches for it inside and out. I didn't know who did it to me, they gate crashed the party looking for trouble with anyone, it never mattered if it was out of order, they just did it.

I think the Police on the whole do a good job in Manchester. They do the best job that they can under stressful circumstances. Fuck me they're not even able to shout at the yobs to keep order as they'll be upsetting the higher ranked dibbles, as it's all about political correctness, and the kids know they have the upper hand. Although I don't know if I respect them because I've had quite a few problems with them over the years. At the end of the day they're doing the job that they're being paid to do.

To be honest my main regret is that I fucked about at school. I regret that I never took my driving test or learned how to drive. The freedom of being on the open road has to be top. I also regret that I never saved my money, going out and spending it all on clothes for all those years pegged me back I suppose, but saying that the women always took first place back then. Look after the pennies and the pounds will look after themselves – that's what my Mother always told me.

At the moment I'm still in limbo as to where my life's heading but I'm sure something will be coming up soon, and I'll be back in business.

'GED THE RED'

There are so many clichés that stand out. One of my favourites is "God loves a trier". Now when that's said of you it's nice knowing you're making the best effort possible at whatever the project may be, even if it looks doomed to failure, but here in Collyhurst we add our own spin to certain sayings hence "God Loves a Grafter".

In my opinion the lads who ventured over the water living the jibbers' life, following the motto "To Pay is to Fail", are the salt of the working classes; proper Manchester Mavericks. Ged and the lads are typical Manc grafters; work hard, play hard and get the job done even when there are barriers on every corner. I first met him when working on Hot Shot's book The Story of a Little Red Devil. Ged was close to Gorton's 'Young Munichs', active from '85 to '95. I always think a maverick is a person who's willing to venture into new places looking to earn a crust and go where few others dare to tread. These pages I was lucky enough to get via a chance meeting with him at the Munich Commemoration in 2017.

Imagine it's the opening scene of The Apprentice, and as Prokofiev's score from *Romeo and Juliet* fades out, the camera cuts to Alan Sugar, about to deliver the week's task. Hopelessly stuck in the 80's, he persists with his facial stubble much as he once persisted with the notion that Chris Armstrong was worth £4.5 million as, stoney faced, he announces to the contestants: "This task will require you to design and publish a magazine to commemorate a major sporting event. You will oversee the sale of this item at said event, which incidentally will be in Europe somewhere and confirmation of exact location, time and date will come approximately two months before, if you're lucky; two weeks before if you're not."

Even to the most cynical viewer, this would seem a tall order, however it would make a bloody good episode. In the mid 2000's this task was the task we took on but with no TV cameras.

MANCHESTER MAVERICKS

Back then, European clubs didn't produce a match programme for Champions League games, as they were not part of the culture for the continental match-goer. This was true for the majority of big European teams at the time; AC Milan, Real Madrid, Porto, Benfica and Roma all subscribed to this tradition, add to that list one of the biggest attractions for any UK based football fan, FC Barcelona.

A pal who never missed a United game pointed out this omission and also highlighted the window of opportunity available to anyone resourceful enough to fill the void. Despite having zero publishing experience, it made perfect sense for me to set about putting together and supplying a match programme for their big European games.

We were adamant that it had to be of a decent quality, and it was always the intention to offer something that was worthy of someone's Euros, and on a par with what was on offer at home. And so we began the ascent of the steepest of learning curves.

Extensive research was required on players, as were match statistics and any historical relevance to the particular match. Content needed to be sourced and in many cases written up first hand.

The term 'Publishing software' went from being a meaningless phrase to being our essential tool which were, again, sourced and subsequently mastered, as was the printing process itself.

"Transferring a PDF from RGB to CMYK at 300 dpi" soon became common phraseology and even more importantly, made perfect sense. Printers had to be found and after much research there were a couple who were more than sympathetic towards our need for extremely tight deadlines and they asked few questions. Most were glad of the work in the face of ever diminishing demand for printed products.

As treacherous an undertaking as this sounds, at the time it all seemed very simple. What could possibly go wrong?

After initial success covering United's European aways, a logical progression was to branch out and cover other UK teams whenever they played on the continent. There would usually be a stand out tie that would fire the imagination of fans, meaning they'd travel in higher numbers than usual and create more demand, such as Arsenal's quarter-final in 2006 against Juventus.

This was also the case when Rangers played at Barcelona's Nou Camp in the group stage of the Champions League in November 2007, and we decided to produce a mag for this game. Rangers had won their only European trophy, The Cup Winners' Cup, in 1972 there so this was regarded as a pilgrimage for many of their fans.

Rangers have the nickname 'The Teddy Bears', which was some kind of Glaswegian rhyming slang. This was extended to the 'Barca Bears' and t-shirts and flags were common, emblazoned with teddy bears wearing sombreros. We'd also featured the '72 match in the mag.

We'd gone over the day before and landed at the same time as the Rangers team. They looked defeated as soon as they got off the plane and we grabbed a reluctant David Weir for a photo as the team walked through customs.

We weren't sure who he was until we'd checked in our own mag, and he looked like he was about to burst into tears on the photo.

The city was rammed and every street and square was packed with drunken Rangers fans, ticking every box for nobhead behaviour by the Brits abroad stereotype. Despite getting dipped on the Metro, the day went pretty well and we sold all the mags.

With Celtic now drawn against Barca in the first knockout stage the following March, there was no reason why we couldn't repeat the success we'd had in November, so planned for it accordingly.

The intention was to plan the operation with a business-like approach; any outgoings were totted up versus the potential income in a spreadsheet. After every possible expense was considered (with printing, flights, accommodation and even refreshments for the lads doing the graft accounted for) it was still looking lucrative.

As street sellers we were vulnerable to anyone wanting to shift snide notes and at the time there was a glut of snide 50 Euro notes knocking about. There was no way we could check the validity and all the transactions were quick and usually in crowded places. We'd been stuck with dodgy 50s before as I'd found out to my cost at the M&S currency exchange back in town.

Unbelievably they let me keep one, which must have been against every protocol going. However, it allowed us to be familiar with at least one security feature on the 50 Euro note: if the number 50 didn't change from brown to purple in the light then leave well alone.

In full on Apprentice mode we came up with various ideas to try to sell as many as we could, and one was to try and up the profile of the sellers so that it looked more official.

We opted to use that universal symbol of perceived authority; the hi-vis vest and duly acquired 4 from Arco in shiny yellow; orange was not an option. We thought this would be a masterstroke; the idea being to knock together some ID passes which stated we were from the Barcelona branch of the Celtic supporters club. This would add legitimacy that the item we were selling was the closest thing to an official publication that they were going to get for the day.

Barca didn't do one, so we would.

A team of four had worked on the Rangers match, and we'd keep the same line-up for Celtic; 'T' was a pal I'd known for years, and he'd done similar sorts of grafting at gigs and occasionally tickets at the football; 'SB' was a lad who lived near me, a family friend who'd grafted at gigs and sports events before, whether it be t-shirts, posters or tickets. He could also speak Spanish and knew Barcelona well.

As the actual selling on the street and at football grounds wasn't something that came naturally to me, having lads who'd done it plenty of times before was a big help. 'T' was an expert at this sort of thing and could walk into the middle of twenty pissed-up lads and command their attention to the point where they'd buy something they weren't really that arsed about. He had no problem fronting it out with anyone who wanted to try and take the piss, and would use put-downs Bernard Manning would've been proud of.

I'd known Dave W from my early teens growing up around

North Manchester. At 19 he went on holiday and never came back. He got a job at a bar, learned Spanish and stayed over there, eventually ending up in Barcelona with his own place. I got in contact with him when I found out where he was now based, and thought he would be able to help us getting around. It also allowed us to have an address where we could send the mags prior to the game, so we could get more in circulation.

He loved it when lads from home came over, and would go out of his way to show them a good time; taking us to all the best places where the tourists didn't go, like the small bars around the Diagonal area. I was frequently told that Barcelona was a drinker's city, and this was something that Dave W embraced, still in holiday mode 15 years later.

He wasn't the most natural seller though, and once swapped some mags for cans of San Miguel outside the Nou Camp with a group of Rangers fans.

Come 4th March, all seemed to be in place for a tight, successful operation. The mags were back from the printers and two parcels had been despatched via UPS and received by Dave W. We'd got our overflowing rucksacks through customs with no mither, and all three of us arrived in Spain safely. Dave W met up with us the night before and took us for a night out around Port Olimpic.

We stayed in the same Hotel that we did back in November, which was close to the airport. It had a shuttle bus to the terminal every 10 minutes, so it was perfect for us when working the fans coming off the planes. We got the bus at 8 in the morning all kitted out in new Hi-vis vests with passes clipped on and made for the arrivals terminal. We looked official, like we were meant to be there.

There were scores of coaches lined up ready to take the new arrivals off to the city centre, so 'SB' and 'T' positioned themselves in between the arrivals exit door and the short walk to the waiting coaches, while I made for the taxi rank at the other end of the terminal so all angles were covered.

Within a few minutes of the first fans stepping from the exit doors 'T' was leapt upon by plain clothes police and taken to a waiting car for questioning. This wasn't in the business plan. We'd been here four months before and done the exact same thing so what was the issue now?

I removed the Hi-Vis vest and jumped in the taxi queue, moving to the back when my turn came round. After about half an hour, 'T' turned up ashen-faced, and soberly told us we had to leave. They'd taken his name, address, passport details and all the mags he had in the rucksack. He'd been released but was told he'd be arrested if caught again.

Luckily he didn't have too many Euros on him otherwise they'd have been confiscated too.

For some reason the Police had taken great offence to his ID pass, and made a big deal by waving it in his face whist ranting at him in Spanish. We were really proud of these passes so couldn't understand the hostile reaction, but there was no doubt they had to go. It was a piss-take that they'd taken the mags too, but we didn't have a case to ask for them back.

We got the shuttle bus back to the hotel, checked out with all remaining mags and made our way to the city centre in the hope that this restriction was isolated to the airport. Las Ramblas was a place we knew well, and we had worked there several times before. As with most people on arrival in Barcelona we'd start off in the Café Zurich at the junction with Placa de Catalunya, and it was full of fans doing the same thing. Dave W met up with us there, together with the recent delivery to his address, having already topped himself up from the previous night. We did some selling around the gathering fans at the Cafe and left Dave W in charge of all the bags whilst carrying on with his one man party. 'SB', 'T' and I ventured out to work both sides of the Ramblas.

Within a few minutes, 'SB' was gripped outside a bar by Police and Enforcement Officers as he was trying to sell to Celtic fans inside. They took his details, and as he could speak Spanish he got more of a grilling. He kept to the line that he was giving them away and therefore wasn't actually selling anything, yet the mags and any Euros he had on him were confiscated. They were insistent on asking who he was with, why he was there and also made it clear to him what the city laws now involved with regard to street trading.

When Rangers had been here back in November, they'd completely trashed the city; pissing in shop doorways, sleeping in the streets and verbally abusing locals was stuff we'd all seen first hand and was pretty much the way they would behave in Manchester six months later before, during and after the infamous UEFA Cup Final at City's ground. This had pissed off the residents to the point where they'd changed local by-laws in fear of the other half of Glasgow inflicting the same treatment. This meant no drinking on the street and crucially a ban on unauthorised street selling.

So that was us totally fucked.

Enforcement Officers (EO's) were now allocated to areas where fans would usually congregate. They were assigned to assist the Police and were fully kitted out with 2-way radios, earpieces, white shirt, black tie and pants and, as is the case with most reputable organisations, hi-vis vests.

We made our way back to the Café Zurich, packed up and planned what to do next. Pessimist that I am I wanted to get the next plane home, but to the credit of the others they were having none of it and just saw it as another obstacle to get over. If we could get into a fanzone, then there would be a large concentration of fans and we could go about our business under the cover of the crowds, and there was one at Placa d'Espanya two stops away on the Metro.

We relocated to a bar in close proximity, and found Dave W who was by now completely smashed from his early morning session. The Fanzone was five minutes walk from the centre of the square itself, so we were in a good place just out of harm's way.

There were now a few hundred fans milling around by the taxi rank and Metro station looking for it, and 'T' set out to do some selling. I made my way to the fanzone and found that it was practically empty. Football fans don't like enforced fun and the fanzone was exactly that, with it's fairground games, flat beer and "We Are the Champions" (Mercury not Pickering) seemingly played on a deafening loop. They were charging to get in which scared a few off, and the ones that did go in spent their time asking themselves why they were there. I made my way back to the bar to see Dave W out cold with his head flat on the table.

'T' came legging it in without his rucksack to tell us he'd just been chased by EO's down the street. They'd grabbed him but he wriggled away and left them holding only a rucksack. There was no way he was getting caught a second time, so had to do some running for the first time since Hough End in the mid 90s. I had a look down the street and walked towards the square to see if he'd been followed. The EO's were about and although not coming in our direction they were clearly mobilised, with their radios in full use. Chances were they'd be looking for the rucksack owner plus any accomplices, so it was time to vacate the bar.

The bar man was now getting fed up of us coming in and out whilst not buying much, and Dave W was not a good advert for business. A Celtic fan wearing a foam cowboy hat let off an air-horn directly over his head to wake him, but he never so much as flinched. We dragged him to his feet and decided to make a break for the taxi rank, under the cover of the crowds. It was too risky to try and flog anything here and by now we were all pretty spooked, so getting away to somewhere quiet was the priority. If we were caught it would've been the end of the trip, especially with the development of the Police now confiscating Euros, so we decided to split up and meet up later. Even if we lost all contact we were on the same flight early the next morning so would meet up at the airport. I thought it best to abandon the city centre all together and made my way to the stadium to see if I could shift any mags there.

As the distant sound of Tina Turner drifted from the fanzone speakers, my three business partners could be seen weaving conspicuously through the crowds. Dave W was prostrate, not even semi-conscious, resembling a life size rag doll being carried by his two comrades in what looked like a scene from the Battle of Little Big Horn. 'SB' was carrying his arms whilst walking backwards and 'T' had an ankle in each hand whilst giving directions, cox-style through the melee. The intention for a discreet getaway was not going to plan, but somehow they managed to make it to a taxi unscathed.

GEO THE RED

On arrival at the Nou Camp it was pretty much like OT in the daytime of a European game, with stalls setting up and a couple of hundred fans milling around, so I plotted up at a fence lining the road on the approach to the stadium. As soon as I took out the mags a stallholder selling scarves bellowed at me in Spanish, what I took to mean "fuck off", then started waving what looked like a permit at me. I abandoned the idea of getting a pitch and moved further away from the ground towards the bars around Collblanc.

I was in contact with the others by mobile and the three remaining lads had plotted up at a bar we knew just off Las Ramblas that was hidden away down a side street. We'd learned the hard way that pre-paid SIM cards were the best way to communicate via phone. Astronomical bills accrued from previous European trips would take a big chunk from any hard-earned profit.

They told me that 'SB' had been gripped and instead of having his name taken and mags/euros confiscated they'd taken him away in a van, presumably to the Police Station. Out of frustration he'd taken a gamble on Las Ramblas being less on top than earlier in the day, due to the large crowds gathering there, and left the cover of the bar to try and shift some of the ever-depleting stash. It was a ballsy idea, but according to 'T' he was gripped within 30 minutes. It would have been easier for all of them to just plot up, get pissed and put it down to one of those days when things didn't quite go to plan, but amazingly none of them did.

'SB's' arrest was a massive worry; I couldn't see the Police releasing the same person a second time for doing the same thing they got lifted for in the first place. My first thought was that I knew his Mum. If he didn't get out in time for his flight, what the fuck was I going to tell her? Then, like the hero I am, I focused all concern on myself. On realising that he had my phone number in his phone, and how useless I would be under any sort of questioning, an overriding sensation of what could be described as bricking it washed over me. I would be classed as the mastermind of an international forgery ring preying on innocent football fans. They probably had a special wing in Catalan jail for English criminals; I would be "cast down with the sodomites",

MANCHESTER MAVERICKS

Shawshank style. After giving my overly-paranoid head a wobble, I decided to do what my business partners usually ended up doing on these trips: head for the nearest bar and hit the Estrella.

As the day went on, the fact that you were abroad (usually in the sun) triggered the holiday gene; the spreadsheets went out of the window. The days when I would be pulling lads for drinking at ten in the morning were long gone, due to being told to fuck off numerous times previously, so it was a case of 'when in Barca, do as the Barcelonés do', and the only one I knew was Dave W.

Due to the heavy Police presence it made sense to follow a plan of going into bars which were full of Celtic fans and try to sell some, as it wouldn't be obvious what was going on. The first bar I went in was packed with Green and White shirts, with the majority in full voice.

"He plays on the left...he plays on the right....Aiden McGeady makes Scotland look shite" belted out, which I took to be a compliment to United's own version. But one song stood out. It was to the tune of Matchstick Men and Matchstick Cats and Dogs, where great Celtic players from over the years were reeled off:

"And they gave us... someone, Dalglish, Macari and Paul Mcstay" etc etc then end up with "And all those football greats ...went through those Parkhead gates..." It sounded mint, although I didn't catch Lee Martin's name in there.

My Protestant heritage must've been just visible enough to provoke mild curiosity, as a couple of lads approached me asking what was in the rucksack. After they'd had a look through the programme it proved to be an opening, and as they flashed it around the bar interest spread to many of the other drinkers. As in the majority of cases, when they actually had a look through it they realised it was of pretty high quality. I must've sold 30 odd within a few minutes. For the first time my rucksack began to feel lighter, which was always a good measure as to how well we were doing. Marching all day with 200+ A4 magazines on your back in Mediterranean heat would take its toll, and the weight issue was a problem we never quite managed to solve. We'd toyed with using thinner paper, but the quality of the mags was compromised and it ended up feeling cheap.

Throughout the day, I kept getting a faint smell of what I thought was cat piss. At first I thought it was a bloke I was next to on the Metro, but then I kept getting a waft of it in bars or even when I was walking on the street, and it was definitely getting stronger. I know certain places have their own smell, like Grimsby or Rhyl for instance, but wasn't aware of Barcelona having one. Whilst plotted up in the bar I realised it wasn't the Barca streets and nor was it any of its residents. Two days previously, when leaving home for the flight, I'd left all my stuff (passport, bag, flight tickets and the mags) together downstairs in the living room, pre-packed ready for a speedy early morning getaway to the airport. I'd bought a new Nike rucksack for the trip and this was something to which our cat must have taken exception, because she subsequently decided to mark this strange, new smelling item with her own signature. Cats don't have access to permanent marker pens so claimed it the only way she knew how, and did so on the padded part, which is meant to be in contact with the wearer's back. As the day had gone on, the heat and sweat had gradually coaxed out the smell from the rucksack to the point where it radiated like radioactive waste. Scrubbing it in the toilets would fend it off for a while but I knew I'd have to bluff it out if it got raised. Denial would be the best form of defence.

I tagged along with a group of fans to get nearer the ground. As expected, the majority of them were ticketless, so a programme was a good way to tell their mates they'd got in, or to at least prove they'd been very close. I pitched up in a bar where the match was on and reasonably filled with Celtic fans. Being pretty much half cut by now meant that my usual inhibitions about bowling into a group of football fans on my own to try and sell them something were put to bed for now. This was something 'SB' and 'T' never had an issue with. I was now using the few Spanish words I knew and ordering beers by asking, "Una botella de cerveza, por favor", and even stretching to, "Por favor, una botella de cerveza", just to freshen things up. This also helped when people asked where the programmes had come from; I lived in Barcelona and was selling them for someone there. If I'd said I was from Manchester they would have instantly lost interest, no matter how authentic an item it was, suspecting it was some kind of scam. Whilst going along with this drunken facade to a couple of fans I'd latched on to, they asked me to find out where the cigarette machine was.

This would be easy: 'machine' = 'maquina'? Cigarette? That had to be 'fuego', which is something to do with smoking I thought, plus I was sure that someone said the word 'fuego' to me when I was smoking near to the airport terminal door.

"Donde esta la maquina en fuego?" I shouted across the crowded bar. The barman carried on serving but kept looking at me with what could be described as a Latin shrug. I went for it again, thinking the only obstacle to getting an answer was the background noise. "Esta la maquina en fuego" I asked loudly, but this time with added arms stretched out in case he didn't realise it was a question. The barman looked at me as if I'd told him I'd just found Christ.

A Spanish customer who was sat on a stool at the bar turned round to me with that same look of incredulity and answered me in broken English, to add insult to injury.

"Hey mate, what do you want?"

I told him that I wanted the location of the Cigarette machine, to which he pointed out,

"You are saying 'the machine is on fire! the machine is on fire!'"

Evidently, his English wasn't as broken as my Spanish.

Part-way through the second half I received a text from 'SB' saying he'd been released and was in the McDonald's close to Collblanc station. It was fantastic news and I made my way over, where I found him together with an upright and now semi-coherent Dave W. 'SB' had been through a tough time. He was taken to a police station and told he'd been detained pending a court date, and they set about questioning him using the 'bad cop, bad cop' technique.

"So you were just given these magazines by a stranger in a bar?" 'SB' held up a lot better than I would've, and stuck to the line; that he'd come across them through a chance meeting. As implausible an excuse as it was, they still just wanted shut of him, so released him on the understanding that he left Barcelona in the next 24 hours. Hopefully we'd be out in less than 12.

After the match, we made our way back towards the ground and as we approached it the sea of departing fans, scarf and flag-sellers appeared on the street as if from nowhere. It looked as though this was a window which the street sellers had been waiting for and every few yards a seller appeared, working from bin bags full of hats, scarves and flags.

We took the remaining mags and hit both sides of the street, feeling safe in the knowledge that everyone else was doing it. For the first time that buzz of selling came back, as we rattled out the last hundred or so mags in quick succession. Over the day, we'd probably lost over half of what we'd produced to the Police, so this late rally pulled us out of the shit. Up until then we were in the position of not even having enough to pay the lads for the graft they'd done.

'T' texted to say he'd been in the ground for the match. I don't know how, but his Irish roots had got the better of him and he'd managed to find his own way in to see the game. The chance to sing the Fields of Athenry with a load of pissed up Paddies was too good to turn down. Celtic lost the game 1-0 to an early Xavi goal and lost the tie 4-2 on aggregate, meaning they were out of the Champions League at the first qualifying round.

We stuck to the plan and arranged to meet back at the airport, while Dave W made his way back to his apartment with the prospect of work the following day. Check-in time was 05:00, which gave us plenty of time to make the journey from the city, and once at the airport we'd be out of harm's way. A count-up of takings showed we'd come very close to breaking even, which left me feeling a little deflated. A massive amount of work had gone into producing the mags, and that's before we'd even attempted to sell any.

However as check-in time approached there was no sign of 'T'. Texts and calls went unanswered and the sense of doom I'd carried for most of the day grew. As the clock turned to 5am a dishevelled 'T' appeared, wandering aimlessly across the departure hall. He'd been there for a few hours but out of sight, asleep in the disabled toilet.

'T' suffers from sleep apnoea, whereby the sufferer loses breath during sleep, manifesting itself in loud noises that sound like choking and sometimes shouting. He'd been woken by the sight of a security guard forcing the lock on the toilet door. The alarm had been raised by a concerned cleaner who'd heard shouting from the disabled toilet cubicle. What they didn't realise was that he wasn't in distress; just fast asleep.

The disappointment from what felt like an unsuccessful trip was only lifted by the relief to be on our way home and away from Barcelona. It had been a day to forget; it felt like all the hard work was for nothing, plus the stress of all the Police involvement. 'SB' put things into perspective whilst on the plane home, "When you take on things like this it's amazing if anything does go to plan". He was right; a few hours ago we'd had two of our lads arrested and lost over half the mags we'd brought over, but still got out unscathed. He paused mid-sentence then offered: "Can you smell cat piss round here?"

"Can't smell anything pal".

We didn't know it at the time but we'd be returning to Barca for the semi-final in April.

DAVID BLATT

Living in Europe the bonus for me was that I was able to see British teams play in Europe and mingle with the visiting fans. I would just hit whatever town the teams as I'd sell whichever team was playing.

Dortmund was brilliant as they turned the squares into a fan-zone. I was over the moon when I moved back to Manchester and was able to get a stall in United's fan-zone, after a season they hired a film team to catch all the reactions from the supporters and stick it up on you tube and send it live at times to the big screen inside the Red Square's fan-zone.

I was asked to help out with chatting live to the fans coming out of the stadium as I was a dab hand on camera, I'd done a filming course at Salford Uni. Suppose it's normal that you get quite a few top people on camera who look out for the cameras to give their thoughts on the game and this is how I met David Blatt. After a few weeks I found out he's not only a writer about United but hasa top book published by Empire who had reprinted Grafters and later my brother Mark's book 'Grafters: Mancs Abroad'.

I read his book and was very impressed, so I'm sure it's easy to understand why I got David to pen in some pages whilst the going was good, I'm sure they'll be a mint read.

As a child it wasn't long before my mother came out with a line that only mothers could ever come out with.

"If you sit in front of the television all day, you'll end up with square eyes."

Didn't parents get away with murder in those days?

Still, at the impressionable age of seven you believe everything your parents tell you and since I didn't want to succumb to this new disease that doctors had yet to find a cure for, it fell to my Dad to find a solution.

So what was the answer? You've guessed it – football.

Now this is quite interesting because my Dad didn't actually like football. Poor man. He paid lip service to Aston Villa, but only because, as a sergeant, he was posted to an Italian prisoner-of-war camp in Aston, Birmingham during World War Two. Some of the local squaddies followed 'The Villa' and I suspect it was more a case of joining in so as to be accepted than some dark, recessed longing for the Claret and Blues.

So, what was our first match? Leyton Orient v Brighton & Hove Albion in the old Second Division in 1956, of course. You see, the "O's" were the nearest league team to my home in Ilford, Essex, so it was logical they would be the first team I actually saw live but I want you to know that I didn't go all the way. Not on a first date. It was okay, I suppose. It was cold and everyone seemed bigger than me. I remember one team played in royal blue and one team played in orange. Orange! Mmmmm... nice. So that was the team I supported that day. It was only as we came out of Brisbane Road that I overheard a conversation that led me to the conclusion that I had mistakenly supported Brighton & Hove Albion in their away colours. Still, no lasting psychological damage was done – the game ended 2-2.

For the next two years my Dad took me to the Bermondsey Triangle of First Division clubs, namely Arsenal, Tottenham and West Ham. At these larger grounds the weather was colder, people were taller and I saw even less. So as you can see. Lots of dates. The odd kiss, but I never went all the way.

Then one day at Highbury it all changed. Even walking to the stadium I could feel the electricity in the air. I began to tingle. Inside the ground I entered a new dimension. WOW! The noise, the atmosphere. And when the teams came out – that ROAR. This was foreplay above and beyond anything I had ever experienced before.

"What team's that, Dad?"

"Why, that's Manchester United, son."

"Well Dad, that's the team for me."

At last – penetration! That all encompassing feeling when you know everything has finally come together. That spark that had been missing suddenly exploded in front of me, inside me and all around me. I was in love. This really was the first day of the rest of my life.

The speed, the skill, the see-saw of scoring and emotion. I actually saw some of it between mens' heads, shoulders and backs. To this day I can look anyone in the eye and say, "I saw Duncan

Edwards play" yet I can't recall which one of our players he was. I was eight years old for Christ sake! Only years later would the terrible significance of that match truly hit me. Duncan had the power, grace, balance, beauty, strength, character and talent to be considered the greatest of them all but he was taken from us too soon. Nevertheless that first time experience set me up for the roller coaster ride that is Manchester United.

Fast-forward several years and my love for the club had grown. It was time I went 'to hers' so to speak. Living in a London suburb that time forgot, I felt that the world was passing me by. Certainly girls were. Fortunately fate was to take a hand in the unlikely shape of my long-lost cousin, Michael Krazney, who revealed the awesome power behind the combined forces of Aladdin's Cave and Doctor Who's Tardis that lurked in the form of the Manchester United (London & District) Supporters Club.

David Blaine, David Copperfield, Dynamo, even the gross Paul Daniels would not have been able to work out how a teenager on little more than pocket money could travel from London to Manchester and back and get a ticket to see pre-Eric's Disciples on Earth but the Manchester United (London & District) Supporters Club could. And so on a momentous day in the spring of 1967 I got up at 5am without waking up Andrew, my younger brother, otherwise I would have been slapped by my Dad. I left the house an hour later armed with my brand new leather-look plastic United sports bag overflowing with United scarf, sandwiches and a flask of piping hot Heinz tomato soup (the word "cool" hadn't yet entered the Ilford vocabulary).

The tube journey from Gants Hill to Charing Cross seemed to take an age. "What if I miss the coach?" I thought as excitement and knots grew in my stomach that I usually associated with the magazines under my bed. Eventually yours truly was hovering on the pavement outside Charing Cross tube station, Embankment entrance. Gradually other red clothed members of the same tribe as me congregated in twos and threes. I remember being taken aback by the complete spectrum of ages around me. I thought I would only be surrounded by guys my own age but there were children with their Dads and men even older than my grandfather.

MANCHESTER MAVERICKS

And there were girls.

That was something I hadn't bargained for. Conflict of interest? No, not really, 'cos fortunately they were both dogs.

"Is it a bird? Is it a plane?"

No, it was the coach rising like a phoenix that was to take us to Old Trafford, centre of the planet. At 08.00 I clambered on board, unaware of any system or pecking order and sat down in the middle next to a short, fair-haired kid with more acne than me. It was his first time too. We started chatting nervously, neither one of us wanting to appear like away-day virgins. By the end of the season he had developed, swan like, into a fully fledged Hoolie, attaching himself to one of the "Cockney crews", whilst I took the cul-de-sac route to nerddum. Just thought you'd like to know.

At 10.30am we stopped for half an hour at Watford Gap services on the M1. If the Manchester United (London & District) Supporters Club was Aladdin's Cave, then Watford Gap was the London Dungeon in disguise. Congealed, tepid and rock 'ard – and they were just the one hundred year old Hell's Grannies serving behind the counter! For a cocooned youth from the suburbs this was an eye and bottom opener. Dogburgers sped in from one orifice only to extract themselves with aplomb from the opposing orifice moments later, leaving little or nothing for my stomach to work with. I got back on the coach an older, weaker and wiser young man.

As we drove down the legendary A5 through Brownhills someone came round with tickets for the game, which incidentally was against Leicester City. Not yet wise to the layout of the ground, my new chum and I chose tickets for 'The Edwards Stand'.

Finally we were traversing the A56 through Altrincham and towards heaven on Earth. Suddenly there was air of expectancy as we passed the world famous "George Best" boutique, a full season behind Carnaby Street but, what the heck! How we cheered. How the two, cool looking sales assistants took the piss.

Groups of Reds started to get off at various pubs along the way before the coach finally pulled into the special car park. As I disembarked I remember taking in a deep breath.

"Manchester air. I was made for this place."

Eighteen years old and I'd finally arrived home. I can't explain the emotion. Tears filled my eyes so I avoided peoples' gaze. This was not the time or place, in front of fellow worshippers, nutters and fanatics to appear like a Southern softie but inside I was welling up. A meat and potato pie for 12p became my staple pre-match meal for years until I discovered the Chinese shop next to Lou Macari's fish & chip shop did Indian curries!

I shuffled down the Warwick Road, my senses filled with noises and smells. I bought a genuine fake Manchester United scarf from one of the stalls then just stood in the front car park and breathed it all in. I queued for hours to enter the Souvenir Shop but had no money left to purchase anything. Around 2.00pm I made my way into the stadium and up flights of stairs before emerging into glorious sunlight and viewing the green, green grass of home. More welling up ensued.

As I took my seat half way up near the half way line I saw and heard the most wondrous thing. Down away to my left the Stretford End was in full voice. I immediately realised I was in the wrong place. Why didn't anybody tell me when I bought my ticket on the coach? Naïve or what? I was finally in the stadium of my dreams and yet I was out of it, you know what I mean? I looked around me. Ordinary people. No, this must never happen again. I want to go mental. I want to lose it. Never had the feeling been so strong or felt so right. While the girls in our school doted on the Beatles, we related to the Rolling Stones. They had an edge. They were unsafe, and best of all, your parents hated them, consequently the Stretford End was the only place to be, among the dangerous and unhinged.

Finally, with the ground full to bursting, a roar went up and the teams came out onto the pitch. I was shivering. I was shaking. And there were no dirty magazines in sight. The match passed so quickly, yet in just one game I learned what every United fan has come to accept for generations. If there is an easy way or a hard way to win a game, United nearly always choose the latter. A brilliant 5-2 victory of breathtaking football over Leicester City, including a double by the King, Denis Law, the 5th being a

MANCHESTER MAVERICKS

glorious chip over the world's greatest goalkeeper, Gordon Banks. Sandwiched between, literally, was a brave goal by David Herd, as two Leicester players sandwiched him and broke his leg. Bastards. He was never to play regularly for the Reds again. How was I to know I was witnessing his last proper game? Manchester United, Glory and Angst. Wasn't it ever thus?

The journey home was a blur of images swirling round my head. I desperately tried to learn the songs I had heard that day, so that when I eventually emerged from Gants Hill underground station at 1.00am on Sunday morning I was able to sing them at the top of my voice all the way home. Judging by the number of lights that came on as I passed, I felt pretty sure I was impressing the local neighbourhood. Life now was just beginning.

As a Cockney Red, living and working in London, opportunities for staying overnight in Manchester were virtually non-existent, especially in the early days when I came and went on the coaches run by the Manchester United (London & District) Supporters Club.

With kick-offs at 3.00pm (remember them?) our fleet of coaches would leave the Embankment entrance of Charing Cross underground station at 08.00, arriving around 1.30pm at Old Trafford. A few Reds would ask the driver to drop them off by The Gorse but for the majority of us, The Dog & Partridge was our home from home. It was the first time I had ever encountered mass singing and chanting BEFORE a match. It was dark and dingy but totally 100% United and a wonderful place to be.

When I first started to go up to Old Trafford in my late teens, being let loose in the souvenir shop was my priority. Working my way up the corporate ladder within the Advertising industry, wearing a tie was *de rigeur* so every home game was an opportunity to peruse the shop for items to wear or carry that wouldn't make this particular writer look like a complete toss-pot away from the match-day experience.

For most of my time travelling with the London & District Supporters Club right up to the early 80s and notching up 30 to 35 games a season, I could sleep safely in my bed (or anyone else's for that matter) confident in the knowledge that while many

Manc Reds would be queuing overnight or from some unEricly hour in the morning, I had a guaranteed ticket.

Of course, there are exceptions to every rule, and if ever I was not successful I could rely on my known supplier, tall, bespectacled Tim. A nutter who also lived 'dawn sarf', he could be found at every game with his 'colleagues', offering tickets 'for a drink'. Obviously some drinks were more expensive than others, but one thing I will say for all the touts I saw regularly at games, I was never sold a fake. If they weren't cruising up and down the Warwick Road they could be found in and out of the Dog and Partridge.

One of Tim's greatest successes was the European Cup Winners' Cup quarter-final tie against Barcelona at Old Trafford in 1984. Having lost 0-2 in the Nou Camp, I believed, as did 58,000 other United fans, that we were in for something special that night. Without a ticket I took my customary half day off work with the corresponding reduction in my career prospects and arrived outside Old Trafford about 90 minutes before kick-off. A tour of the touts led me to Tim. A price of £35 was agreed. Remember, this was around 35 years ago so pretty expensive but I think you'll agree, it was one of the shrewdest purchases I ever made in my life. Recognised as the best atmosphere ever witnessed at Old Trafford, anyone who was there will never forget it as United turned over the Catalans with a 3-0 triumph in front of a seething home crowd.

A flip side was the 1968 World Club Championship second leg at Old Trafford. Beaten 1-0 and kicked off the park in Argentina, a game in which Nobby Stiles had been singled out for 'treatment' before retaliating and getting sent off. This was just two years after Rattin's antics as Argentina captain upon his sending off in the infamous World Cup quarter final at Wembley, and anti Argy feelings were running high (and have done, on and off, ever since).

In the return leg, Juan Sebastian Veron's father, Juan Ramon Veron, opened the scoring for Estudiantes as early as the 7th minute which dampened spirits considerably. However, by continuing their dirty, vicious tactics our level of hate and passion rose and

MANCHESTER MAVERICKS

The Stretford End was soon heaving with animosity. In the 75th minute both Best and Medina were sent off. The whole ground was in uproar, then in the 90th minute Willie Morgan equalised and we all went ballistic. Two minutes later and a scramble led to our second goal. Just as we were all orgasming the referee blew the final whistle and nobody knew if we had levelled the tie or whether it was all over (it later transpired he had blown before the ball crossed the line!). It was one of the most unsatisfying endings to a match I have ever experienced, and that includes beating Sunderland away 1-0 while City beat QPR 3-2 in "Fergie Time" to win the league.

We were all seething as we exited the ground. There were reportedly only around 300 Estudiantes supporters in the ground that night, but we were after every single one of them. I then spied Tim as we marched along the side of the railway station by the ground. He spotted a couple of fat, well-dressed, middle aged Spanish speaking gentlemen exiting one of the executive entrances. He strode over to them and under the pretext of asking them for a light, punched both of them in their respective stomachs. I suspected their layers of clothing that cold night had reduced the full effect of the blows, but we all felt slightly better. It was nothing but a hollow gesture, we had to get our anger and animosity out of our systems.

The Dog and Partridge has held many memorable events, but one particular significant moment was back in April 1999. Neck and neck with Arsenal, United were stuttering in pursuit of the Premiership. Andy Walsh, in his capacity as head of IMUSA, had arranged a meeting in the pub prior to our crucial home game against Aston Villa. He gave a rousing speech in support of the team, and he and his fellow members gave out leaflets for us to distribute along Sir Matt Busby Way before the game to as many United fans as possible, urging them to rise up as one and together we can sing the club to victory.

A hard earned 2-1 victory was as much a testament to us as the team, (in my own mind anyway). We could do no more. Until the next game that is.

I was too young to go to Wembley when an unfancied United

DAVID BLATT

beat overwhelming favourites Leicester City in 1963. After an underwhelming league campaign Denis came alive in the final and five years after the awful Munich disaster, United were back!

Yet between 1963 and 1976 I experienced eight (yes, 8) losing semi finals in all tournaments. That does something to a man, I can tell you. When my non-United mates went to Wembley with their teams I would sometimes be offered a ticket but I'd refuse. How could I go to Wembley if it wasn't with United? Forget it. So when Gordon Hill got the first of our two goals against Derby at Hillsborough in 1976 I saw the rest of the game through a veil of tears. My personal dam had broken.

Years of watching rival supporters frolicking around Wembley and now it was my turn. We all agreed to meet at Trafalgar Square at 10.00am. What did we find? Gangs of Millwall, Chelsea and others looking for stray Reds, so that was a damp squib start to my first Wembley final with United. Add Bobby Stokes offside goal and that crowned an underwhelming day I had waited 13 years for.

Tout Tim kept me in FA Cup Final tickets down the years: from £25 for the Southampton Final in 1976, to £35 for Crystal Palace in 1990. In all that time I never experienced aggro on the day in or around Wembley itself, save the League Cup final against Liverpool in 1983. Normally it was understood that a Wembley final meant calling something of a truce but for the Neanderthals following Liverpool that counted for little.

Walking back after the match to Preston Park, we encountered large groups of Liverpool fans on the lookout for individual United fans. We were outnumbered so we gave them a wide berth. To this day I still wonder where our fans were that day.

Chelsea can be just as bad, as anyone attending their 4-0 thrashing in 1994 can confirm. They even caused havoc just walking up Wembley Way for the Charity Shield season opener in 1997. Scum.

It's a given that Old Trafford is my favourite building. I was so proud when the Cantilever Stand was constructed so United could host matches in the 1966 World Cup finals. We had the most futuristic stadium in the country. Architecturally, we've added piecemeal and I can no longer claim we have, aesthetically at least, the most beautiful stadium, but on an emotional level, nowhere else comes close.

When my first book came out in 2004 I flew to Manchester from Cannes for the launch. Andrew Searle from Parrs Wood Press had got me a full page editorial coverage in the *Manchester Evening News* that day. I bought a copy and sat in St Peter's Square opposite the Victorian glory of the Midland Hotel. That was a special moment and the image of that building in the background will forever be stencilled in my brain.

As a Cockney Red I can't claim to have socialised in and around Manchester much. We always drove back straight after matches, first on the coaches then under our own steam, so I won't pretend to look cool and name the coolest places. Hope you understand.

As for music, well the world record for selling out a concert is held by The Stone Roses reunion at Heaton Park. How cool is that! Unfortunately, as a Cockney Red, for me the vast majority of awesome concerts I have attended and let it all hang out since the 60s have taken place in and around London or festivals like Glastonbury, Isle of Wight, Monsters of Rock, Download and so on. Although a few years ago my wife and I caught the best girl band in the world, All Saints, headlining the Manchester Pride concert over the August Bank Holiday (okay, my daughter's in the band. Biased or what!) A great night was only dampened by trying to find somewhere to eat afterwards. Why do all local eateries close before midnight? What's all that about!

Going back in time, my wife and I also attended the BBC Radio 1 Roadshow in Manchester in 1997 which was headlined by All Saints and the Shirehorses. I had a lovely conversation with Mark Ratcliffe after their performance. For a Bitter he was mightily gracious about the girls and we had a great conversation about football. I always loved Mark & Lard. They are sorely missed today.

Last but not least, in November of last year I caught All Saints at the Manchester Academy. A brilliant concert, aided by the low ceiling which amplified the sound and blew me away. Then after the gig I accompanied my daughter, Melanie as she deejayed along with Tim Burgess of Charlatans fame at an all-nighter at the Deaf Institute.

I know Carling don't do weekends, but having beaten Fulham 4-1 earlier that afternoon, and then finishing the night at the girls' hotel, The Lowry, it came pretty close to the perfect Saturday night, Sunday morning.

I've been lucky. As a teenager I grew up in the 60s: The Beatles, Rolling Stones, The Kinks, The Hollies, Four Seasons... pop music has never been as good as this since. Then in the 70s I was in my twenties and we had Pink Floyd, Led Zeppelin, Allman Bros Band, Jethro Tull, Bob Dylan, Neil Young, Melanie, Rory Gallagher and Frank Zappa... this list is endless. The best era for music!

I also regularly saw the Holy Trinity live. George Best, Bobby Charlton and Denis Law. I loved them all, for different reasons. We were all Denis in the playground. Lightning reflexes, he was a scruffy urchin with his shirt outside his shorts and sleeves too long as though he always wanted to wipe his nose on them. Meanwhile Bobby would glide across the mud (not much turf then!) like a ballet dancer, then unleash a shot so unstoppable the world would freeze as one of his thunderbolts screamed through the air and lodged in the back of the net.

Then there was George. We couldn't be George because he got the girls that were out of our league, but he made today's debates about who is the world's greatest footballer redundant. Ronaldo or Messi? Pele or Maradona? Anyone who saw George Best play week in, week out knows he was the greatest of them all. He was chopped down mercilessly by the likes of Tommy Smith, Chopper Harris, David Webb et al, yet got up like a rubber ball and skinned them alive. He performed at the highest level at home and away. He did it with a heavy leather ball and on mud encrusted pitches. Imagine if George had been playing today...

One United player that touched my heart was Stuart Pearson. When he scored and raised his right fist in the air, his smile would fill the whole stadium. Another was Gary Neville. He was 'us' on the pitch. A United fan through and through. Never blessed with the greatest ability, he did what any one of us would do, practice day and night just to be allowed to put on the famous Red shirt. And when we scored, he was one of 'us' again. No-one will ever forget his celebration when Rio scored his last minute winner against Liverpool at Old Trafford. While the rest of the team ran to congratulate Rio, he ran in the opposite direction just to kiss his badge in front of the Liverpool supporters. How we would all have loved to have done that!

I still have the T-shirt.

SIR MATT BUSBY

The three people who stand head and shoulders above all others for me, in the 20th century are Nelson Mandela, Spike Milligan and Sir Matt Busby.

Forget Manchester United. Whatever Sir Matt Busby would have done in his life, he was a special man. Anyone who ever met him would say the same. I was lucky. I met him a few times over the years. As Max Bygraves would say, "Let me tell you a story…"

"Fergie out", "Atkinson Out", "Sexton Out", "Kenyon Out", "Glazers Out", "Lights Out", "Way Out", "Far Out", "Out Demons Out", "Get Your Tits Out", you've heard them all down the years I'm sure.

But "Busby Out". No, I don't think so.

I don't think I ever heard anyone say this. I first saw the Reds on a long, never to be afternoon of the Babes last game on British soil, the immortal 5-4 victory at Arsenal. I would subsequently see them whenever they came to London until that fateful day aged fourteen when I discovered one of the three United Supporters' Clubs in London. My geography class at school saw an immediate improvement as it brought the road atlas to life.

ACT 1

One Saturday during the 1966-67 season saw the Red Army descend on Ipswich. Now I don't know about you, but getting up for work is as natural as a salmon swimming against the current in its desire to spawn, but getting up to see the Reds – piece of cake!

My system? All I would think about when I went to bed

was Manchester United. I fell asleep thinking about Manchester United and, guess what, I woke up (just like that) thinking about Manchester United. I was an Ad man's dream.

Ipswich away was a bonus for a Cockney Red. I could stay in bed an extra two hours as the train didn't depart until around 10.00am from Liverpool Street station. Needless to say I got there miles too early yet there still seemed to be hundreds of United fans milling around. And then I realised why. Without any prior warning THE TEAM was spotted walking through the concourse on the way to the train.

ROOAAR!

We all steamed over to them. The players, to a man, looked at us with disdain as they fought to extricate themselves from the masses and seek refuge in the arms of the first class compartments.

"Working class, moi?" each expression exclaimed, as they disentangled themselves from our hero worshipping mauling.

All except one. The Manager, Matt Busby.

Sandwiched between two luggage trolleys he proceeded to have a word and shake the hand of every single one of us, or so it seemed to me at the time. Eventually I pressed my soft, clammy hand into his whereupon he said unto me.

"Hello. What's your name, son?"

"David" (Sir, Your Honour, God. I mean, how do you address THE man?)

"And where are you from David?"

"London, sir... but... but... (quick, quick, think of something to say before the moment is lost for ever.) I go every week!"

"Wonderful David. We need more supporters like you. Good luck."

And so it came to pass that the man and his right hand were gone. Time stood still. In my world there was only silence. I looked at my hand. HE had touched my hand.

No, he had actually SHOOK my hand.

"I will never wash this hand again," I thought as the outside world began to infiltrate my senses.

A moment later I was back to normal as I joined the crush to board the train. We spent the entire journey running up and down the corridors of the train, singing and chanting, banging each and every window through which we caught the glimpse of a player and wondering why they never acknowledged our presence.

ACT 2

Three weeks later, after a game at Old Trafford, the Manchester United London & District Supporters Club held its Annual Dinner & Dance at Belle Vue. Rumour had it that one or two of the players had promised to attend.

If the truth be told, the "do" was a bit boring. But then at around 9pm the mood changed as a couple of players were spotted nervously entering the room. As a committee member of one of the official supporters clubs I was a bit more reverential in my behaviour than I had been three weeks previously. OK. I agree, I was a bit wet but then I realized that the great Matt Busby was also with them. My heartbeat quickened as I crossed the dance floor to take it upon myself to welcome them to our humble "do".

Before I could say a word, Matt Busby smiled and said: "Hello David. Nice to see you again."

I turned into an Instant Goldfish! My mouth opened and shut but nothing came out. My eyes welled up with stinging tears. I was so embarrassed, awestruck, overcome, immobilised, in love and incomprehensible that I was unable to speak. GOD had remembered my name. From three weeks beforehand when I was just one little "oik" amongst thousands of Reds (Sorry. Did I say hundreds before? Well, passage of time, artistic license and all that) pressing our flesh against him.

Over the next thirty years of licking and grovelling I must have had over a dozen conversations with the man. And he always remembered my name. Extraordinary.

It got to the stage that when, as a shareholder, I regularly attended the United AGM, Sir Matt would enter the room yet I would resist the temptation to join the throng which descended on him like a swarm of locusts. I would pretend to continue to converse with whoever I was speaking to at that moment until, with the start of proceedings imminent, fellow shareholders would begin to make their way to their seats leaving Sir Matt room to breathe. He would then catch my eye, and HE would come over to ME and we would have a little chat, whilst all around I was aware of expressions which translated into... "How the hell does HE know HIM?"

So, along with Nelson Mandela and Spike Milligan, Sir Matt Busby was one of the greatest human beings of the twentieth century. I'm almost inclined to say Sir Matt Busby was perfect, but human beings are not perfect.

But if perfection were possible, the term used by scientists, biologists and Tomorrow's World to explain this phenomenon would be "Busby".

"Busby Out." I don't think so.

WRITING ABOUT THE REDS

I used to buy copies of *Red News*, the original United fanzine, on the supporters club coaches en route to matches. I loved the way the anger, piss-takes and passion mirrored my own feelings for United. The editor, Barney Chilton, asked for contributions for a book he was going to publish about the greatest day and night of our lives, namely May 26, 1999. It was an outpouring of emotion like a dam that had just burst. It felt like an exorcism (whatever that feels like) a cleansing of the soul.

And it felt good.

Barney then asked me if I'd like to write for the fanzine. Being a lot older than most, I started to put down in print all my recollections and interpretations of past matches and mayhem.

And it felt good.

Then one day Barney suggested I write a book. I said, "**** off!. Who'd want to read that?" In my opinion, Fever Pitch by Nick Hornby was the best book ever written from a fans' perspective (sorry Colin). It contained passion (admittedly, not something you associate with an Arsenal supporter), campaigning zeal, facts and figures, and a writing competence I could never hope to compete with. But Barney said I write in a sort of self-depreciating style that some would find appealing.

MANCHESTER MAVERICKS

He talked me round, so I got all my articles that I'd written for *Red News* up to that point, put them in chronological order, wrote pieces that filled the gaps, and that's how "MANCHESTER UNITED RUINED MY WIFE" was born.

At this time, early 2000s, I was living and working in Cannes in the south of France, so sending off a synopsis, a couple of sample chapters and a covering letter to all the leading publishing houses in the UK and the USA cost a fortune. At that time Publishers wouldn't accept submissions by e-mail so I had to print out over 100 sets, then post them all from France.

It goes without saying, but I'll say it anyway, most didn't even bother to respond, let alone send a rejection notice. Plan B was then to send sets to specialised Sports Publishers. This drew two possible leads, Manchester's own Parrs Wood Press run by Andrew Searle and one from a fellow FSA (Football Supporters Association) committee member who also published a QPR fanzine and ran his own small publishing company. It was a hard choice but in the end I went with Andrew, as I hoped he would have more contacts in the Manchester area, which despite the claims of ABUs everywhere, is where the vast majority of United's match going fans reside.

By combining our respective expertise and contacts we sold around 10,000 copies. It was even on sale in the Megastore, which surprised me, because if anyone from United had actually read the book, they would have run me out of town. We were about to discuss a second edition when the specialist bookseller Sports Pages went tits up and brought Parrs Wood Press and countless others down with them.

A contact of Andrew's, Simon Lowe of Know The Score Books, picked up the mantle and a second edition was published. This sold a further 1,700 copies before they also went tits up without your truly receiving a penny. Thought I'd get that one off my chest.

Now without a publisher, I recently produced an updated Kindle e-book edition on my own which I have just brought out and is currently available on Amazon. So you know what to do, don't you!

The follow-up was a bit different.

Apart from sex and drugs and rock 'n roll, and Manchester United of course, one of my great passions is travel. My wife and I had often talked about travelling around the world, but how could anyone on a normal salary, with a mortgage, two kids and a football team to support make that a reality?

Then in 2009, with the sale of Ronaldo, and to a lesser extent Carlos Tevez, I thought it would take Sir Alex at least two seasons to fashion another Premiership winning and hopefully, Champions League winning team together so, as Elvis Presley once sang, "It's now or never."

My wife and I agreed to sell our two bedroom flat in London to finance our dream, only by this time the recession had kicked in and we lost £100,000 in the value of our property. In the end we sold up in December, paid back the naughty bank, made ourselves homeless and with the remaining equity bought 2 Round The World air tickets. We knew we could never ever get back on the London housing ladder but we felt this was a once in a lifetime opportunity and fuck the consequences.

We pushed it to the max. Round The World tickets are amazing value for money if you plan it well and adapt to the conditions. The maximum length of time you can use a RTW ticket is one year, so we travelled for one year. The maximum number of scheduled flights is 16, so we made 16. The maximum number of stops per continent is 4, so we mad e 4, and so on…

My not so secret mission was to watch, live, as many of United's 60 odd matches in the calendar year of February 2010 to February 2011, together with England matches in the World Cup until their eventual elimination. By a combination of pubs, bars, streaming, internet cafés etc I detail in THE RED EYE – A United Fan's Distorted View of the World, every single match and my attempts to watch them all. Not all were successful, but the agonising before and after, as well as the matches themselves, offers the reader a unique perspective for watching Eric's Disciples on Earth in the four corners of the planet, at any unholy hour of the day or night, whether in an urban hell hole or halfway up the Andes.

MANCHESTER MAVERICKS

*Author David Blatt in Medellin, Columbia
outside a shop with a familiar name.*

On top of this I had to cope with a wife who really, REALLY hates football, and was no help whatsoever in making my mission a success.

Prior to flying off I'd ordered 100 "LOVE UNITED HATE GLAZER" stickers which I systematically stuck in places around the world, from the statues in Tienanmen Square, Beijing to the entrance to Anchor Wats, Cambodia. From the ticket office in front of the Taj Mahal to a plaque inside the Maracana Stadium in Rio. It had to be done and I was the man to do it.

It was also my mission to meet as many Reds as possible around the world, to see if Manchester United meant as much to them as it meant to me. I suspect I knew the answer in advance but I wanted find out at first hand.

★

Between 2000 and 2006 my wife, youngest daughter Jasmine and myself lived in Cannes in the south of France, and since

DAVID BLATT

August 2011 my wife and I have been living in Ibiza, so going to Old Trafford requires military precision. Nice airport, a twenty minute drive from Cannes, was easy. By booking around 6 weeks in advance I could purchase flights all year round between £25 to £60 return, less than the cost of petrol driving from London to Manchester and back as a Cockney Red. Then by sharing the petrol costs with mates… happy days. But Ibiza is different.

Since the recession, all subsidies from the Ibizan authorities for flights have been cancelled. In our first winter there were no return flights at all between Ibiza and the UK, whilst flights via Barcelona were expensive and connections not conducive for the weekend with work on a Monday. Hence severe withdrawal symptoms for the past eight years.

With my youngest living in London, depending on the day and time of the match, I tend to fly direct to Manchester on the Friday, then take the train down to London after the game. Rail fares in the UK can be horrendously expensive, especially London to Manchester on weekday mornings with departures before 09.30 but I've discovered if I go on the Virgin Trains web site I can book a single fare on a Sunday for as little as £15 as long as I book one month in advance. Now that I've retired I fly back on the Monday. That's civilized!

So as you can see, I have to be careful and plan my games well in advance, although I always make the *Red News* Annual Dinner in May a must. I also make a weekend of it, so I look for any gigs I can get to or films I've missed. I tend to wander round the Trafford Centre during the day (sad) and The Printworks or the Northern Quarter in the evening.

On the day of the game you'll find me standing along Sir Matt Busby Way, along with the fanzine sellers come rain or shine, giving out flyers for my two books. Before my last game I actually sold paperback copies of "The Red Eye' to unsuspecting Reds, many of whom would question my parenthood or offer me a free haircut without anaesthetic. My faith in human nature was restored as just before kick-off I had sold out!

AFTERWORD

In May 1963, FA Cup Final day, I was warmly invited in by our neighbours, The Dudsons. It was a full house, with everyone tuned into this amazing black and white, crystal-clear TV set with an outer-space aerial placed perfectly on the top. Everybody was overexcited and it was a great final, with The Lawman (Denis Law) scoring a top goal and ending up Man of the Match as United beat Leicester 3-1. It's hard to explain how big those finals were back then; at times they came over as a bigger buzz than the European Cup Final or the World Cup, as the build-up went on for weeks in advance and gripped the nation. Back in the 60's I'd be grafting at Old Trafford, minding bikes in my Granddad's back alley, selling *Manchester Evening News* and *Football Pink* newspapers. At our school if you behaved and did well in class the Sisters would give you a ticket for the Man United Reserves home games, so I'd get to see all the up-and-coming talented players along with the old pros making comebacks from injuries. Back then it was rare to see women at the football. I think this probably had something to do with the atmosphere around grounds at that time; it was never friendly and often violent.

A few years later, and just like everyone other kid inside Collyhurst flats, we played football virtually 24/7. In openings, on the cobbles, any spare patch of grass and inside the local sand-park attached to Willert Street Police Station. The games played here were organised by the best players among us with teams being evenly matched, and outsiders looking for local talent came along regularly to scout for their teams. In the summer of 1967 two United scouts called at the Vickers' home to inquire about the bubbly blond-haired lad they saw in the sand-park flying past defenders. Mrs Vickers said "well my two lads don't have blond hair but our Donna has!" As soon as they found out she played for Saint Michael's Boys' team she was asked if she'd like to take some trails for The Corinthians Ladies. Even Granada TV got involved, interviewing her for Scene at Six. Donna became a mini celebrity

AFTERWORD

back then and we all loved the press she got, having played with and against her. She hung her boots up aged 38 and moved to Australia where she now coaches girls.

So with Donna in mind, I loved it when United formed a women's team this season. I was well chuffed, with our first game away at Liverpool in the cup played over the Mersey at Tranmere's stadium. There was a good crowd there to see United bang in the winner in the last ten minutes. A few weeks later I fancied going to watch them in Leigh's rugby stadium and the ladies won with ease. Unfortunately the weather was proper piss poor; non-stop wind and rain pounded me and I had no choice but to get offmans early. I was soaked and feeling ill. As soon as I got into Manchester I went and bought a bottle of strong cough syrup and stayed indoors till Monday, thinking I'd done the right thing chilling out at home alone. To be honest I knew something was adrift and my doc said it was a stupid move as fluid had built up over my lungs. So he gave me antibiotics and said come back in four days if it's not cleared up. It never did, so the doc said, "Okay I'll double the dose for the next 4 days". However I got mixed up, thinking he meant take double the amount after he'd already doubled the strength of tablets.

Come Monday morning I was carried over to the doc's by Gagzy, who I've known for 55 years so is akin to my brother. No surprise, within half an hour I was in a taxi off to North Manchester hospital for x-rays. The docs said the pictures were not clear enough, that they needed to have the clearer CT scan, so said stay in overnight and redo another CT scan next day again to get a even clearer picture. Then the docs were asking me to go home, eat well, chill out and come back in a week to have surgery on my right lung, to get rid of the poisonous liquid that had pancaked it flat as. It took a full week in ozzie to clear the shite and then I was told to go home and wait for a letter asking me to call back and check the scans. If there was any fluid still knocking about, they'd simply insert a small thin tube into the front of my stomach which meant I could release whatever is left at home. It all sounded fine by me, no big ting!

So the next Monday morning a letter landed asking me to go

to ozzie again. I thought "nice one, time to get it sorted", yet the next day another letter came from another hospital up in Bury asking me to go there on the same day at the same time. I phoned both ozzies and they said the Bury appointment was the main one, forget the other.

As soon as I landed in the department a crystal-clean nurse came out right on time, asking me to come into the office. The main doc was there, sporting a dull kipper with two student nurses sat on either side who looked even more worried.

I'm not sure where this came from but as soon as I sat down I got a cold shudder and blurted out "Listen Doc what's the bad news? Is it the big C?" You see, I'd always worried about the times in the late 70's when we got an extra £20 a day for chopping away at deadly asbestos with just Jay cloths wrapped around our mouths for protection.

"I'm sorry to say, Mr Blaney, that yes, you have got cancer and it's very bad. I'm also sorry to say we've no idea where it's come from and sadly, Colin, we don't have time to find that fact out."

Fuck a Brick!

The fact is that protocol in all hospitals demands that when it's terrible news like this, you are supposed to have a close friend or family member with you for back up. I just put it down to a mix-up and dropped it from my mind. 15 minutes later I was in a taxi with steroids, sleepers and a bottle of Morphine. All that came to mind was the Irish fella who appeared on Who Wants to be a Millionaire? He had come over the water to film a few months before but, having a wee drink problem, he had bottled it the first time. The next night at the studio he got his act together. Soon Chris Tarrant was asking him if he was steady, and believe you me this chap was chilled. When asked what he would buy if he won the jackpot, as cool as the lager you sup he replied, "Well Chris, in my local off-licence there's a £100 bottle of whisky sat up on the top shelf. I'd love to have the pleasure of a wee dram of that tomorrow".

So as I was coming back into Collyhurst I asked the driver to pull over at my Local Offie. I nipped in and bought a bottle of the best Andy Pandy from the top shelf, VOSP Remi. It cost me the

AFTERWORD

small fortune of £75, and in my world that's a full week's night boat from Cairo (Giro). I also picked up a pack of Carlings, Stellas and Magnum ciders, and once in my flat I phoned up a friend and stuck in an order in for Thai weed, Sticky Black, a chunk of Pollen and 5 grams of cannabis oil.

Three days later I was in the worst state health-wise of my life, and believe you me I've been in seriously bad states; coming off the booze and drugs, "Sleeping with the towels" we called it, and this would take a week or up to ten days to recover. I even had deep and dark thoughts for the very first time, and realised I must have been depressed besides being so ill.

I say that as I'd never had any idea what being depressed consists of or feels like. A letter from the hospital landed that same morning saying I'd three months to live. I felt like a man on Death Row. Maybe I'd read too many true crime books back in the day, fuck knows! The only thing I noticed that day was the weight had plummeted from me drastically.

It was definitely time to pull my Salford's up and get a fucking grip, sharpish. All I thought about was those close to me: Syl, my two brothers, my Sister, my son and two granddaughters, besides all my close friends and exes. I kind of understand why Jeremy Kyle slags off Facebook, it's got a lot of downfalls, but in my case it's worked, with 5,000 friends who are mostly all United heads who like to know what I'm up to on Match days. It goes without saying that I sell a few books and Inter-City Jibbers T-Shirts as well, and so I thought "Fuck it, I'll just go public with my Cancer problems", and of course the response was the kind that gives you faith in humanity.

What gave me the much-needed lift and told me to act the right way was thinking back to 1970, when I was in and out of police stations like they were my second home. I was finally sent down by the Juvenile Court for three months. I was a 14 year-old schoolboy who had grown up way too quickly and I was soon brought back down to earth. Those three months were the hardest, longest, toughest test of my youth. A few years later I spent just over a year banged up in Borstal, but honestly that was a walk in the park compared to 3 moons spent in the Detention Centre. All told I've spent 10 years locked up all over the place, and looking back the time in DC was what I termed my apprenticeship in life. I know a day's always 24 hours but those three months were so long. I'm hoping the three months I've been told I've got left will stretch out as much in my mind.

Getting back on track had to be my sole priority, so I sacked the drink and smoking but decided to use the Cannabis Oil daily. I just stick it up where the sun don't shine and it brings my anxiety down to a nice level.

Now as I write it's Black Friday, so I'm off to buy some new clobber and prepare for my first session of chemotherapy next week. It doesn't take much to work out that I'll be getting the strongest blast they can dish out. Then three weeks later, coming into Crimbo, I'll get another dose. The week after the new year I'll have a CT scan to see if there's a wee chance the treatment is helping to freeze the cancer and stop it spreading, as they know it's impossible to cure. If so I'll have another four sessions to round it off. In my books I'm a Collyhurst Cowboy who's ready to throw himself on the slab and tell the doc to give it his best shot!

Now I'm not going over the top here with wishful thinking, but believe you me I'll be the happiest Manc on planet Earth if I were to be able to attend my book launch for Mavericks. I say that because it will be around Easter time. If not and it goes the other way it's easy for me to accept that I've lived a full life as a Grafter for over 25 years, which supplied me with total pleasure. I seriously have to pinch myself to know it's true; I've lived such a wonderful and fulfilling lifestyle, and then to completely change my life around by becoming a writer has been the cherry on the cake. I even think I made my family proud.

I have lots of moments in my life that made me proud, but there's a few that stick out: 1963 in Saint Malachy's Church, having my first Holy Communion; 1965 making my football debut v Saint Patrick's up at Monsall's Red Rec next to where Newton Heath once played; 1967 passing my trials for Manchester Boys; 1969 passing my trials for Manchester Youth Federation (Youth Clubs); 1974 bearing a son, and then having two granddaughters. Then much later on in life and after six years of writing, finally

AFTERWORD

getting a book deal and all that came after it. I'm proud of my work outside the books as well: in the media; having the chance to feature in the hit film The Casuals shown at the Football Museum; doing TV; putting together a Photography exhibition inside the Royal Exchange; being part of a writing team for the play Up on The Roof, and being asked to play two parts in the production itself, which was shown again at The Royal Exchange with Syl watching me in the wings.

So the Grafters book was followed by 'Hot Shot' and 'The Undesirables'. I also did a bit of telly on Channel 5's 'Pickpockets and Proud' and Channel 4's series 'Secrets of the Pickpockets', 'More Secrets of the Pickpockets' and finally 'Secrets of the Pickpockets Abroad'. Just reading these achievements back makes make me proud.

More importantly knowing my mother's still on the ball as I write now and that we remain a tight family unit brings everything into focus. I'd like to take time out to thank all my close friends who've been really upbeat and loyal with me over the last few months helping me come to terms with cancer.

Special thanks to David Adamson for all his interviewing, editing and proof-writing with the Mavericks and Empire Publications for sticking with this project for the past 15 years!

Lastly, I know it's gonna be one hell of a battle to stem the illness, but my head's in a good place and remember, "Health is Wealth", and never forget to live each day as if it's your last, no matter what happens.

MUFC all Day!

Colin Blaney